Kino and Kinder:
A Family's Journey in the Shadow of the Holocaust
by
Vivien Sieber
ISBN: 978-1-914933-17-2

Published By: -

i2i
PUBLISHING

i2i Publishing. Manchester.
www.i2i.publishing.co.uk

For Peter and Paul

Acknowledgements

Putting together this story has only been possible due to the huge generosity of family, friends and strangers, some of whom have become friends during the process. What started as a random collection of letters, unpublished manuscripts and Peter's report on the hostel, has grown into this book.

I need to acknowledge the great help I've had from many people along the way.

It is unlikely this book would have come to fruition without Tim Hume's generous input and constant encouragement, as critical friend, editor and proofreader.

Helen and Heinz Rupertsberger, curators of the Jewish database for the Josefstadt area, were tremendous help with regard to Vienna. They answered my many questions about the Palast Kino and were kind enough to research and send me papers from the Wiener Stadt-und Landesarchiv (1939-1969). They also created the initial summary and timeline of events. Others who helped included Hubert Steiner and Christian Kucsera of the Archiv Der Republic, Susanne Claudine Pils of the Wiener Stadt-und Landesarchiv, Elisabeth Streit and Günter Krenn of the Austrian Film Museum and Michaela Englert of the Admiral Kino.

Joan Carus and Mary Wealleans, (Windermere Public Library) gave me valuable background on Windermere and the hostel. The 2013 photograph of South Wood is courtesy of Matthews Benjamin, Windermere.

All the women I contacted from the original hostel, have been generous and helpful with their comments and recommendations. In particular, the late Elfie Reinert, for her recollections of life in the hostels and for commenting on the chapters describing them.

In Oxford, Marieke O'Connor helped with translation whilst Margaret Staff proofread early chapters.

Thanks, are also due to Lionel Ross, the proprietor and publisher of i2i Publishing and to his senior editor, Mark Cripps who has bravely edited this book helping to make it much more readable.

Paul Hodges has done so much, including general encouragement, image manipulation, IT support, proofreading and bag carrying. He demonstrated enduring patience with the process and with me.

Contents

Prologue

Oxford: A Few Large Boxes

I have always known that my grandmother, Paula, was born in Brno, Czechoslovakia (now the Czech Republic), that she moved to Vienna to run a cinema, the Palast Kino, owned by her family, and that she and my father, Peter, were Jewish refugees. They both managed to escape to England from Nazi occupied Vienna in 1938, joining Peter's half-brother Erich, while the majority of Paula's family died in concentration camps. Paula was fifty-four and spoke no English when she arrived, penniless, in London. She became one of the two matrons in a hostel for refugee girls in Tynemouth.

When the Kindertransport began in 1938, a group of Jews in Newcastle formed an ad hoc committee to establish a hostel to give temporary homes to some of the rescued girls when they arrived from Europe. The committee raised the funds to set-up and maintain the hostel and support the children until they could be collected by their parents. Although the initial expectation was that the hostel would give temporary shelter to the children, in reality, it operated for seven years from 1939 to 1946. The hostel was forced to relocate from Tynemouth to Windermere when war broke out with only three weeks' notice. About forty girls stayed in the hostel; it was home to twenty-five of them for the duration.

Peter gained a scholarship for refugees to Newcastle University, was interned in the Isle of Man and Canada during his first year, and finally graduated with a BSc in Electrical Engineering. He was then the first enemy alien to become an officer in the Royal Navy, was involved in minesweeping as well as the D-Day landings and went on to serve in northern Europe on intelligence gathering missions for the Navy.

In 1999, keen to record the contribution from the Newcastle committee that created and funded the hostel, Peter contacted as many of the hostel girls that he could trace and asked them to complete a survey describing their experiences during their time in the hostel. By now mature women, several wrote movingly of being separated from their parents, their journey to England and life in the hostel. Not all were positive about their experience; indeed, one wrote that as she was still so traumatised by these events, she could not contemplate completing the questionnaire. Naturally, each of their experiences were different as were individual reactions to those experiences. Much of their writing is interspersed throughout this book as individual quotations. All were writing in their second language and their text has only been minimally edited.

In 2000, Peter used these responses to write a report, 'The Newcastle-upon-Tyne hostel for Jewish refugee girls. In recognition of the Hostel Committee who initiated the Hostel and managed it, and of the Newcastle Jewish community who supported it' (the report is shown in the Appendix). Peter acknowledged the help that he had from the women brought up in the hostel, notably from Elfie Reinert, in tracing individuals now spread across the globe.

When Peter died, in 2000, he left a few large boxes with an apparently random and poignant collection of photographs and documents along with Paula's old attaché case, which was covered in stickers from the places she had visited and contained another collection of letters, documents and photographs. There were also a couple of Peter's unpublished manuscripts based on Paula's and his own lives that he wrote during the 1970s. A notebook containing a detailed contemporaneous diary that recorded Peter's internment in the Isle of Man, the sea crossing to Canada and his time in Canada was an unexpected find. I also inherited Peter's meticulous notes and the responses to his 1999 survey. Peter was keen to acknowledge the kindness of Dr and Mrs Freedman in giving him a home, enabling him to join their family in Newcastle when he was an undergraduate and beyond. His writings appear throughout the book.

Recently, I contacted a few of those women who are now in their eighties and nineties. I was fortunate enough to meet Elfie Reinert in her home a couple of times when she was most generous in answering my questions, correcting my understanding and checking draft chapters. Some, I contacted by phone, others by e-mail. All have been generous with their reminiscences and comments and a number of them have been included in the book. Sadly, there are fewer now than when I began this project only a few years ago.

This book began, rather by accident, when I tried to understand what had happened or, at least, what had probably happened, to my family. A visit to Vienna changed vague questions into a tangible project. I must acknowledge the enormous help I have had from individuals at the Austrian State and City Archives, the Film Museum and the curator of the Jewish database for the Josefstadt area.

Hopefully, this book allows the people involved, from Peter to some of the girls Paula cared for in the Newcastle and Windermere hostels, to tell their own stories. As the Austrians maintained meticulous records, it has been possible to reconstruct much of what happened to the family left behind in Vienna in 1938, and to the cinema (and the individuals that appropriated it) between 1938 and 1946. Documents from the archives and correspondence show Paula's ten-year battle to regain ownership of her cinema.

I have learnt a great deal along the way researching and writing this book. Although I already knew the basic structure of my immediate family, my parents, grandparents, half-uncle and aunt, all the other relationships were vague. Whilst annotated family photographs helped me to build a basic family tree, they did not include dates of birth or give an indication of how these people had spent their lives or indeed, when and how they died.

During my research for this book, I have spent a lot of time using Geni (My Heritage) which is similar to Ancestry. Geni is a virtual database that already contains over twenty-three thousand pieces of information that have been uploaded by ordinary people. The software identifies shared information, linking individuals to present searchable family trees that then show the kinship relationship between the searcher and individuals. Users can create entries and edit information about existing entries to build and modify their family tree. Additional information, like copies of birth, marriage and death certificates can also be uploaded. It was only when I began to search for Paula Ticho that I discovered just how extensive the Ticho clan was. Indeed, there were so many entries, I could not follow a generation across my screen when I attempted to scroll. I became confused as my mouse slipped. In the end, I printed each individual screen and then used Sellotape to stick the pages together. I then spread the long scroll along a table, weighting down the end with books, unrolling it to read the relevant section. Although this exercise took time, it did give me an insight into how large the Ticho family was and still is. Some of my ancestors were quite famous; most were not. The Sieber/Schiebers are a much smaller family.

The information Geni holds relies on people having the interest and time to make entries and upload information about their families and it is inevitably incomplete, mistakes happen as some nuggets of information end up in the wrong place. Helpful curators manage sections of the tree that generally correspond to their family interests. With help from the patient curators, I have updated Geni as I learnt more about my family. New information appears all the time as more records are digitized. Every week or so, Geni sends me an email with updates of new matches from my search along with a monthly update on changes within my family tree. It is fascinating to suddenly view the tree, something I have now studied for a while, from the perspective of a distant family member.

When I became more interested in finding out what had happened to the family my grandmother had to leave behind in Vienna in 1938, I found more specialised sources. I began to search the JewishGen databases that include records of millions of Jews and information organised by communities across Europe, North Africa and the Middle East. JewishGen is an offshoot of the New York based Museum of Jewish Heritage, one of the many living memorials to the Holocaust. The minimum information I needed to begin to search these databases was the names and place of birth of the person I was seeking. JewishGen also maintain the terrifying Holocaust Databases made up from the lists that carefully recorded the details of arrests, transports and genocide of those captured by the Nazis.

To complicate matters, the way names were written was often different even on official documents, 'K' or 'C' were frequently used interchangeably, for example in Karoline/Caroline. When the politics of a region changed, as new countries were formed following the First World War, the names of towns and cities changed along with the language. Many places ended up with varied spelling in a number of different names. Several people had multiple names, depending on the language in use at the time. Louisa and Laura are the same individual at different times. Street names were and still may be spelt differently, for example a street that features heavily in this book may still appear as Josefstrasse, Josefstädterstrasse, Josefstädter Strasse, or Josefstädter Straße. For consistency, I use the last to describe this street throughout the book, as it is the current official form.

GenTeam is another database managed by volunteer historians and genealogists that specialises on Austria and neighbouring countries. Detailed information and documents are available from this site. Whilst FindBuch concentrates on information about confiscation and theft of property by the National Socialists and Austrian restoration efforts. Of course, there is increasing overlap in the information held between the different databases and the same document appeared following searches in multiple databases.

The United States Holocaust Memorial Museum, one of the larger 'Living Holocaust' projects, has collated oral testimonies including survivors of concentration camps, children saved by the Kindertransport and some of the people in this book. Links to these testimonies are included in the resources sections at the end of this book which gives links to the databases and other sources of information should readers want to explore issues raised by this true story or to begin their own research.

There is also a bibliography that lists some of the many books and references that have informed this book.

I try to present the evidence for this story as I uncovered it but the errors and assumptions are obviously, mine alone.

Although this is a story about my family, it is in no way remarkable for the time. Sadly, persecution and genocide continue today as families are forced to flee repression and bloodshed and become impoverished refugees. Whilst they travel in the opposite direction, perilous sea crossings on small boats and tragic drownings are still common.

Section 1

1880 – 1938:
Pre-World War I to World War II

Chapter 1

Brno: Manchester of the Habsburg Empire

Capital of Moravia

Let me begin with a little context for those unfamiliar with Boskovice, Neu-Rausnitz and Guru Humorlui, the tiny towns and ghettos of nineteenth century Middle Europe. Briefly, Czechoslovakia was only created following the Great War in 1918, by the amalgamation of the Bohemian Kingdom (Bohemia and Moravia), Slovakia and Carpathian Ruthenia. The Kingdom of Bohemia was first ruled by the Hapsburgs and then the Austro-Hungarian Empire, as part of the Crown Lands. Bohemia and Moravia were important industrial and agricultural centres throughout the eighteenth and nineteenth centuries, exporting goods and food throughout the empire and particularly in Vienna. Prague, which is now the capital of the Czech Republic, was then the capital of Bohemia, whilst Brno was the capital of Moravia. Brno became increasingly important as industrial processes moved production from small home-based craft work to large-scale factory manufacture in the latter part of the nineteenth century.

Laws, dating back to the Middle Ages, controlled the number of Jews allowed to live in towns, as well as preventing them from owning property. In contrast to Bohemia, where over fifty per cent of the Jewish population lived in Prague, in Moravia, Jews were spread across villages and tiny towns. Largely prohibited from living in cities, the Jewish population was forced to live in segregated communities in poor housing that was often destroyed by fire. Disease spread rapidly through the overcrowded inhabitants of the ghetto.

The law also prevented Jews from working in the professions and many other types of employment, but home working and trade were permitted. Many men relied on working as itinerant peddlers, pushing their handcarts from village to village, to support their families. Others were tailors and artisan craftsmen working in their already overcrowded homes to make goods that were often sold in the markets in the central squares of Brno and Olomouc, the university city and ecclesiastical capital of

Moravia with strong links in eastern Czechoslovakia. Ghettos sprung up close to towns and cities so that goods could be more easily sold in their market squares. Boskovice, which contained one of Moravia's larger ghettos, was thirty-five kilometres north of Brno, so inhabitants could tramp into the city to sell their wares. Life within the ghetto was autonomous; the population had their own mayor, police force, fire brigade, and schools that were generally built beside the synagogue and yeshiva, a place where people come together to study the Jewish religion.

Jewish emancipation began with the relaxation of land restrictions. In 1848, Jews were allowed to live where they wanted and could move out of the ghetto and in 1867, they were permitted to buy land.

The Ticho family
During the 1870s, Yitzchak Zvi Ticho was one of the first to take advantage of the new law when he bought a house on Masaryk, Boskovice's main square. A distant cousin of mine, Charles Ticho described Yitzchak Zvi Ticho's shop in a recent article in the *Jerusalem Post*. Although the front of the house was outside the ghetto, facing the square, the back door opened straight into the ghetto, allowing escape, if required. The family lived on the first floor above their shop, called A.J. Ticho - Drapers, that sold textiles and sewing supplies to people visiting the busy market. By and large, families had to be self-sufficient. Clothing was generally made and repaired by the women of the house where a few were lucky enough to have sewing machines, whilst others were outworkers for local factories. The demand for fabrics and haberdashery was constant and trade at the shop was brisk.

When the railway reached Brno in 1838, the line connected the city with Vienna and the empire. The effects of this new connectivity were almost immediate; people and goods were able to move rapidly, trade flourished and the city expanded quickly. As the industrial revolution reached Moravia, factories were built along the Svitava and Svratka valleys, as water was needed to drive the huge wheels that powered them. The Jewish community quickly recognised the opportunities mechanisation offered to the textile industry. The collated history of Jews in the Boskovice community from the fourteenth century to modern times is a community project organised by JewishGen. It shows that along with the Tichos, the Schwarz, Eisler, Czaczkes and other leading families from the Boskovice ghetto established factories outside Brno. The Ticho Brothers factory was one of the first to mechanise the production of garments, early examples of ready-made clothing. Textile factories employing thousands of people, spread along the valleys outside Brno. Brno became known as the 'Manchester of the Hapsburg Empire' and was recognised for producing high quality fabrics and garments that were sold across the empire, as well as being exported to Paris and London.

By the end of the nineteenth century, members of the extended Ticho family worked in most aspects of the textile trade. While Yitzchak Zvi ran his shop on Masaryk Square, his brother Bernard, moved to Brno and set-up his own draper's shop in the Krautmarkt, the main square in Brno. Bernard expanded rapidly and was soon running three shops on different sides of the market square, a prime location in the busy city. One of the shops was at right angles to the Reduta Theatre, the oldest theatre in Europe. The shop even appears on a 1919 historical video of Brno.

Postcard of the Krautmarkt, Brno. The Ticho shop is white and set back from the other buildings below the Parnassus fountain.

Bernard lived with his wife, Bertha and their growing family, above one of the shops. Number eighteen was at the bottom corner of the square that sloped steeply up towards the Parnassus fountain. Paula, born in 1889 and the youngest of four, was an appealing child. Her strong dark hair had a natural curl, long lashes surrounded huge brown eyes and she could be impossibly charming. Inevitably, she was indulged by her elder brothers, Alfred and Ernst. Her sister, Selma, was nine when Paula was born and enjoyed the responsibility that often falls to an older sister of caring for a younger child.

Infant Paula Ticho. Brno, 1889.

Paula was confident and prospered at school, understanding from an early age the importance of hard work. Whilst she was not greatly interested in the detailed history of the Austro-Hungarian Empire, when she was interested in something, she learnt quickly.

With a good ear, she was naturally good at languages and became an excellent mimic. She enjoyed drawing and reading, and her writing was fluent, characterised by strong slanting letters formed with a broad nib. Whether she learnt basic arithmetic at school or in the shops, she could add columns of figures quickly and accurately. She was born with a natural sense of style and always made the best of herself. A bit of lace here or a ribbon there, easy to come by if your parents run the best drapers in town, made her hair and dresses stand out from the ordinary. Although she was tiny for her age, as she grew up, Paula filled a much larger space. In contrast to her quiet sister, Selma, Paula was outgoing and flamboyant; she positively relished an audience. Whilst Selma was patient and enjoyed detailed work, Paula applied herself with ferocious energy.

The elder brothers were already in Vienna; Alfred, studying architecture at Vienna University with Ernst studying engineering. The boys also made sure to find time to enjoy the many theatres, vaudeville, and bars the vibrant city had to offer. Everyone gravitated towards this capital of a vast empire.

In Brno, the family lived in the spacious apartment spread over three floors above the shop. The kitchen and living rooms were on the first floor with the formal dining room and adjacent living room overlooking the square. These rooms had impressively high ceilings and their wooden parquet floors were covered in richly patterned Persian carpets. The rooms at the front of the house were joined by tall interconnecting wooden doors. The dining room, with its large table, was the hub of the home as this was where the family ate. Meals were particularly jolly when Alfred and Ernst returned from Vienna for high days and holidays. Everyone talked at once, apparently, not listening to one another. On the second floor, Bertha and Bernard's bedroom also overlooked the square. The girls were in rooms close to their parents whilst, when they were home, the boys slept in small rooms at the top of the house.

At home, the family spoke German with a little Yiddish, Czech was reserved for servants and the market. Closely aligned to the Hapsburg Empire and Vienna until 1918, German was the dominant language in Brno and wider Moravia. Performances at the Reduta and other theatres were in German. The closing days of the empire were a riot of languages; the upper classes spoke French and haut Deutsch (High German) along with a little locally useful Czech, Hungarian, or Polish and associated regional dialects. Depending on location, peasants spoke a Moravian regional patois, Yiddish, or a combination of dialects. By the time Paula left school at fourteen, she could speak and write excellent German, spoke French with a Parisian accent, along with some Czech (though in later years, she likened speaking Czech to a throat infection) and a little Yiddish. She had an uncanny knack of matching the accent of the person she was speaking to; haut Deutsch for a duchess, Czech dialect for a servant.

Paula Ticho at fourteen years of age, Brno.

Pupils left the district school when they were fourteen. Most started work in local textile factories, whilst others became apprenticed to a recognised trade. Boys who were either clever or whose parents could afford it, went to the gymnasium (grammar school) until they were eighteen. Girls normally left school at fourteen to become domestic staff or factory workers. Paula was expected to help in the home and the shops and in due course, to find a suitable husband. She made her impatience with cooking and cleaning very clear.

Paula's elder sister, Selma, as a young woman in Brno.

Paula could be so charming when she wanted her own way, whether it was to do something she liked or not to do something she disliked. Rather than spend time on mundane domestic chores, Paula was very happy to work in the shops, making eye-catching displays in the windows and on the counters.

She learnt about fabrics and quickly mastered the huge Singer sewing machine, powered by a single large treadle that needed a steady rhythm to produce even stitching. She quickly acquired the knack of it and became an excellent seamstress. Working in the shop taught Paula the importance of maintaining accurate records and she began her lifetime habit of keeping ledgers in large, hardbacked, ruled notebooks. More importantly, she recognised the importance of presentation. It soon became clear that she enjoyed talking to customers, helping them to find what they wanted to buy.

Bernard quickly noticed his daughter's knack of spotting things that would appeal to customers and that would sell well. Paula began to accompany him on his trips to Vienna and Prague. He enjoyed her company as she was always lively, often mimicking other passengers on the train.

Cosmopolitan city of culture

When Emperor Franz-Joseph opened the Ringstrasse in May 1865, he had replaced the city's medieval walls with magnificent buildings to create a great city that rivalled Paris. The ornate buildings, built in classical style with multiple stories, were designed to give an illusion of height and embellished with pilasters, friezes and occasional caryatids. Buildings in Vienna are a bit like their famous whipped cream 'schlagobers', light and frothy. In place of the austere city walls, the Ringstrasse became a series of great public buildings interspersed with formal gardens and the area was further augmented when great families built their palaces along the Ring, the Ringstrassenpalais. Vienna was a city to promenade and to be seen and admired, whether in the ornate chambers of the opera house or the many theatres dotted round the city or wandering in one of the formal gardens scattered through the city. Fashionable women, aware of the latest styles from Paris, dressed to perfection and Paula wanted to join them. By comparison, Brno, although only a few hours away by train, seemed a provincial backwater.

Capital of a great empire, Vienna was a city of culture and trade that attracted visitors from all over the world. At the turn of the century, Vienna was a cosmopolitan city, reliant on imports from across its empire to feed its inhabitants and sustain the high living standards that many of the wealthy enjoyed. The city was liberal and the arts flourished, supported by patronage from the emperor and many wealthy families. Several of the great banking families were responsible for the construction of wonderful palaces: the Rothschilds, Ephrussis and the Bloch-Bauers and were also patrons of the 'Fin-de-Siècle Vienna' supporting literature, music, art and architecture. They financed the 'Secession', famed for promoting Klimt and Mahler, the director of the Opera House, both examples of how Jews had become part of Austrian society. Members of this rich Jewish society were assimilated to the extent that many thought of themselves as Austrian first and Jewish second.

Paula aged seventeen. Brno, 1906.

Young love

Of course, Paula soon met a young man who rapidly fell in love with her and she returned the sentiment. Oskar was the middle child of Leopold and Marie Stössler's seven children. Like his father, Oskar was born in Neu-Rausnitz, a small town about twenty kilometres east of Brno, whilst his mother was born in Vienna. Like Boskovice, the Jewish ghetto in Neu-Rausnitz was established during the mid-fifteenth century after Jews had been expelled from royal cities. In the mid-nineteenth century, half of the population of two and a half thousand were Jewish. The community was autonomous with its own synagogue and school. The family must have been religious as Leopold's grave in Vienna noted that he was chief cantor and an honorary citizen of Neu-Rausnitz. Leopold died in 1920, aged eighty-three years-of-age.

The two families must have been very different as Oskar's parents would have been highly observant, attending synagogue regularly where Leopold led the services and they must have adhered to the strict rules of a kosher diet at home. Oskar would have received a formal education at the ghetto's Jewish school. In contrast, Paula's family were Jews who attended the synagogue regularly but did not maintain all the traditional aspects of the faith. While they may not have maintained all the strict kosher rules of Orthodox Jews, the household did not eat pork. They were assimilated into society. Whilst the Stösslers were traditional Orthodox Jews, the Tichos were active members of the Jewish community but they were not excessively observant. Leopold was a respected pillar of his community in a small town whilst the Tichos were successful drapers in Brno, the capital of Moravia.

Oskar was captivated by Paula's beauty and her vivacity. If Bernard had reservations about Oskar, his misgivings were quickly dispelled by Paula. In any case, Bernard had been in the habit of agreeing with Paula since she was about twelve. If there was a disparity between the two families, Paula didn't care. Oskar was attentive, handsome and charming and he would take her to live in Vienna. If Leopold and Marie had reservations about the match, Oskar was in love and regrettably, had not cared to follow their advice for many years.

During his strict Orthodox upbringing, Oskar had rebelled; hours of Hebrew class had not appealed to him as he had neither the interest nor the patience to study. Oskar escaped to Vienna and found work there as a minor clerk. His leisure time was generally spent in bars and in the company of pretty women with the result that he was handsome and charming but shallow. He was thirty when he married eighteen-year-old Paula. He had already spent half his life living in Vienna and surely must have appeared highly sophisticated to his young bride.

The wedding ceremony in the central synagogue was traditional: the couple stood under a canopy known as a huppa. Leopold led the chant. Paula walked round Oskar five times before the rabbi recited the seven blessings. Bernard provided a lavish celebration, along with a generous dowry, enough to set the young couple up in comfort in an apartment in Vienna. Paula shone, her huge smile lighting up the room as she and Erich danced. Their honeymoon was a brief trip to one of the Austrian lakes.

Trouble sets in rapidly

Undoubtedly for Paula, the move to Vienna was a significant part of Oskar's attraction, but the marriage soon experienced problems. They lived in a tiny apartment in the Vienna suburbs, with little furniture and only very basic amenities, as Oskar appeared unable to afford better. Used to spending money as he liked, Paula's dowry dwindled rapidly. Oskar, pleased to be seen with a beautiful younger woman on his arm, spent the money intended to furnish their apartment on fashionable clothes for himself and entertainment. Paula quickly became pregnant. She hated being fat and ungainly, knew little of what to expect from her confinement and was afraid of pain and of losing her tiny waist. Confined to dingy surroundings, with few shopping trips or visits to the cinema, Paula complained constantly. In turn, Oskar returned later each evening. On the brief occasions they were together, they argued.

A baby is born

Paula and Oskar's son, Erich, was born in an unexceptional nursing home in Pater Street, in Vienna's second district, Leopoldstadt, the Jewish quarter, effectively an island between the Danube and the Donaukanal. After a week, Paula and the baby returned to isolation in the drab apartment. Her mother sent layette (baby clothes) and bedding for her grandson. Tired and lonely, Paula complained or asked for money every time she saw Oskar. Erich was only a few months old when her doctor shyly indicated that to avoid infection, she should restrain from intimate contact with her husband. To make matters worse, one night, Oskar walked past Paula's bedroom door to visit the young maid's room at the end of the corridor. Hardly waiting to pack, with baby Erich in her arms, Paula took a taxi to the station and the train back to her family in Brno.

Paula was only twenty when she returned to Brno with her baby son Erich. In just a couple of years, she had evolved from an eye-catching, headstrong girl into a beautiful young woman. Her parents were kind and tried to hide their disapproval of both the marriage and her exit from it. They could not understand the situation. Paula was too proud to tell her mother how her husband had caught gonorrhoea during one of his many liaisons. The Viennese court awarded Paula a divorce in 1914. She was restless as Brno's provincial small-town attitudes were stifling; she had no interest in domesticity and found a clinging toddler an imposition on her freedom.

Chapter 2

Vienna: Capital of a Great Empire

Mesmerised by the Kino

As soon as she was old enough to go to the cinema, Paula was fascinated by it. She always enjoyed the travelling cinema when it came to Brno and rapidly became a regular patron of the first permanent cinema in Brno, the Centrál, when it opened in 1907. She found the whole experience mesmerising, from being conducted to her red plush seat by the smartly uniformed usher with a torch with its beam shaded to prevent disturbing other customers, to the hushed anticipation as the pianist began the accompaniment to the film itself. Once she started travelling to Vienna, there was the Lichtspieltheater, the first cinema in Austria, which had opened in 1902, and many other cinemas to visit.

She visited the Centrál so frequently that she was noticed by directors of the budding Czech film industry, and as a result, she was invited to take a screen test. This caused her a great deal of fuss: what should she wear? How should her hair be arranged? She drove her mother, sisters and maids crazy as whatever they did, nothing was good enough or right. She did not want to appear like a naive village girl in front of the sophisticated men from the cinema. Nor did she want to look like a street girl! Should she wear fur, lace, velvet or brocade? Dresses were tried, hastily thrown off and discarded. As the pile of rejected garments grew, Paula's temper increased exponentially. Her family did not understand the pressure she was under. She thought they were all stupid not to see what an opportunity she was being offered. It would be more than a pity not to make every effort to look her best. Finally, probably just to restore peace and to save the maids further ironing, Paula was permitted to borrow her mother's pearls, fur wrap and the cream silk blouse with collar and cuffs made of beautiful hand-made lace. At least the maid then knew what would need ironing for the great day.

It was bright and clear when Paula looked out over the Krautmarkt. Too nervous to eat a good breakfast, she dunked bread in hot chocolate before excusing herself to prepare for the screen test. A little lace was needed for her hair; could one of them just run down to the shop and collect some suitable ribbon or lace to make a bow? A dab of her mother's rouge to highlight her cheekbones, perhaps a little lipstick?

The tests were successful and the directors invited Paula to take a minor role in a film they were planning, but her father forbade it as, in his view, films were not a proper or suitable career for his daughter. No doubt, life in the Krautmarkt apartment was difficult for everyone until Paula got over her disappointment.

The family buys a cinema

Stuck in Brno with a small child and her life stretching before her, Paula realized what she wanted to do with the rest of her life; she would return to Vienna and buy a cinema. Unfortunately, she had no money, nor did she know anything about buying, let alone running a cinema; but that was what she had definitely decided to do. Paula knew her own mind and was quick to act once her decision was made. She knew how to use her beauty and how to charm her father. She was determined to persuade him to buy a cinema and Bernard was used to doing what Paula wanted. Helped by her architect brother, Alfred, she produced a business plan. Times were good for the Tichos, the shops were doing well as the town continued to expand and demand for clothes, fabrics and haberdashery made them particularly profitable. Eventually, an agreement was reached. The family would buy a cinema; Paula and her sister, Selma, would move to Vienna to run it. Selma would work in the box office and manage the accounts, as well as acting as a discreet chaperone. For some time, Paula's son Erich remained in Brno and was cared for by his grandmother.

One of the family stories that took me a long time to understand was the one in which my great grandfather Bernard sold a shop but only realized enough cash to buy a pair of shoes!

Bernard and Bertha sold one of the shops, possibly because it was becoming too much to manage as they were getting older, or because they needed to release capital in order to buy the cinema. They followed the popular advice of the time to be patriotic and buy government bonds. However, their value was eroded by inflation. The Great War ended in November 1918 and one of the consequences of the Treaty of Versailles was that the Central Powers were forced to pay reparations for the war. Germany left the international gold standard which, in turn, led to hyper-inflation. The economies across middle Europe were so closely intertwined, that rampant inflation spread across Austria and Czechoslovakia. Paper money was reprinted at ever increasing values, as banknotes lost their value; there were even photographs of piles of valueless banknotes, wheelbarrows were needed to transport them, banknotes were even used as wallpaper. The 'shop to shoes' story was explained, inflation had eroded the value of the capital realized from the sale of the shop leaving only enough to pay for a pair of shoes. Life really was difficult for everyone.

The Palast Kino
The building that housed the Grand Palace Cinema, Josefstädter Straße 43 – 45, was designed and built in 1913 by the architects Ludwig Sommerlatte & Johann Marschall. It is a pretty building with the central façade set back between two pillars that are topped with small domes. Wrought iron railings run between the pillars creating small balconies. On the upper floors, stone garlands incorporating clown-faced gargoyles, swags and bowls of fruit run under the windows between the two pillars. Behind the façade, the complex, like many similar buildings in Vienna, are a series of blocks each containing several individual flats, built around an open courtyard with a single entry from the street. Apartment blocks came with a concierge who monitored the comings and goings of the occupants and their visitors; it was their business to know what was happening inside every apartment.

As was usual in Vienna at the time, the flats were let for moderate rents. Sommerlatte and Marschall appear to have owned this development as they remained the landlord. Rents were strictly controlled in Vienna in the 1920s and 1930s. Few individuals owned their homes and even opulent flats were rented cheaply on long leases. As inflation continued to erode the value of the currency, rents became cheaper. The first recorded owner of the cinema, Katharina Fleischmann, lived in a flat in one of the blocks behind the cinema. The original French name, Palace Grand Kinotheater, was replaced by Palast Kino for patriotic reasons in 1914. Documents from the Vienna city archives and cinema museum show that: Bernard and Bertha Ticho bought the Palace Grand Kinotheater for two hundred gold kroner in 1915. At the time, it was the second largest cinema in Vienna and could accommodate seven hundred and six people in the main hall and circle above. It was extended in 1934, creating a second balcony, increasing the capacity to seven hundred and eighty-eight.

The building above the cinema in Josefstädter Straße with wrought iron balconies and figurative stone carvings.

Paula chose the films, agreed the accompanying music with the pianist, and was very much the public face of the cinema. She had an instinctive knack of understanding what films her clients wanted to see and would enjoy, as well as charming film company agents to let her show them. Selma kept the business running by her meticulous management of routine matters, which were of course, far too mundane for Paula to notice. Quiet Selma managed the finances, staff and practical matters. They all worked hard and the cinema became a success; often it was the first to screen a title that would then become successful elsewhere in Vienna. The whole family contributed to the cinema: Alfred, an architect, designed the foyer and sweet shop and in 1934, expanded the balcony to add an extra eighty-two seats to the overall capacity of the cinema.

Interior: the patrons sat facing the curtained silver screen.

Over time, his flair for interior design and love of the simple functionality of Bauhaus design introduced a sparse elegance throughout the cinema. Alfred's expertise became recognised more widely and he began to work as an interior designer for other clients.

The Palast Kino was run by the two women, and it was a success. Paula's passion, her uncanny ability to choose films that people wanted to see and her ability to turn every visit for the cinema going public into an enjoyable experience rapidly made the Palast Kino a very successful business. Again, documents from the city archives show that Bernard died in 1919 and was replaced by Bertha as the owner. In turn, Paula's sister Selma became the managing director when her mother died in 1924. The cinema is then shown as being owned by the Ticho family.

The balcony and additional seating Alfred installed. The bright light, top centre, is from the projection box.

Austria struggled to rebuild its economy following the ravages of influenza and the Great War. The virus that caused the Spanish flu pandemic between January 1918 and December 1920 spread rapidly between soldiers on the trenches in France and spread to their families when they returned to their native towns and villages as the war ended. Caused by an influenza virus, closely related to the one that caused Bird flu in the 1990s and 2000s and not unlike the coronavirus, SARS-CoV-2, which caused the 2020 Covid-19 pandemic. Spanish flu eventually spread across the globe, infecting about twenty-five per cent of the world's population, with mortality rates between three to five per cent; there were probably between forty to fifty million deaths overall. In his fascinating book, *Contagion and Chaos*, Andrew Price-Smith explored the possibility that the Spanish flu pandemic originated in Austria rather than, as is normally assumed, France. He argues that as an unknown virus swept across Austria in the spring of 1917 and the pattern of infections differed from that seen in other countries; this might have been caused by an early outbreak of the virus. Spanish flu probably shortened the course of the Great War as mortality was particularly high in Germany and Austria where the population was already weak. The Austrian population was starving, living conditions were insanitary and overcrowded. Hospitals were already full of war casualties, overcrowded and unable to maintain hygiene. Antibiotics had not been discovered, intensive care and ventilators were still to be invented. Many were sick and did not recover.

Alfred Ticho, (Paula's brother). Vienna, 1936.

As the cinema prospered, Paula's confidence grew and she blossomed accordingly. Voluptuous, tiny but flamboyant, Paula enjoyed the attention she attracted as the public face of Palast Kino. She enjoyed clothes, followed the fashion and bought well. Every evening, she would greet customers as they arrived at the cinema dressed in full evening dress. Paula loved living in Vienna; she enjoyed society, she knew she was unique; few women ran their own business in the 1920s. Lively and beautiful, she was flattered by male attention and had several affairs. Paula may have been small but she had a huge capacity for drinking Tokaji, the sweet wine from Hungary. Several gentlemen were left in a stupor and had to be carried out during the private dinners she hosted; they had perhaps hoped for more from these occasions. Not troubling to be discreet, her gentlemen friends would visit the flat in Gonzagagasse where she now lived with Erich and a maid. With the curiosity of a teenager, Erich may have watched his mother with her male friends through the keyhole. He was old enough to be disturbed by these visitations and become increasingly unsettled. At the turn of twentieth century, Vienna was the birthplace of Freud and psychoanalysis. Unfortunately, not knowing any better, Paula sent Erich, not to Freud but to a conservative critic of psychoanalysis.

Selma (Paula's sister) in front of the Palast Kino, 1937. The display shows photographs from the films showing that week.

Gestapo HQ

Paula, Erich and a young maid, lived in a flat at 1, Gonzagagasse 7, close to the Danube Canal and the old Jewish quarter at Leopoldstadt. Gonzagagasse is made up of tall, five-story blocks of apartment buildings. Shops are at street level. The buildings are well proportioned, some with ornate decorations. The street is bisected by a small park that today has a well-equipped playground for small children. The buildings beyond the park are relatively recent, replacing ones damaged by allied bombs during the 1940s. The brutalist concrete block that now stands on the site of Paula's apartment proudly calls itself a residential house of the community 1959 to 1960. Gonzagagasse runs into Morzinplatz which is now a long rectangle of grass and paths alongside the tram lines that run along the bank of the Danube. The Hotel Metropole was a magnificent building, designed by Schumann and Tischler, built for the 1873 Vienna World Exhibition. Photographs show a large, imposing building close to the riverbank, richly decorated with Corinthian columns and caryatids. Following the Anschluss in March 1938, it was confiscated by the Gestapo and became their Vienna headquarters, the largest Gestapo headquarters outside Berlin. Terrified prisoners were taken to the basement jail directly from the street, using the Salztorgasse entrance. Prisoners were beaten and tortured, often for weeks, to extract confessions. Many were sent straight from the Gestapo headquarters to one of the concentration camps to work as slave labour or to the gas chamber. A few returned to their families, badly beaten, often broken by the torture they had received; others committed suicide rather than face further abuse. In time, the headquarters also become the central collection point for Jews before they were deported to concentration camps. Allied bombing damaged the building and it was finally destroyed around 1940 by bombs and the fire they caused. The surviving ruins of the hotel were torn down to eliminate any memory of the building. Alone, above a few concrete steps, on the edge of this empty piece of lawn, is a monument, made from granite mined from the Mauthausen concentration camp.

Carved into it are these words, translated into English:

*Here stood the House of the Gestapo. To those who believed
in Austria it was hell. To many it was the gates to death. It
sank into ruins just like the 'Thousand Year Reich'. But Austria
was resurrected and with her our dead, the immortal victims.*

A row of Stolperstein, each with the name of someone who
was arrested and killed, is set into the pavement in front of the
memorial. Stolperstein began as an experimental art project in
Germany when the first Stolperstein were installed in the
pavement outside Cologne City Hall in December 1992. A
Stolperstein, literally a stumbling block, is a brass plate, the size
of a granite steppingstone, engraved with the name and dates of
a victim of Nazi or other persecution, set into the pavement at the
last place a victim lived freely. This is usually the home where
they were taken, collected or arrested. The art project that Gunter
Demnig began has now spread across many countries. In 2018,
there were over seventy thousand Stolperstein, making them
globally the largest disseminated memorial.

Just outside the Jewish quarter, Gonzagagasse was
convenient for the cinema as Paula could easily take a tram to the
Ringstraße . She would alight at the stop outside the Burgtheater,
the imposing Baroque building, home of the Austrian National
Theatre, which stands opposite the town hall, the Rathaus. Once
she had crossed the Ringstraße, it was then a pleasant walk
through the Rathaus gardens before finally reaching Josefstädter
Straße. On wet days, she probably took a second tram up
Josefstädter Straße. Some mornings, Paula would stop at one of
the many Viennese coffee houses. Sometimes, she would take tea
in a café before going to the cinema for the evening performance.

Cafés were more than a place to simply sit and have coffee
and a cake. They were communities; you greeted those you knew
formally and were introduced to others; gossip was exchanged
and business was conducted in civilised surroundings. While
some worked alone at the small tables, others talked business and
struck deals. Importance was placed on manners, greeting
acquaintances and friends formally; raising hats, kissing ladies'
hands, and bowing to other gentlemen was expected.
Appearances were very important in 1930s Vienna. Café
Landtmann, possibly the finest coffee house in Vienna, opened in
1873 and was refurbished splendidly by Ernst Meller in 1929.

Patrons had the choice of small tables and straight, dark wooden chairs in the centre of the magnificent room or in a private padded banquette ranked along the wall; there was a space for everyone. As it was only round the corner from the Burgtheater tram stop, it became Paula's favourite coffee house. The clientele was glittering and international: Freud, politicians, actors, musicians and luminaries from the cinema were among the regular customers. The famous film director, Otto Preminger, visited regularly and it is probable that Paula first became acquainted with him there.

Once a week, she would meet her fellow cinema owners when they would select the films that each cinema would be showing during the following week. Unusually, the Palast Kino changed films twice a week. Visits to the Sascha studios in Siebensterngasse 31 to preview new films and screenings were common. These events were festive; the studios created coffee houses or Parisian dance hall scenes where actors, dressed as waiters, would serve refreshments. This gave Paula the chance to talk to other cinema proprietors and to meet the film makers. Sometimes, film distributors organized screenings for cinema owners and critics in specially selected cinemas across Vienna.

The Palast Kino was often the first to show the most successful films. Films were in black and white, short and silent. A typical showing would have a few short films and a newsreel, each accompanied by the pianist playing popular tunes. Paula would work with the accompanist to choose the music that would be suitable for each of the films at the start of the week. There would be three or four showings per day.

As well as running a successful business, Paula was a beautiful young woman, a stylish extrovert who dominated a room. She had many admirers and adored their attention. Vienna is famous for charm and manners that were, and to a large extent still are, formal. On meeting and departure, a man would bow, take the woman's hand, and kiss the back of it while saying, "Kiss your hand, dear lady." Fresh flowers would be sent as corsages to be worn at a ball, or as a thank you following an entertainment. Men were careful to walk by the kerb to shield women from mud and other detritus thrown up from the street by passing carriages. Before the Great War, motor vehicles were rare, horses pulled carts, trams and carriages. Roads and pavements were inevitably dirty. A few older men might still wear a sword or sabre strapped to their right hip, a reason for them to be careful when walking. Doors were opened for women assiduously. Most men would wait to allow another male through a doorway before passing through it themselves, nodding as a mark of respect. Manners were such an essential part of Viennese culture; they were deeply ingrained at an early age.

The traditional interior of Café Landtmann with neat tables and chairs remained almost unchanged in 2019.

Leaving Selma in charge of the cinema, Paula would make brief visits to spas to swim and socialize or to go to Brno to visit her aging parents. Travel from Vienna was easy as an extensive train network had developed across the Austro-Hungarian Empire in the nineteenth century. She enjoyed the relative informality of the small spa towns. Although men exchanged their dark suits for pale linen ones and Panama hats replaced Hombergs, they always wore polished shoes and ties and manners remained essential.

Paula wearing a daring, short-skirted flapper dress
at a spar in Vöslan in 1921

Public transport began in Vienna in 1883 with the introduction of horse-drawn trams and steam-powered trams that ran from Hietzing at the western end of the city to Mödling at the southern end of the city. Both gave access to the Vienna Woods and alpine meadows beyond. Electric trams were introduced in 1899 and the network was well developed by the early twentieth century. The Austrian Film Archive has made some fascinating videos available, one taken from the front of a tram as it moved round Vienna in 1906.

Horse-drawn vehicles - carriages, drays, carts, trams - shared the noisy and chaotic roads with electric trams, and pedestrians, while men repaired the cobbles and others collected waste, presumably from horses. Men wore long, dark coats and hats, which they raised as they passed friends and acquaintances, holding a walking stick or umbrella in their other hand. Women also wore long, dark coats or long skirts with shorter coats and huge hats. They appeared to be Edwardian ladies. Many carried an umbrella or parasol. The second video shows the Vienna streets between 1920 and 1930. There were now more cars than horses but the roads were still relatively quiet. Men still wore long dark coats and hats, carried walking sticks, or umbrellas and walked briskly whilst the women wore much shorter skirts, a few in pale colours and many of their hats were cloche style rather than the decorated dinner plates of twenty years earlier.

The journey to the Vienna Woods and outlying villages, like Grinzing, was a simple twenty-minute tram ride. At weekends, particularly when the weather was warm, people would flock to the countryside. Walking and swimming were popular, as was visiting the Heuringer, outdoor bars selling cheap local wines from grapes grown on the hills above the village. People sat and chatted and, in the evening, local musicians would play and some couples danced. Others walked to the top of the hills to admire the views of Vienna nestling in the valley below. A tram that operated between Vienna and Bratislava even made day trips possible.

Paula, posing in something fluffy.

Chapter 3

Gura Humorului: A Rising Star

Another ghetto and a spa

Gura Humorului in Bukovina province was a beautiful, small town set in a valley between two rivers, the Moldova and the Humor, with the Carpathian Mountains as a backdrop. Located in the extreme southeast of the empire, in the middle of central Europe, it was a traditional market town. The economy was based on timber from the richly forested foothills of the Eastern Carpathians surrounding the town. Wood was always needed at a time when towns and railway networks were expanding rapidly. Whilst Gura Humorului sits at the confluence of rivers with forests rising steeply on either side, below the town, the Moldova valley widens creating flat, fertile land that is easily cultivated.

Bukovina was annexed by the Austro-Hungarian Empire in 1774 to create an important trade route between Galicia and Transylvania. Bukovina became Romanian after the First World War and was split between Romania and Ukraine following the Second World War. On the route that connected Vienna with Chisinau and Odesa in Russia, Gura Humorului prospered. To meet the empire's ever-expanding need for wood, both for building and to fuel the steam engines that increasingly powered factories, road and rail networks were built into the forests of middle Europe. In 1889, a rail service, part of the two hundred and twenty-eight kilometres of lines built by the Orthodox church to expand logging began serving Gura Humorului. Although traditionally, some timber was transported by floating it down rivers, the beech trees that grew abundantly in the area produced a dense trunk which was too heavy to float and could only be moved by road or rail. The arrival of the railway transformed the economy. Given its picturesque location and favourable microclimate, Gura Humorului also became a popular summer resort and spa, particularly for travellers from Eastern Europe.

As in Brno, Jews were not allowed to live in Gura Humorului before 1835 when the law was relaxed and they were allowed to settle in towns. The town was small, with a population of two hundred families, about seven hundred individuals, living in two hundred simple timber buildings. There were only five Jewish families. Thirty years later, the town had expanded rapidly and become a regional centre so that the census also included the inhabitants of outlying villages. The 1867 census recorded eight hundred Jews, who contributed approximately thirty per cent of the two and a half thousand inhabitants. The Jewish community was made up of around thirty extended Orthodox families who observed the traditional rights and ceremonies. Many were manual labourers, craftsmen working with local wood, some were itinerant traders, selling wares from village to village, whilst a few prospered and set-up timber mills. If you replace the flat acres of arable fields with wooded hills, village life was probably similar to that of *Tevye the Dairyman*, Sholem Aleichem's stories that were possibly the first Yiddish writing about life in Eastern Europe and were later retold in the popular film, *Fiddler on the Roof.*

Initially, timber mills were small, powered by water from the rivers. Then, as industrial processes spread, large steam-powered mills that could process tons of timber were built. Three families, the Kleinbergs, Kahns and Schiebers became prominent towards the end of the nineteenth century. The first records of birth and death in the town were made by Schulem Schieber from 1856. Like the Tichos in Brno, who made their living from varied aspects of the textile industry, the extended Schieber family made good livings from timber. Hermann Schieber's father, Chaim, shared ownership of a mill with his brother Berl Schieber. Although the records are sketchy, Chaim and Berl had sufficient finances to contribute towards rebuilding the local synagogue following a fire in 1899. Their donation must have been significant, as the synagogue is named Schiebershe, after the family. At one stage, the brothers were publicans as they held the alcohol license for the town. Else Reisner, a cousin of Hermann's, left a vivid description of her happy childhood in Guru Humorlui in an oral history, deposited in the US Holocaust Memorial Collection. She noted that whilst her grandparents were Orthodox, her parents, Fanny and Freda Askenazi were not, as they had moved away from the strict observance of Jewish law.

Else said her parents were first cousins, so it is likely her husband was Berl's son Freidrich.

Else described Guru Homorlui as being in the Crown Lands. Clearly, she thought her family were very much part of the empire. Her parents moved to Vienna when she was five, to give her older sister the opportunity of gaining a better school education, whilst her grandparents remained in Guru Homorlui. Chaim also encouraged his boys to get a good education and professional qualifications. Chaim's family moved to Vienna in the early 1900s when Hermann and his siblings became students at the university. Chaim remained in the timber trade, opening sawmills in woods on the outskirts of the city. Following the Russian invasion of Bukovina during the First World War, Else's grandparents fled to Vienna as impoverished refugees. Penniless, they moved into Fanny and Freda's small apartment.

Hermann qualified as a Doctor of Jurisprudence in 1913 and became Dr Schieber. However, war broke out the following year shortly after he had started his law practice. He was called up by the army and served as a captain. Unusually for a Jew, he was awarded the Iron Cross. If he was troubled by memories of the trenches, he did not share the horrors he had seen with those around him. Hermann was a very private person; people sitting close by would have no idea what he was thinking. In company, he was always courteous, sitting amiably, without contributing much to the conversations going on around him, and always leaving a good impression on his departure. His brother, Josef, did well in the war and was made a member of the Frans Josef Bande, which seems to be similar to the British award of a knighthood.

Hermann was forty when the war ended and then he had to rebuild his practice almost from scratch. He took a lease on a large apartment at 3 Schreyvogelgasse on the corner of the prestigious Universitätsring. Viennese rents were strictly controlled and became cheaper as inflation soared. Hermann used the flat as both a home and an office where he met clients, the grandeur of the building adding to his status. His career developed quickly and soon he was working on major cases for the Government as a Judge Advocate with all the attendant prestige.

A respectful, growing love

After a succession of brief, unsatisfactory affairs, Paula met this young lawyer who was rising rapidly through the ranks of his profession. Paula and Hermann were introduced to one another by mutual friends in the German spar town of Baden-Baden. There was an instant spark, a mutual attraction, and in addition, they each understood and clearly respected the other's profession.

This picture of Hermann was possibly taken to mark his qualification as Doctor of Jurisprudence in 1913.

Paula and Hermann's courtship was of two adults that blossomed into love. Their time together was, of necessity, limited. Whenever possible, they met in Baden-Baden. Hermann's behaviour towards Paula was entirely proper; he took her to good restaurants, to the opera, and dancing at select nightclubs. He treated her with respect and bought her roses and other pretty things. Their relationship developed slowly, they became lovers and went on holiday together. Inevitably, Paula became pregnant and without telling Hermann, she arranged to have an abortion. If Hermann was to ask her to marry him, it was because he wanted to; not because marriage would have been the honourable solution to the pregnancy. Eventually, he took her to meet his family and proposed. Paula charmed both of his parents. Chaim was impressed by her lively business sense and his stepmother was delighted to see Paula enjoying the many cakes that had been made for her benefit.

Hermann in military uniform, 1917.

The only objection to the match was Hermann's family name, Schieber, which had multiple unfortunate slang connotations. During the Great War, it meant 'pusher' which described the many black-market racketeers selling everything from basic food and clothes to luxuries. Paula was delighted to be asked to marry Hermann but she said she could not possibly marry a man called 'Spiv'! In March 1920, Hermann changed the family name to Sieber, as did his brothers and sisters.

In June 1920, Paula became Frau Dr Sieber when they were married in the Central Synagogue.

The Sieber/Schieber family. (Left to Right) Front row: Fanny, Adele, Mitzi, Chaim, Rosa. Back row Manu, Hermann, Senig. Vienna, June 1925.

A perfect honeymoon

Their honeymoon hotel in Venice was on the Grand Canal. A sixteenth century villa decorated with frescos, ornate mouldings, crystal chandeliers and plenty of gold leaf with a spectacular view of other beautiful villas across the Canal. Unusually, there were gardens with shaded paths and quiet places to sit. The ballroom was huge and ornate. Paula glowed with happiness; her diamonds glittered as they danced under the chandeliers. After a few days, they retreated to the recently opened Des Bains Hotel, another huge and ornate establishment that, as it was slightly further from the centre, was cooler during the day and had several swimming pools. Hermann took great pleasure in watching Paula swim. Taught to swim by her brothers, she was naturally a strong swimmer as her short, broad body was ideally suited to breaststroke. They spent many happy and relaxing hours cruising between the Venetian islands. Hermann bought her a necklace when they visited Murano, the glass island. The restrained purples and dusky greens of the hand-blown glass, offset by gold, emphasised her handsome face and eyes. After a month, they had to return to Vienna, their respective duties and the Schreyvogelgasse apartment.

Happy home for a growing family
Beethoven's house, Pasqualatis, on the only hill in Vienna, is a pretty, rather simple, baroque building on three floors with dormer windows in the roof. It is located next door to Schubert's smaller house. A sign on the ground floor makes it clear that the museum is only open at restricted times. The staff in the shop have nothing to do with the museum and so should not be disturbed. The shop sells Beethoven memorabilia, cheap tat for tourists. One side of Pasqualatis looks down on the Liebenberg-Denkmal war memorial, beyond that the Ringstraße and the university. The front looks down onto Schreyvogelgasse. The beautiful Viennese palace built by the Ephrussi family, described by Edmund de Wall, in *The Hare with Amber Eyes,* is just around the corner from Schreyvogelgasse.

I, like other members of the family when visiting Vienna, have been photographed standing by the entrance to Number 3. The huge pair of wooden doors are more than twice my height, they have carved panels with ornamental iron grilles set in at the top to let light into the hall.

Number 3 Schreyvogelgasse is an historical corner house that even has a Wikipedia entry. Built in 1880, by Ludwig Tischler in the Viennese neo-Renaissance style, it was renovated in 1994. There are five stories with a cornice along the roof that makes it look even more imposing.

The imposing wooden front doors at Number 3
Schreyvogelgasse.

Behind the carved wooden doors, the entrance hall is magnificent with neo-classical plasterwork walls with ornate architraves, pilasters and complex dentil ceiling mouldings. Swirls of plaster tracery flow from flower-filled urns. Even the steps leading to the lift are hidden behind wrought iron railings, joined by columns with matching pilasters.

At the back of the glass and mahogany lift, there is a little seat. Patterns of stylized flowers and leaves are etched onto the glass while the whole lift is encased in a froth of cast iron. The flat is on the fourth floor.

The ornate entrance hall with plaster mouldings, columns and wrought iron railings.

Turn left out of the lift and you are met with a pair of glossy wooden doors surrounded by a simple architrave. Inside, the flat was just as luxurious as the prestigious address and approach indicated. Its generous proportions, high ceilings and patterned parquet flooring were the backbone of what would become a happy home for a growing family. Three large living rooms run across the front of the apartment creating an impressive vista when all three pairs of doors were open.

Hermann had taken little trouble over furnishing the parts of the flat he used as living quarters as his needs as a bachelor were simple. He gave Paula carte blanche to furnish the flat as she wished and they spent many happy hours visiting department stores and antique shops. They chose huge Persian carpets with geometric patterns in rich reds and blues. Both liked the Biedermeier style, so they indulged in furniture with fancy carvings and curly ends. Together, they bought gilt mirrors with intricate plasterwork, chandeliers and pictures. Paula's mother sent huge stuffed eiderdowns covered in paisley-print cotton satin, bolster pillows and a couple of sets of damask table-linen, with matching napkins, very suitable gifts from a draper. Hermann's parents sent an antique wooden bookcase and a particularly fine Hamadan carpet; ideal gifts from someone in the timber trade. Their kitchen china, bought in the local street market, was the traditional Meissen Zwiebelmuster with its distinctive blue and white onion pattern.

Looking up at the intricate wrought ironwork on the lift.

In the first few months of their marriage, they delighted in their collection, adding comfiture pots each with a semi-circular hole in the lid to accommodate a silver spoon whilst the knob was formed into a small rose; the cake plates had frilly edges and ribbon plates made with an open lattice weave ceramic.

Zwiebelmuster butter dish with frilly edges and distinctive blue and white onion pattern.

Their many brothers and sisters generously gave them a new dinner service, hand-painted Meissen, along with cut crystal glasses for entertaining.

Of course, there was a vitrine, a glass cabinet, to display their treasures. The front was a door made of four narrow glass panels, separated by narrow bands of turned mahogany as were the two sides of the cabinet. The back was mirrored to allow the rear of the ornaments to be displayed back into the room. The three Meissen figurines took pride of place. Each was a delicate painted girl with flowers on their frocks, one held a basket of flowers, another a posy, whilst the third had a little brown and white dog at her feet.

There is a family story that one of Paula and Hermann's wedding gifts was a Kokoschka which Paula found so disturbing that she gave it away. Looking at Kokoschka's *Still life of Mutton and Hyacinth* in the Belvedere, I could understand why Paula might not have kept the picture. A tortoise is climbing across a skinned rabbit, there is a mouse in the foreground and a glass fish tank all displayed on a table as in a classical still life.

Hermann's law practice grew both in the number and importance of cases that he was asked to handle. He had worked on a number of cases for the government by the time he married Paula. His title had been elevated to 'Juris'. Unusually for a Jew, he often acted for the government on cases of national importance. To accommodate the family, and possibly more importantly, to retain privacy for both clients and family, Hermann took an extra couple of rooms in the adjoining flat adjacent to their living room. A doorway was constructed between the living room and the rooms that became his office. Whilst his journey to work was short, it did at least, provide some separation between home and work.

A new arrival

When they returned from the honeymoon, Erich joined them along with Seffi, a woman from the Tyrol, who would take care of the family and the flat. Hermann's original apartment became the family home. They settled into their new life happily. Soon, Paula was gloriously pregnant. Unlike her previous experience, this time, pregnancy suited her, enhancing her voluptuous figure, and making her skin glow with happiness. Hermann was tender, enraptured by the obvious changes to the body he loved. Paula continued to work in the cinema, choosing films and music, and was charming to staff and customers alike. Selma continued to sell tickets and order the coal, working from her tiny glass-fronted booth by the front door that was both her office and the hub of the business. Increasingly, Paula would spend her afternoons resting back at the apartment. Erich often arrived to escort his mother home on his way back from school. The school day may have been short but there was plenty of homework Erich should have been doing in the afternoon. Erich was already scared by the pregnancy, worried by the erosion of their former intimacy and a little jealous of his stepfather. During his vacations, an increasingly unhappy Erich could only watch as his mother became more wrapped up in her marriage and the child developing inside her. Erich spent less and less time at the apartment, preferring to spend time with school friends, whose tolerant parents would invite him to accompany them on vacation. Peter was born in June 1921, a year after the wedding.

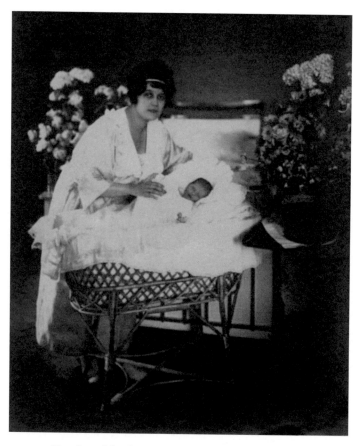

Paula with the new-born Peter in his crib
surrounded by flowers. Vienna, June 1921.

Hermann's first child was delivered in a luxurious nursing home in the countryside not far from the city. For Paula, this was so very different from Erich's birth in Prater Street. Photographs show the well-wrapped baby in a pretty crib with a radiant Paula, in masses of fine cotton lace, surrounded by huge floral arrangements.

The boy was to be called Peter Georg Sieber. The proud father was dispatched to the registrar's office, and he returned with the birth certificate. In his excitement, Hermann had forgotten to register the middle name; Paula was furious. The baby remained Peter Sieber as Hermann refused to return to the office to re-register another name.

Erich Stössler holding Peter Sieber. Peter would
have been around one year old. Vienna, 1923.

Two weeks after the birth, Hermann collected his wife and son in a taxi. He had flowers delivered so that the apartment looked and smelt like a florist shop. In the saloon, there were vast containers of lilies on tables, on the bureau and on the piano. Baskets of Paula's favourite flowers, lily of the valley, filled the bedroom. As soon as his family was fit to travel, Hermann took them to Baden-Baden.

The Sieber family paraded along the walks and promenades with a nurse pushing the perambulator. Seffi had not accompanied them as she normally returned to her family for the summer. She would re-join them in Brno at the end of their vacation along with Erich who was already with his grandmother. Paula was happy in the spa. As a strong swimmer, she enjoyed the treatment pools and admiring glances from onlookers. She had always liked being noticed and now with her handsome husband and healthy baby, she certainly was, in colourful new clothes by day and positively sparkling with sequins and jewels by night. Glowing from fresh air, they probably spent more time sitting in cafes than hiking in the countryside as they were both more café habitué than Alpine walkers. Paula and Hermann enjoyed being together, with nothing more important to do than deciding how they should please themselves next. The evenings were warm and the hotels and restaurants where they ate usually had tables outside. Musicians and flower sellers moved between the tables, adroitly keeping out of the waiters' way. The pavement was warm from the sun and the air milky with summer smells.

Married Life

As was usual for the maid, Seffi's room was tucked behind the kitchen. Early in the morning, she would go and buy fresh rolls, leaving quietly without disturbing anyone. Hermann would take his simple breakfast: coffee and rolls, on his way to his office in the adjoining rooms. Paula, often late back from the cinema, would have her breakfast of bread, butter and jam with milky coffee with baby Peterl, a term used mostly by his mother, on the bed. As Peter grew, Seffi would give him sweet rolls to dip into a cup of hot chocolate to keep him occupied and let his mother sleep on.

As the family grew, their respective businesses prospered. Hermann gained new clients, his seniority and reputation growing as he was engaged on increasingly more important cases. Herr Dr Juris Sieber and Frau Dr Sieber had an excellent social life, meeting friends and colleagues in coffee houses, restaurants, theatres and private night clubs. Café Landtmann was literally around the corner from their flat. They met many people from the film world there. Paula introduced Herman to

Otto Preminger as he visited regularly for large cups of mocha coffee. It was an exciting time to be in Vienna. The arts flourished, the great Burgtheater and the Opera House were experimenting with new works and staging the classics in novel ways, as well as the many independent theatres, cabaret, and vaudeville.

Paula in a fur coat with a magnificent
white fur collar, beads and lace.

Viennese balls restarted slowly after the war. The most prestigious, the Opernredoute, was held in 1921 to raise funds for pensions for theatre staff impoverished by the war. Sascha Films took a box at the 1922 Opera Ball; Paula and Hermann were amongst the guests. Vienna State Opera House is a magnificent building with ornate ceilings, mirrors, marble staircases, balustrades and plenty of gilt. The architect may have shot himself on the opening night, when it became apparent that he had forgotten to include toilets in his grand design, but this omission had been rectified many years earlier. For the ball, the stalls seats were removed and replaced with a dance floor, identical floral swags hung from the front of every box and the entire building was decorated with flowers. Damask tablecloths, silver cutlery, and crystal glasses were laid out on tables in the boxes. The catering was on a lavish scale.

Paula in apricot tulle and ostrich feather headdress
in shades of orange and apricot.

The Sascha box was lively, champagne and Tokaji flowed. They watched as the debutantes in white gowns paraded alongside their youthful partners in white tie and tailcoats. Paula was particularly resplendent in a short, sequinned gown with a skirt made from several layers of silk tulle in shades of apricot. Her headdress was crowned by apricot and coral ostrich feathers and the whole ensemble adorned with chains of pearls and dangling bracelets. Hermann, as always, was perfectly turned out as befitted the occasion. Once the formal part of the evening was over, the couple danced together with obvious delight. The diamond ring he'd given her to commemorate little Peterl's birth sparkled brightly along with her other jewellery. Paula loved dancing, particularly with Hermann. He basked in the attention his fabulous wife attracted, secure in the knowledge that whilst she might flirt with other men, it was him she really loved.

Paula dressed to kill!

They took holidays at fashionable spa towns, visiting Baden-Baden often. Seffi and baby Peter would accompany them while Erich would stay in Vienna or visit his grandparents in Brno. Hermann, formally dressed as ever, in a dark suit and wing collar, would take a morning walk while Paula played with Peter and prepared for the day.

Paula, Peter and Erich posed by the lake at Kitzbühel at the Grand-Hotel. Paula drew an arrow on the picture by Peter.

Sitting on the same bench each day, an elderly gentleman would come and sit by him. On learning he was a lawyer, the gentleman would tell a long, convoluted story in anticipation of a legal opinion that he duly received. After five days, Hermann presented the gentleman with a bill for the advice given on the third bench to the right of the park entrance in Baden-Baden. He was not bothered further. For her thirtieth birthday, Hermann presented Paula with a small country house, their schloss, a summer castle, where the family spent happy months together.

Peter with his paternal grandmother Adele Schieber
at Baden bei Wein.

A terrible tragedy

Hermann had survived the trenches of the First World War
fighting for Austria only to be hit by a taxi driven by a drunk
driver. The car careered across the road, mounted the pavement
and hit Hermann. It took eight weeks and three days for him to
die slowly and painfully of gangrene. Peter, aged five, was taken
to visit his father in a sanatorium where he was floating in a
saline tank. Over time, parts of his leg were amputated to stem
the infection. The child was left with an image of his father more
shrunken at each visit that stayed with him throughout his life.
Hermann was forty-eight years old. They had only been married
for six years. Paula was utterly devastated and bereft but, with

her sister and Seffi, she had her sons to look after and a cinema to run.

Ironically, six weeks after Hermann's death, a parcel, embellished with the government crest arrived. It contained a scroll appointing him as Judicial Council and silver insignia on a blue ribbon (to be worn on formal occasions). It was unusual for a Jew to be awarded this government title that was only used to honour senior lawyers. Despite the belated recognition, Hermann's practice was worth little. The important government work and the work he had been doing for a bank were personal and could not be transferred to another lawyer.

Hermann Sieber. Vienna, June 1925.

A court case followed in February 1928, and the driver from the Bellcar Autotaxi Company was found guilty and sent to jail.

Following a civil case, the company was ordered to pay damages. Paula was only awarded a small amount, as she already had an income from the cinema. Peter was to receive fifty schillings a month, which would be worth about three hundred and eighty-five euros a month today, until he reached fourteen, which then would increase to seventy-five schillings a month (four hundred and twenty-five euros today) until he was able to support himself. By comparison, their maid Seffi, was paid about sixty schillings a month. As Peter was a minor, his funds were held and managed by the court. Paula had to see a judge and justify any request for funds before they were released to her.

Chapter 4

Vienna: Two Widows Meet

An unwilling student

Paula and a ten-year-old Peter. Vienna, 1931.

Studying at school was not Peter's strength as he recalled:

> There was school from eight to one in the morning, bits of homework in the afternoon, cycling in the Prater with my best friend, Fritz Pfeiffer. I belonged to a swimming club and went there two or three times a week. In winter, there was skating in the city park and looking at girls from a scared distance.

Peter was not excessively studious at school, following his interests rather than the curriculum. Paula was a busy single parent with limited formal education herself; she had not known how to advise Peter on his studies nor did she discipline her little Peterl. The interview she arranged with a boarding school had been a disaster. When asked if he enjoyed riding, Peter had been positive about bicycles but contemptuous about horses. Unfortunately for Peter, the school prided itself on an equestrian tradition. In 1932, he sat the entrance exams for the grammar school (Gymnasium), passed and was enrolled in the Handelsakademie, specialising in business studies. The school was built in 1904, only a few blocks along Josefstädter Straße from the Palast Kino. More austere than its neighbours, the Art Deco façade with panels of grey highlighted in gold, the building stood out. It was a logical choice of school for Peter who had no clear idea of what he wanted to do. Missing his father, he was attracted to the idea of following in Hermann's footsteps and becoming a lawyer. The Handelsakademie was probably the wrong school for an aspiring lawyer, as it was not a highly regarded academic Gymnasium. The Austrian education system was clearly demarcated in a hierarchical structure with the elite Gymnasium at the top, above technical schools. Although it is now the highly respected Vienna Business School, in the 1930s, the Handelsakademie gained Gymnasium status despite the curriculum including technical subjects such as typing. A high proportion of the students were Jewish, who hoped to follow the tradition of working in the family business. His friend from the flat next door in Schreyvogelgasse, Fritz Pfeiffer, already went there. It was convenient for the cinema. Unless he was with Fritz and some of his other friends, Peter usually stopped at the Palast Kino on his way home from school. He was indulged by staff, particularly Frau Strand who ran the sweet shop and usually managed to find him something to nibble from her stock. Florian

Fischer, the projectionist, was always kind to Peter, showed him how to change reels of film on the huge projector, how to use his beloved Rolleiflex (a twin lens camera introduced by the German company, Paul Franke and Reinhold in 1929) and shared his passion for photography. In the 1930s, photography was a specialist occupation.

Studio photograph of Peter at Semmering. Winter, 1927.

There were many professional photographers with studios who would take formal pictures. Mounted in stiff cream frames, people would give them to their friends as keepsakes. Paula clearly frequented a couple of studios as a number of these pictures still exist. Less formal holiday pictures, taken by roving photographers, were printed onto postcards to be sent to friends. Peter's knowledge and interest in photography would have been unusual for a boy of his age.

Of course, Peter would stay for performances and managed to see the newest and best of the films. Once the late afternoon performance was over, Paula would often accompany him home to Schreyvogelgasse so that she could change into a formal evening dress before returning to welcome guests to the evening performance. Part of the attraction of the Palast Kino was the elegant Frau Dr Sieber, charming her visitors in the foyer. Peter would stay in the flat, would eat the meal Seffi provided and do his homework.

As he grew taller and more concerned for his mother's safety, he would often return to the cinema to escort her home after the last performance. Without a father and with a working mother, Peter's childhood was rather solitary. His relationship with Paula was unusually close. He adored her, taking his responsibility for her wellbeing very seriously from a young age. One consequence of Paula's strong matriarchal influence on Peter was that he did not think gender was a barrier to doing anything. Whenever Peter's uncles visited them in Vienna, they always asked how he was getting on at school, though Uncle Alfred was generally more interested in how his swimming and rowing were coming along than academic matters.

The photograph is from the front of Julius Hass' 1936 identity card. His occupation was given as cinema director.

Paula's sister Selma had married a quiet man, Julius Hass. The picture on the front of his identity card shows a man with a kind face. It was dated 1936 and his occupation was stated as cinema director. Another picture shows him sitting in a grass field, possibly at a picnic, smiling gently. Peter was obviously fond of his Uncle Julius as he left the following note pinned to the identity card:

> Uncle Julius Haas married Selma. I was very close to him. A great sportsman. Fished and exhibited fish at the Paris Exhibition. Taught me rowing. He was an early skier and used the 'Telemark' technique for downhill skiing.

> He was a pioneer in radio and early wireless receivers which filled a room and ran an early radio-electrical shop. Advised (unpaid) the cinema.

Peter's closest friend, Fritz Pfeiffer, lived in the larger, adjoining flat that overlooked the Ringstraße . His father was an entrepreneur, good at making money, with many contacts in Vienna and across the continent. Fritz was a large, unruly boy with unkempt, curly hair who often got Peter into trouble. As neighbours, the boys spent a great deal of time together in each other's flats. The expanse of parquet flooring in the Pfeiffer's huge hall was also too tempting. They would move the huge Persian rug to one side and play skittles with the family's pet dachshunds, sliding the poor dogs across the smooth wood towards a target. Apparently, the dogs enjoyed the game, tucking in their already short legs and using their tails as rudders. Tails wagging, they would run, nails scratching at the floor, back to the boys to be tossed again. As they grew older, walking the dogs became a good way of surreptitiously looking at girls.

In time, Paula collected a circle of male friends and admirers. Paula realized that some of Erich's problems may have stemmed from seeing her male visitors in the Gonzagagasse flat, so she rented a small apartment to entertain her few lovers away from their home in Schreyvogelgasse. Of course, she had a number of close male friends who did visit the apartment.

There is an envelope of photographs of three of Paula's close friends. Dr Winterberg who was a medical doctor is shown in a formal picture. He is balding, has gentle eyes behind round-rimmed spectacles, and is wearing a tweed jacket. There is also an informal snap of him in a physician's white coat sitting on a sofa with, improbably, a parakeet on his knee.

Paula's friend, Dr Winterberg, who was the nearest
to a male role-model for Peter.

On the back of the formal picture, Peter wrote:

My deepest friend there.

There are also a couple of photographs showing Paula seated at an outdoor café with Dr Winterberg and another couple. On the back, in Paula's writing is 'Karlsbad 16.8.1929'. Paula is dressed in black, alleviated by a little white. Dr Winterberg seems to have been a kind man, who gave Peter time.

He took him to galleries and theatres and was probably the nearest to a father figure for this rather solitary boy, asking him about school and suggesting books he might enjoy reading.

The second friend was Herr Ingenieur Sumbul. There are three pictures, one of him proudly staring at the studio wall in a rumpled three-piece suit and frameless spectacles. Another shows him seated in white tie evening dress with a prominent decoration hanging from his left breast. It is dated the twentieth of February 1929, Paula's fortieth birthday. The third is a postcard, dated March 1932. He was in Arosa, Switzerland, standing in snow with mountains behind. In this picture, he is wearing a long, dark overcoat, over a dark suit and tie, hat in his left hand and he is supported by a walking stick in his right hand. In all the pictures, he appeared to be a strong, confident, imposing man with thick, dark wavy hair and rather thick lips.

Peter wrote on the back of the picture of Herr Ing. Sumbul in evening dress:

Proposed to Mother.
Helped us in 1938.
Industrialist, Yugoslavian (Belgrade I think), Honorary Consul.
He helped Jewish causes and charities.
A memorable man.

Herr Ing. Sumbul had built the small engineering works in Belgrade that he had inherited from his father into a large company, employing over three hundred employees who worked on major civil engineering projects such as building railways. He travelled widely on business and only visited Vienna from time to time. They enjoyed each other's company whenever they could meet. The entertainments he organised for Paula were lavish, such as a box at the Opera followed by a late supper. Although it was barely ten years old, the Kabarett Simpl, was rapidly becoming celebrated for its entertaining programmes of song, dance and political satire. Paula took him to the Simpl on Wollzeile to see Armin Berg perform on the small stage. Sumbul was enchanted the first time he descended to the tiny, smoky auditorium to the friendly cabaret and enjoyed the singing and vaudeville in this intimate club.

Herr Ingenieur Sumbul. Vienna, twentieth of February 1929.

Peter was introduced to him at the Schreyvogelgasse flat:

There was a lot of extra dusting, polishing and baking. I was told that as a visitor was coming, I was to wash behind my ears, wear long trousers and stay in my room until called. Seffi was wearing her best black dress with the white lace apron.

I was called into the sitting room and saw a handsome, tall man taking the space of two people on the chaise-longue. He was too big for any of the spindly chairs. As instructed, I said:

"Good evening, Herr Ingenieur" and in the deepest voice I had ever heard he replied:

"Good evening, Peter."

We talked about swimming and skiing while Seffi served copious amounts of cake.

The third set of pictures are of Rabbi Fiegler. The largest is a formal photograph of him in Rabbinical dress, with a black cap and embroidered stole around his shoulders, framed in a doorway. Mounted in a cream frame, it shows a man who looked rather like a young Sigmund Freud, with a neat, white goatee and piercing dark eyes. Another picture of him in dinner jacket and bow tie, shows he was bald. The final photograph, taken in Karlsbad in August 1936, shows him dressed in a formal dark lounge suit and striped tie but he looks thinner and careworn.

Peter wrote on the back of this picture:
'Rabbi Dr Fiegler (Adored Mother. Came to Vienna from Czechoslovakia to do my Bar Mizvah)'.

One of the stories Peter regularly told about his childhood was of the Christmas meal Paula shared with Rabbi Fiegler. As was usual in Austria, the celebration was held on Christmas Eve. Also, as was usual, the centrepiece of the meal was a huge baked carp. Unfortunately, as Seffi brought the fish into the dining room, the platter it was to be served from cracked and most of the fish ended up on the floor. The Rabbi ate the single portion that had been salvaged whilst Paula had bread and ham.

Paula, leaving Selma in charge of the cinema and Seffi in charge of Peter, managed to take holidays and travel. She was a regular visitor at spars like Karlsbad in Czechoslovakia, which is currently called Karlovy Vary, and the German resort Baden-Baden; nineteenth century resorts with thermal springs, formal parks and large hotels. The excellent rail network was a legacy of Austria's former empire. It was easy to travel from Vienna to Czechoslovakia, Southwest Germany or the Austrian lakes. Indeed, a tram service operating over the eighty kilometres separating Vienna and Pressburg was opened in 1914. Pressburg, once the capital of Hungary, was included in Czechoslovakia when the new nation was formed following the First World War when it was renamed Bratislava. The Vienna tram was suspended during the Great War as one of the main bridges linking the countries was destroyed by a bomb. Following repairs, the service recommenced.

In the mornings, Paula would enjoy recuperative treatments and being pampered in the spars. She rested, shopped for elegant gowns or sat with friends in cafes in the afternoon and spent the evening dining and socializing. Occasionally, she met Rabbi Fiegler in Karlsbad. Perhaps, their shared Czech origins made it particularly attractive to them. There are photographs of Paula with a teenage Peter posing in front of the ornate Market Colonnade, built in 1892 and designed in the Swiss style by Austrian architects, Ferdinand Fellner and Hermann Helmer. It is white with intricate, carved wooden pillars and ornate fretwork arches over the doors. The building is curved, echoing the curve in the river it faced. Inside, there are three thermal springs. Peter had grown and was now about the same height as Paula. They looked relaxed and smiling. The next picture shows Erich, smart in a bow tie, white bags and correspondent shoes, Paula in the centre and Peter, who had grown since the last photograph, was stooping to remain level with Paula. They were again grouped in front of a colonnade in formal gardens but none of them look particularly relaxed.

Another very different set of photographs, clearly taken by an amateur, record Peter and Paula's holiday in France in August 1937. Instead of the stiff and formal professional photographs of subjects posed before staged backgrounds, these pictures show street scenes with scruffy children. The houses were tall, along the narrow streets common in the Mediterranean. One shows a banana plant and another, a simple fishing boat tied up in a waterway. Peter clearly enjoyed the opportunity to use his Rolleiflex to record his travels. Whenever Paula and Peter were away from Schreyvogelgasse, Seffi would visit her family in the Tyrol. She would always return with huge jars of preserved fruit, hams and vast cheeses.

To mark his entry to the gymnasium, Paula had Peter's room refurbished to suit the young man he was becoming. Since the successful refurbishment of the Palast Kino, her brother Alfred had been getting work as an interior designer, so he was commissioned to redesign the room. Alfred quickly disposed of the Biedermeier and ordered bespoke units modelled on the famous Berlin Bauhaus. The ornate, over-curly furniture was replaced with functional oak units. The storage unit, fondly called a compactum, had a set of drawers, with small green spherical handles, above a pair of cupboards, with identical green spherical handles. There was a flap that could be lowered to create a writing table and bookshelves ran along the top of the unit. A matching table and a simple chair, with rattan back and seat on a metal frame, were provided for Peter to do his homework. There were also a couple of armchairs for Peter to use when entertaining his friends. There are a few photographs of Peter sitting in the room with a young man, both always in jackets and ties, seated at the table or in armchairs. There is one picture of him with Karl Urbach, both looking very serious. As in all grand Vienna flats, occupants could summon a servant by pressing the bell switch in their room. The bells from every room connected to the kitchen and hence, to Seffi. Paula's rule was that Peter was not to use the bell when he was alone, but that he might summon Seffi to ask for coffee and, no doubt cake, when he had visitors. Another visitor of about Peter's age was

Hermann Bondi. Peter and Karl spent a lot of time together as their mothers were close friends. His mother, Alice Urbach, was to play a key role in Paula's life.

Another happy couple

Paula's elder son, Erich, neither enjoyed nor did well at school. He was flippant, lacked respect for authority or his teachers and had little interest in learning.

Some of our funnier family stories were associated with Erich's essay writing. Asked to write an essay on 'my feelings on climbing a mountain', his response, 'If only I'd got to the top', was not well received. Paula was summoned regularly to the school following one transgression or another.

Inheriting his mother's looks and outgoing personality, Erich enjoyed charades, dressing up and acting. Erich's childhood sweetheart, Karla, left school at fourteen. Whilst education was considered essential for Jewish boys, most girls had little formal education. Her parents were wealthy, as they had inherited substantial sums from her mother's banker father. The only expectation was that, in due course, she would marry. Karla was short, with dark, curly hair and dark eyes. As a child, she had scratched the cornea of her right eye when, chasing a cat down a garden, a rose branch whipped across her face and a thorn snagged her eye, leaving her with limited vision. Still, she was jolly and given to wearing bright colours. She was expected to help with the apartment and accompany her mother on social visits until she found a suitable husband. The card game, bridge, was very fashionable in 1920s Vienna. Although most coffee houses employed someone to run games and instruct clients in the finer points of the game, Karla would have learnt privately. A table or two would be set and played at in many of the private apartments Karla's mother visited both morning and afternoon for coffee, cakes and gossip. Karla quickly showed interest in the game and joined private classes arranged within her mother's circle as her aptitude became clear. Unlike Paula or her mother who wore ankle-length dresses during the day, Karla's skirts, stopping just below the knee, were daringly short.

At nineteen, Karla was pregnant. Paula arranged everything; Erich was sent to work for an Austrian engineering company's office in England whilst Karla had a secret termination. Paula said that she would agree to their marriage if, after a year's separation, they found that they still loved one another. They corresponded whilst Erich was away, were delighted to be together again when he briefly returned for the winter holiday and were still very much in love on his return. So, in April 1933, they married at the Central Synagogue, Vienna.

Erich and Karla on their wedding day. Vienna, April 1933.

Karla's parents arranged a lavish reception at the Sacher Hotel, home of the famous Sachertorte. Everyone dressed for the occasion: diamonds sparkled, champagne and Tokaji flowed. It was clear that Karla and Erich were in love as they shared secret smiles and their happiness with the guests.

Peter observed:

> Karla's parents had been lavish. It was in the Sacher that they held Karla and Erich's wedding breakfast. I remembered them well, dressed for the occasion, beaming proud happy parents and hosts.

Erich made a number of trips to England during the months following their wedding and they finally moved to London in December 1933. Erich became the sales representative for an Austrian engineering company.

Vienna's Mrs Beaton

Alice Urbach had, from early childhood, been fascinated by cooking. She used to spend time in the kitchen watching the cook prepare family meals. Food was scarce following the First World War and cooks had to improvise, replacing eggs with root vegetables in cakes, substituting roasted acorns for coffee. Alice learnt far more than just the rich recipes of traditional Viennese cooking which would stand her in good stead in the future. Paula and Alice were introduced via a mutual friend as they had much in common: both were widows with children to support. Alice's husband, Max had been a doctor but he was a compulsive gambler who had lost most of her inheritance before dying, leaving her widowed with two boys and little money. So, needing to earn enough money to support herself, Otto and Karl, she used her culinary skills to set up a catering business.

Alice lived around the corner from the beautiful Baroque palaces and formal gardens of the Belvedere in the third district to the southeast of the city. As with those behind the cinema on Josefstädter Straße, there was a large central garden with blocks of flats around the perimeter. Alice had a large flat. At first, she ran classes from home but soon she needed a larger venue as the demand for her classes increased. She began offering classes from the test kitchen of a local cooking shop on two afternoons a week, but once again, demand outstripped availability. Her next expansion occurred when Alice came to an arrangement with a local hardware store. She used an empty room at the rear of the store for classes whilst the store stocked the novelty utensils she used during her demonstrations. Although this was not the smartest area of Vienna, the curb was lined with expensive cars, parked for the duration of the class. Alice also lectured at the Café Landtmann, around the corner from Paula's Schreyvogelgasse apartment. Alice modestly attributed part of her success to the many women who needed to learn to cook as ingredients became available and plentiful following the shortages resulting from the war. As a result of the food shortages during the war, many women had not had the opportunity to learn to cook from their mothers, or else they had servants who did the cooking.

As her cookery school became increasingly acclaimed, she was then approached to write a recipe book that became a best-seller, *So Kocht Man in Wien (This is How We Cook in Vienna)*. Alice was the Mrs Beaton, Delia Smith, Pru Leith and Jamie Oliver of her day. With much in common, the two women became close friends and met as regularly as their business commitments allowed.

In summer, Vienna is quiet as it is stuffy and hot, and those who could, would travel to the country to escape the heat. As the richer classes moved to the countryside for their holidays, Alice had no-one to teach, so she would rent a large rambling house in the country and other children would join them, providing playmates for her boys and, possibly, income. In 1933, Alice rented a house with a huge garden by Lake Millstadt. Peter joined them for a couple of months. The boys enjoyed the freedom and played out of doors, splashing around in the lake, walking and scrambling up hills. The first year Paula stayed for a week in July and visited for weekends when she could. The boys, particularly the younger two, Karl and Peter, became close friends. Enjoying the freedom offered by the countryside, both boys spent their time on and in the lake becoming strong swimmers and quite competent with small boats. The weather was hot. They spent most of the day outside, only returning to the house for the large meals that Alice prepared. The house Alice rented in 1934, again in Millstadt, had a huge glass veranda built over the lake that was used as the dining room. Sometimes, other members of Paula's family joined them for weekends or longer. Peter was with Alice again for the summer in 1935 as she had taken a house on Wörthersee (Lake Wörth), the largest of the Carinthian lakes tucked between the Alps and the Adriatic. One year, Uncle Ernst and Aunt Muschi spent two weeks with them. Ernst, an excellent sportsman, went fishing allowing Peter to row. Patiently, he taught him to tuck his elbows in and row without soaking everyone. He was a kind coach and mentor to the two fatherless boys. Paula continued to enjoy swimming, particularly once she had a good-looking young man to accompany her as they swam around the lake. Short and solid, Paula was a natural at breaststroke. Peter, growing fast, was as thin as a rake, and a natural at the crawl. Under Ernst's tuition, he developed a lovely style and would glide cleanly through the water.

Chapter 5

Austria: National Socialism Threatens

Historic persecution

Antisemitism has been endemic across Europe for many centuries. Jews had been expelled from cities since the fourteenth century and were restricted to living in ghettos during the eighteenth century. Furthermore, the type of work they were permitted to do was restricted. To some extent, Jews worked in trade and banking simply because these were the only careers which they were legally allowed to follow. For centuries, there had been periodic outbreaks of antisemitism across Europe. Few Jews lived in Russia before the end of the eighteenth century when Russia annexed Poland, though previously some had moved there in search of work. Traditional, kaftan-wearing, observant, Orthodox, Eastern Jews were usually confined to ghettos. Early in the nineteenth century, pogroms began in Tsarist Russia and Jewish ghettos were attacked, their inhabitants killed, goods stolen and homes set on fire. Many were forced to flee, with whatever possessions they could carry, to escape from their tormentors.

Dispersed by these pogroms, many Jews moved west towards Europe and the centre of the Austro-Hungarian Empire. Enabled by the increasing freedoms of the nineteenth century that allowed Jews to buy property and also, live in towns, families like the Tichos and the Schiebers migrated from ghettos into towns and cities. By the early twentieth century, most had integrated into society. Kaftans were replaced with tailcoats and skirts. Many became less traditionally Orthodox in their observances. Over generations, they began to think of themselves primarily as Czech, Austrian or Viennese, but they were still Jews. Some were more, others were less observant of the religious laws and customs. They had become assimilated into urban society in cities like Vienna. In *Good Living Street,* Tony Bonyhady describes how some of the leading families spent the fortunes they had made in banking on grand buildings, supporting the arts and lavish lifestyles. The beautiful Viennese palaces described in *The Hare with Amber Eyes* and the story of Klimt's portrait of Adele Bloch-Baur told by Anne-Marie O'Connor in *The Lady in Gold*, described a rich, opulent society that few could aspire to. In *Last Waltz in Vienna* George Clare describes an affluent, middle-class, Jewish Viennese family, similar to Paula's. Tom Stoppard's play *Leopoldstadt* vividly shows life in another assimilated Viennese family. Some of the richer, Jewish families had survived the Great War relatively unscathed.

Adolf Hitler was born in 1889, in Braunau am Inn, a small town near Linz, close to the German border, and was consequently an Austrian citizen. Because of his father's work, the family moved to Passau in Germany, for a couple of years, where Adolf acquired his distinctive, Bavarian accent, before returning to Austria. He developed strong, German Nationalist ideals at a young age. Adolf's family and school life were troubled. At eighteen, he moved to Vienna to study fine art but failed to meet the entry requirement of the Academy of Fine Arts or the School of Architecture. His money ran out when he was twenty years-of-age and he was forced to live on the streets, taking casual work and selling his drawings of Vienna sights. Living in Vienna in the late 1900s, Hitler was exposed to racist and antisemitic rhetoric which, coupled with his belief in German Nationalism, sowed the seeds of the ferocious hate that was to follow. He moved to Germany in 1913 and despite being an Austrian citizen, fought in the Great War in the 6th Bavarian Reserve Infantry Regiment, probably as a result of an administrative error, as he should have been deported back to Austria when war broke out. Although Hitler was promoted from private to lance corporal, he was assigned to the relatively safe role of regimental message-runner. His regiment fought in a number of battles in Belgium and France including Ypres, the Somme, Passchendaele and Fromelles, all with huge losses. Hitler was wounded in the Battle of the Somme when a shell burst at the entrance of the dispatch riders' dugout. He received two awards for bravery; an Iron Cross Second Class in 1914 which was a common award; and the less common Iron Cross First Class after an open battle in which messengers were indispensable. Temporarily blinded by British mustard gas in 1918, Hitler was sent to a Prisoner of War camp after he was released from hospital in November 1918. He was released in January 1919 and returned to barracks in Munich. Although he had renounced his Austrian citizenship in 1925, Hitler only became a German citizen in 1932.

Defeat in the Great War and the subsequent Treaty of Versailles in 1919, forced Germany to admit to starting the war. Several productive provinces were transferred to other countries, along with the imposition of economically damaging sanctions, and the Rhineland was demilitarized. Germany's territory was reduced and borders were moved: land was returned to Belgium; Alsace-Lorraine was returned to France; substantial, productive, eastern districts reverted to the newly reconstituted Poland; Memel was returned to Lithuania; large portions of Schleswig went to Denmark; Sudetenland went to Czechoslovakia; the South Tyrol became Italian; and a portion of Alpine provinces were divided between the Serbs, Croats and Slovenes. To further ensure that Germany would never again contemplate territorial expansion or develop military strength, the annexation of Austria was specifically prohibited. Germany had to make reparations payments to make good damage caused by the war. When he learned of the conditions imposed by the Treaty of Versailles, Hitler began to develop the idea that he would liberate Germany and make Germany great again.

Hitler was antisemitic at an early age and shortly after his election as Chancellor in 1933, he began to introduce political and legal changes that discriminated against Jews. The anti-Jewish laws he introduced restricted where Jews could work and banned them from employment in the civil service. By 1935, the Nuremberg Laws stripped German Jews of their citizenship and forbade Jews to marry German gentiles. Jews were increasingly excluded from social and political life in Germany. When they could, some emigrated. Although catastrophic for the individuals affected, many of these restrictions went largely unnoticed within Germany. At that time, few Jews lived in Germany; Jews accounted for less than one per cent of the entire population. The majority of Germans living in rural communities would never have met a Jew.

Germany was economically damaged by the consequences of the Great War that led to hyper-inflation in the 1920s. In the US, confidence was shaken by the Wall Street Crash and subsequent Great Depression. Much of the world was in economic turmoil. Empires were breaking down, affecting trade.

Germany was left with hyper-inflation, and little infrastructure or industry remained. Life was hard, food was in short supply and millions were unemployed. Many families were recovering from the loss of their younger members, killed in the war or from Spanish flu which, unusually, killed healthy young adults rather than the old and infirm. Most lived in poverty. With this backdrop, Jews became useful scapegoats and an easy group for Nazi propaganda to target. They were different, rich and often conspicuous spenders in cities, further east in Poland and Russia traditional Orthodox communities were equally different. Jews were blamed for inflation, food shortages, even the Wall Street Crash.

The brown-shirted Stormtroopers formed the Nazi Party's original paramilitary wing; these small groups of elite troops were identifiable by the colour of their shirts. As the Nazi party began to hold meetings that were frequently disrupted by communist and other protesters, these elite troops along with other thugs, enjoyed breaking up these demonstrations. After a particularly robust fight, following a large public meeting in Munich in 1921, Hitler recognised the value of the group and called them the *Sturmabteilung,* the SA or Brownshirts. In contrast to the *Schutzstaffe,* the SS, Hitler's paramilitary organisation that was responsible for the majority of genocidal killings, the SA was mostly composed of violent thugs who enjoyed raping, beating, and looting.

Politics in Austria were febrile. Although the Treaty of Versailles had specifically forbidden union between Austria and Germany, the two countries remained connected by geography and history. It became increasingly difficult to ignore what was happening in Austria's larger neighbour. Antisemitism, though never far from the surface, became increasingly pervasive and visible throughout the 1930s. The descent into the horrors that were to follow was insidious; few recognised the real risks. In 1934, in contrast to Germany where less than one per cent of the population was Jewish, between seven and ten per cent of the population of Vienna were Jews.

The Austrian film industry began to make mainstream films in 1910. Before then, they had only produced newsreels for local consumption. Although there was competition from cheap films made in the US, the Austrian industry managed to release twenty to thirty films a year throughout the 1920s. A few were internationally successful, epic films, like those produced by Alexander Korda and Michael Curtiz, with huge casts and lavish sets. Once Hitler had taken power and Jews were banned from working in the film industry in Germany, some moved to work in the less hostile environment in Austria, while others emigrated to the US. Germany was the main export market for Austrian films in the 1920s and 1930s. In 1933, Germany imposed a ban on importing Austrian films unless Jews were forbidden from working on the film. As a result, the Austrian film industry had no alternative than to stop employing Jews. By 1936, Jews were banned from working in any part of the film industry. To get work, they had to leave the country. Many, like Paula's acquaintance, Otto Preminger, chose to emigrate to the US, others moved to Czechoslovakia, France or England; only a few chose to remain.

Germany's anti-Jewish influence continued to seep across the border, and gradually, living conditions amongst the Jewish population deteriorated. Some lost their jobs and were forced to take whatever casual work they could get. Living became increasingly hand-to-mouth; people had to sell their possessions to pay for food. No longer able to pay their rent, families moved in with relatives.

Jewish children were increasingly segregated in schools, as recalled by Elfie, one of the hostel girls:

> There were only two of us in the same class who were Jewish. They were mainly Catholic in that area but there was one girl who was Protestant but she wasn't Catholic. One day, we just went into school as usual. When we came into our classroom, there were desks with two pupils sharing a desk and the teacher just said, "You can't sit with the others. There is a desk over there for you to sit. You can't mix with the others because you're Jewish." I mean, she wasn't a nice teacher, but she particularly wasn't nice to us and we weren't allowed to mix with them in the playground because they might be contaminated and so, for a while, we had to sit separately.

Lessons were changed in order to emphasise the inferiority of Jews and demonstrate their 'Untermensch' characteristics. If Jews were bullied in schools, teachers did nothing.

Peter noted that gangs of gentile boys tormented Jewish boys:

> There was a group in my own class that made fun of Jewish boys and ganged up on them. Some of the teachers, too, made remarks. Later that year, it became much worse. A group of the strongest in the form started to beat up Jewish boys. One small boy in particular often had a bleeding nose or a black eye. His father complained. Nothing was done about it. One day in the morning break, the little Jewish boy came blundering in, crying. He had a black eye, and a big swastika painted in red on his white shirt.

One week, Oskar Lamac, a music student who was Peter's piano teacher, did not arrive at the flat as usual to teach him. No one knew anything about it. A few weeks later, Paula bumped into the musical director who had initially recommended Oskar as a teacher at Café Landtmann. He told her that Oskar had been killed on the Friday night before the Anschluss. He was in a cheap bar with a friend as they were too restless to study but did not want to be out on the streets. A group of other, half-drunk, students, each wearing a red armband with a black Swastika in the centre of a white circle, came into the bar. Oskar was known at the university for his left-wing views. "We'll teach you about politics, you communist pig," they shouted, as they hit him and his friend with knuckle dusters. The friend collapsed at the bar so they left him and dragged Oskar out onto the pavement. They kicked him to death whilst passers-by did nothing, not wanting to get involved. Ironically, the first-person Paula knew to be murdered by these thugs was neither a communist nor Jewish, Oskar was simply a left-wing student who had expressed his views in public.

Anschluss
Austria is a small country with many lakes and mountains, limiting the landmass available to farmers. Much of the industry, that had once made the empire rich, was located in Czechoslovakia which was lost once the borders were redefined. Essentially, the newly defined Austria was no longer economically viable. The trade between the empire and its

capital, that had ensured supplies of food, clothing, fuel and industrial products were readily available, had ceased. As the 1930s progressed, most of the inhabitants of the city suffered from food and fuel shortages.

The Treaty of Versailles had also left Austria with an unwieldy political system as no single party could gain a majority. The country was ruled by an unhappy series of coalitions between the Christian Social Party and the Greater German People's Party. The latter embraced the idea of German Nationalism and annexation. Through the 1920s there were clashes, which sometimes erupted onto the streets, as sectarian gangs rioted. Possibly influenced by fascism in neighbouring Italy, in 1932, Chancellor Engelbert Dollfuss moved the Christian Social Party towards dictatorship and fascism whilst an Austrian Nazi party, keen for unification with Germany, grew stronger.

The Austrian Civil War, in February 1934, was a series of skirmishes between fascist and socialist groups. A few hundred people were killed and thousands injured during the fighting, and once Chancellor Dollfuss ordered the army to participate, the violence escalated. The socialist leaders of the uprising were tried, and nine were executed. Over one thousand five-hundred others were tried, sentences were harsh and some socialist politicians were forced into exile. The government banned the Social Democratic Party and replaced the democratic constitution by introducing a fascist system, similar to that of Mussolini in Italy, which became known as Austrofascism. Dollfuss' Austrofascism was aligned to the Catholic Church and was totalitarian, rejecting parliamentary democracy whilst the Austrian Nazi party looked towards Germany. A few months later, in July 1934, members of the Austrian Nazi Party, aided by German SS officers, attacked the Chancellery in Vienna in an attempt to remove the Austrofascists. Although the July Putsch failed as a coup d'état and the planned German invasion was foiled, Dollfuss was shot during the commotion and died a few hours later. He was replaced by Chancellor Schuschnigg. In the aftermath, supporters of the Nazi party were arrested, many fled to Germany or Yugoslavia. It is likely that this attack was orchestrated from Germany.

For the time being, Austria remained an independent country, but antisemitism, fuelled from Germany, continued to escalate. Conditions for the Jewish population continued to deteriorate. Schuschnigg, wanting to maintain an independent Austria, attempted to ease relations with Hitler and removed the ban on the Austrian Nazi party and their newspaper. However, it had always been Hitler's intention that the country of his birth should be united with Germany to form the Third Reich. Indeed, on the first page of the book he wrote in prison, *Mein Kampf*, he insisted, 'German Austria must return to the great German motherland' and 'common blood belongs in a common Reich'.

Schuschnigg was weak. His attempts to appease Hitler and maintain Austrian independence failed. In February 1938, the German ambassador in Vienna arranged a secret meeting between Hitler and Schuschnigg at Hitler's mountain retreat in Bavaria. In response to threats from Hitler to invade Austria, Schuschnigg agreed to grant the Austrian Nazi Party political freedom and to make Arthur Seyß-Inquart, Home Secretary. Unable to maintain independence in the face of German and Austrian Nazis, on the ninth of March, Schuschnigg announced that a referendum (plebiscite) on Austrian independence would be held in a week's time on the following Sunday. Hitler responded by demanding that the referendum should be cancelled and mobilized the army. Two days later, Schuschnigg cancelled the referendum. In an emotional speech broadcast on Austrian radio, he announced that the army had been instructed to show no resistance to the German army as it entered Austria. He resigned later that day and was replaced by Hitler's puppet, Seyß-Inquart. On the morning of the twelfth of March, twenty-five thousand German troops and police marched across the border into Austria as the country was annexed by Hitler.

The Anschluss, as the annexation of Austria by Germany became known, was clearly choreographed; troops arrived in Vienna, and Hitler's triumphant parade in the Heldenplatz, the Square of Heroes, in front of the Hofburg Palace which housed the chancellor of Austria, was a clear signal of the danger to come. Massive displays of military power accompanied by rabid crowds of local Nazi supporters filled the city for a few terrifying days. Cries of *'Ein Volk, ein Reich, ein Führer'* (one people, one nation, one leader), reverberated between buildings.

As Peter recalled:

My mother was crying as we left the cinema to walk home. The town had gone wild. There were hordes in the streets shouting and singing. A few hundred yards from the Mozart monument and the Beethoven house, circles of demented men and women danced around bonfires in the street. Triumphant. Primitive. That Friday night, the scum took over. We kept to the side-streets, to the shadows by the walls. Already, we were fugitives in what had been our hometown.

The German army marched in on the Saturday and Hitler entered Austria. A thousand soldiers in impeccable field-grey goose-stepping in ranks thirty men wide along the Ringstraße , the sides of the road solid red with swastika flags. They came from the north, marching towards the Hofburg, the Imperial Palace. Behind the infantry came the motorcycles. Then there were the tanks. Next, came a squad of limousines bearing sinister-black SS and well-tailored medalled army generals.

Then there was one open car. Hitler in brown, standing, his arm raised, to the tumultuous welcome from the crowd. The Gestapo made thousands of arrests. Many thousands cheered. Others killed themselves. Undertakers ran out of coffins.

Horrified, Paula and Peter watched the parades as they moved along the Ringstraße from the flat, unseen behind the huge curtains, too frightened to switch the lights on in the room that had once been Hermann's office. The military precision of the formations of Nazi vehicles and troops was terrifying as they goose-stepped behind the Führer, standing arm raised in his car. The crowd roared. From the top floor of their tall building, they clearly heard the shouting *'Ju-da verr-rrecke! Ju-da verr-rrecke!'* (death to Jews).

How many in that crowd had been secret Nazis before the Anschluss? In his memoirs, published in 1950, the French ambassador, Robert Coulondre described their warm reception of the invading army:

> *The only injuries the German soldiers received on entering Vienna was from the stems of the flowers that were enthusiastically thrown at them as they marched by.*

Later, the crowd became feral, looting Jewish shops and homes, brutally beating young and old in a senseless frenzy of rage cleverly orchestrated from Germany by Hitler and Goebbels. The brutality of those days and the speed of the Nazification of Austria is well documented. In contrast to Germany, where the spread of antisemitism was slow and insidious, in Austria it was rapid and brutal. Jews carried on living increasingly difficult lives. Brownshirts and other thugs, legitimised by Hitler, roamed the streets beating up mostly, but not exclusively, Jews.

Aryanization, the forced transfer of Jewish businesses to non-Jews, moved so rapidly after the Anschluss, it must have been planned well in advance. It involved the transfer of Jewish property into Aryan hands in order to 'de-Jew the economy'. Slowly, Jews were stripped of their rights as citizens and human beings. Silently, Aryans, preferably party members, took the work of Jews. Sometimes, an individual would simply not appear for work, on other occasions, an individual would be taken, which meant being collected by police for a beating, transfer to a labour camp or worse. Cinemas owned by Jews were no longer allowed to show the newest films. On the day Florian Fischer, the projectionist, did not arrive for work, nobody asked what had happened to him. He wasn't seen again. Presumably, he had been taken. A local thug, proudly wearing Nazi insignia, took his place the next day.

Shortly after the Anschluss, the Gestapo confiscated the Hotel Metropole and turned it into the largest Gestapo headquarters outside Berlin. The majority of the nine-hundred staff were recruited from the Austrian police. It was here that people were taken for questioning, interrogation and torture. At first, men might crawl back to their families, beaten, bloody with broken bones and missing teeth. Soon, more simply disappeared, taken by Nazis: the SA and the SS, to collection centres, like the Hotel Metropole, for transit to labour and concentration camps across Germany and Poland.

Auschwitz, Dachau and Bergen-Belsen remain familiar seventy-five years after their liberation revealed the horrors within. Other smaller camps are less well known: Belzec, Chelmno, Majdanek, Maly Trostinec, Mauthausen, Gusen, Sobibor, Ravensbrück, Theresienstadt and Treblinka. The structure, number and management of the camps evolved from

1933 onwards until the end of the Second World War but ultimately, there were a small number of large, specific, extermination camps and many other camps and sub-camps which spread from France to Eastern Europe and North Africa. In many, if not most camps, there were deaths amongst those incarcerated if not through industrialised processes but by the result of appalling conditions and terrible treatment by those running them.

Palast Kino

The cinema was rapidly Aryanized as its management was given to Nazis as the Tichos were forced out. The amount they were paid to run the Palast Kino was reduced each month and each successive valuation of the business was lower than the last. After they had paid their loyal staff, there was little left for Paula and Selma.

Palast Kino programme. Fourteenth of April 1938.
Ironically, the film featured was *Dead End*.

Peter remembered:

One evening, I had a narrow escape on the way to the cinema. Turning into Stadiongasse, just behind the Rathaus at the bottom of Josefstädter Straße , there were two men on their knees scrubbing the pavement. They were watched by a group of stormtroopers. Other SA men were looking around for more Jews to punish. I walked slowly towards them, with my hands in my pockets, whistling a marching song and said "Guten abend" in a Viennese accent as I passed them. They said, "Heil Hitler" as I walked round the corner. I was shaking as I told my mother what had happened, just down the road. She said I had done well. This was a common experience; my friends had similar stories.

Whenever the family met and talked, new stories of things that had happened to friends and neighbours were told, each incident was worse than the last. At first, the horrors of these outrages were described in detail; but as they became more severe and happened more frequently, people talked about them less. Paula tried to protect Peter who was still a child. Peter tried to protect his mother. People cast around for other things to talk about. They snatched at any glimmer of good news. What could they as individuals, or even together, do to stop what was happening anyway? Whole meals were spent talking about anything other than what was happening outside on the streets. Gradually, a collective depression spread across the community. Some had problems sleeping, others found waking up difficult, some smoked too many cigarettes, whilst others lost interest in eating, as fear spread.

Chapter 6

Europe: Escape

Conditions deteriorate

As conditions in Vienna became more hostile to Jews, Paula realized it would be necessary to send her child away to safety. Erich and Karla wrote regularly, saying how well they were doing in London. Though the streets might not be entirely paved with gold, they were happy; there were opportunities for those who looked for them. Whilst not quite London and not quite a village, Streatham was a lovely place to live.

Paula began to collect the paperwork that would be necessary before she could buy an exit permit for Peter. She had to prove that all taxes due had been paid. In Germany, ever desperate for money to fund armaments, the Reich relentlessly increased taxes on Jewish businesses and the exit taxes individuals were forced to pay before they could leave the country. Paula's monthly income from the cinema was less than the tax demanded for Peter's exit permit. Her capital was solely invested in the business with only a small amount invested in a savings account. Fortunately, the bulk of the compensation settled on Peter after the car accident that had killed his father remained untouched. Paula had only asked the court for small sums to be released so the bulk of the capital was intact.

Before he could make the journey, Paula would also have to obtain proof that Peter could enter Britain. Unemployment was high in Britain following the Great War and immigration was tightly controlled to stop foreigners taking jobs. The 1920 Aliens Act required any alien seeking to enter the country for employment or residence to register with the police. All immigrants, including refugees, would have to prove that they could support themselves without state aid. Employers, family or wider contacts would have to send an affidavit, a form guaranteeing that they would not be a burden on the state before anyone could enter the UK. Erich sent an affidavit, a guarantee that Peter would be supported financially and make no claim on the British state.

Peter confirmed:

The form arrived from Erich. My mother took it to the embassy. The queue reached around the block. Every embassy in Vienna was marked by a long queue. When the Nazis started to humiliate and hurt the would-be fugitives in the queues, the British were the first to allow applicants to wait inside the embassy.

With a heavy heart, Paula began to make arrangements to send Peter to his brother in Streatham. At seventeen years-old, Peter was already tall for his age. Paula took him to the Jewish department stores where his father had bought his clothes. At Rothberger, Peter was fitted with trousers, jackets, shirts and socks all in the best quality, warm fabrics. Everything was two sizes too large, allowing plenty of space for growth. They went to Maison Zwiebeck for shoes and a thick coat. Walking through these opulent stores, Paula remembered her earlier visits with Hermann when, as newlyweds, they had chosen furniture for the flat. Paula had to remain calm and to fight back her tears. She was about to be separated from her son for an unknown length of time and she had already lost his father. It had already been five years since she had seen her older son. They bought an attaché case. Peter would take his beloved camera, the Rolleiflex, which had been a birthday gift from Paula's friend, Dr Winterberg, and his typewriter, along with his prayer shawl and kippah.

They visited relatives so that Peter could take his leave. Uncles and aunts produced aufschnitt, although not as lavish as they had been. Spreads of sliced, cold meats and cheese, bread and, of course, strudels and gateaux, were prepared. They said not to worry, Peter would only be away for a short while and they looked forward to seeing him when he returned. Paula managed not to cry at each farewell. Peter was worried about his young Jewish friends: Karl was destined for America and Fritz would be going to England so they should soon be able to meet again.

Peter described his sad departure from Vienna:

A little group came to see me off at the railway station. There were many such groups, each self-contained, quiet, trying to be unobtrusive because strutting between us were SA men in brown uniforms, revelling in their power to frighten, even now to stop a child, arrest a parent.

Aunt Selma was there, Aunt Muschi and Uncle Ernst. Seffi in her Sunday best. Dr Winterberg said, "Good luck in England," and gave me a Mont Blanc pen. I had barely time to thank him before he turned and left. I kissed my aunts and Uncle Ernst and Seffi, and then my mother walked with me to my train. On the way to it, we went alongside another train filled with Austrians going on holiday. A man looking out was watching us. As we passed his window, he spat down at me. The spittle landed on my right shoulder.

My mother tightened her grip on my arm, afraid I would make a scene and wreck in these last seconds the safety she had achieved for me. I walked on quietly, said good-bye to my mother and got onto the train.

Peter, Vienna, 1938. Paula's writing said, 'Marking his departure for England'.

Peter travelled alone by train to England with half a crown in his pocket. Fortunately, English had been one of the few subjects he enjoyed at school and Paula had arranged for him to take extra conversation classes on Saturday afternoons. The hope of visiting his half-brother and sister-in-law in London had been further encouragement to study.

A terrible experience

Alice's younger son Karl was studying medicine and was in the process of applying to emigrate to the US. A few days before his twenty-first birthday, he was queuing to collect the final papers needed to allow him to leave Austria. As he waited, he saw a group of Nazis coming to take him from the queue and had tried escape; he was arrested and sent to Dachau. Near Munich, Dachau was one of the first concentration camps built by the Nazis. Karl was arrested in November; once he was a prisoner at Dachau, his head was shaved and he was made to stand in the cold for hours. A close friend and family member paid for his release and three months later, he left the camp and managed to escape to the US to join his brother, Otto, in Oregon.

Others left Vienna; illegal boats ferried terrified individuals across the Mediterranean Sea to Palestine. Similar dangerous journeys are taken across the Mediterranean today in the opposite direction.

Hostel girls

The girls who were later to be rescued by Kindertransport reported that their education was disrupted and life became increasingly difficult for Jews in Germany and later, Austria.

Annie was brought up in a farming community in Fischach, a village near Augsberg, Germany. She described the conditions deteriorating:

> *In 1934, there was a plebiscite in Germany. They had handed out hundreds and hundreds of little pins on which said 'Ja', which meant vote yes, for Hitler. And everybody wore this little silver 'Ja'. And I remember grave looks. I remember sort of whispered conversations about what was in the newspapers. And no one suspected Hindenburg would appoint Hitler Reichschancellor.*

There were still newspapers who opposed Hitler. And I remember people saying, "The English will not let it happen." But then, Hitler was in and everyone knew it was going to be bad.

I remember being uneasy. You would walk along the street and somewhere, there would be painted a big hackenkreus, a swastika, or people would be nervous. But they were nervous like Jews who always feel under pressure; they were mistrustful of everyone. We did not talk to anybody if we travelled on the train and we were careful not to draw attention to ourselves expect when it came to religious observances where we could not help being different. And there was never a time we did not know it was dangerous, never. We knew it was dangerous, we did not have to be told. We drank it in with our mother's milk – that is what really happened.

And in 1936, the Gestapo came to the village and plastered the Jewish store windows with signs forbidding the transaction of business. And HD tore the sign off his store. We were all inside the downstairs living room of my Aunt Betti, and the front windows looked directly out onto what was going on. The place was deserted. They dragged H out to the smithy and they had him kneel down and they knocked him down and he was kneeling on his hands and knees like an animal. And there were two or three people who were beating him up. My father said, "My god, they are going to kill him!" He was on his way to go out and everybody said, "If you go, they will kill you too. You must not go."

I think there was such a deep-seated belief, I cannot explain, I mean every so often someone would say, "But we fought in the war." They could not believe that this would be anything that would have any permanence. It was simply more than their minds could deal with.

Elfie's family had moved from their village to a flat in Stiemark, Vienna, where they were joined by her uncle and aunt. She described their departure from Vienna:

An aunt of mine who came to live with us. There were illegal boats leaving for Palestine and my aunt and uncle were leaving and taking one somewhere. Obviously, from where the boats were leaving, they were going to Palestine; but they weren't allowed to land in Palestine. They had to leave the boat with little boats and go and land that night. My mother, I think she had kidney problems and heart problems. My father heard that these boats, the big ships were like cattle ships and he decided she'd never survive. So, they wouldn't go. But my aunt and uncle went and they survived and lived for a long time in Israel with my cousin.

Kristallnacht

On the ninth of November 1938, the SA organised a Jewish pogrom across Germany and Nazi occupied countries: Austria, Poland and Czechoslovakia. Riots broke out in cities and towns as synagogues, Jewish hospitals, schools, shops, and businesses were attacked, their windows were smashed and the buildings wrecked with sledgehammers. Jewish men were arrested, some taken to concentration camps, others beaten and released. Shops had their stock taken or destroyed. Local Nazi sympathisers, many of whom enjoyed the chance to riot and loot, joined in. It was a night of chaos and terror and was called Kristallnacht, from the glass from the broken windows found on streets and pavements the following day. It was widely reported across the world, notably in London, and shocked the British Government into recognising the true menace that the Nazis presented. Kristallnacht was the turning point, it was no longer possible to hope conditions might improve but necessary to recognize that Hitler was a terrifying menace.

Elfie remembers that terrible night:

My introduction to Kristallnacht came as I was going home by train from my aunt and uncle's house. Suddenly, I saw big crowds in the streets. I had no idea what was going on until I came to our street and house.

Our store had been closed. JUDE was marked on the windows. My grandparents were in our apartment upstairs. Out in the street there were crowds of Nazis who were beating Jews – old and young. They were made to scrub the streets. One of my uncles went to help an old man and promptly was beaten himself. He was arrested and sent to Dachau concentration camp. His wife, my aunt, was an oral surgeon and had many non-Jewish friends who tried to find out where he was being held. Eventually, my aunt and uncle were able to get visas and emigrated to Shanghai before coming to the US. My aunt had been able to buy my uncle's release from Dachau.

The Nazis came to all the houses looking for Jewish men. Some were able to hide – but not many. When they entered my aunt's apartment building, her Christian doctor friend pretended he was looking for a patient, came to her door with a black doctor bag and put some of her valuables in it. My best friend who lived in our apartment building, with her parents and brother, had her father arrested the same day and sent to Dachau.

Ilse also remembered that night:

On Kristallnacht, they burned all the synagogues except the one in the first district. The reason it was spared was that it was in a very narrow street. Had they set it on fire, it would have burned houses across the street, which they had commandeered for their own private use. They had also burned all Jewish books they took from houses and synagogues.

Life in Vienna became increasingly difficult for Jews. Families had to move in together as individuals were evicted or could no longer pay their rent. Although parents tried to shield their children from the things that were going on, at only ten years old, Elfie realized something bad was happening:

Well, we knew I knew something was going on because when we came to Vienna, we lived in Stiermark and we had a big flat on the first floor of a house where we lived with my aunt and uncle and my cousin who went to Israel. And one day, these two storm troopers came up to our flat and took my parents and my aunt and uncle away with them. My cousin was, I think, she was six or five years older than I and so we were left on our own and I think I just relied on her. So, she must've looked after me and after herself and we didn't know are we going to see them again. We've heard all sorts of rumours that they were being taken away and I don't know how long they were away. I don't think it was very long. I think it was some days and first one came back and they all came back. But secondly, I remember my mother saying they were standing in a queue and one of these storm troopers they would just say you go this side you go that side you go this side. And they were lucky to be the ones that went back home. The others were taken away. So, we were aware of things happening and then my aunt and uncle left to go to Israel with my cousin. And then my parents must've heard that there was a place for me to go to England.

Kindertransport

Reports of Kristallnacht in the British press forced many to recognize the dangers Jews and others faced under the Nazis. Public sympathy, particularly for children across Germany and the occupied countries, led to an urgent debate in Parliament on the twenty-first of November 1938. The plight of children was recognised and the Kindertransport (children's transport) began operations. Temporary exceptions to the requirement for individual affidavits were agreed, but charities had to guarantee that they were able to cover the cost of caring for these children. The children still needed visas. No-one was allowed to enter without proof that they would not be a burden on the state. Charities also had to guarantee a further fifty pounds per child towards the cost of returning them at the end of this temporary arrangement. Groups and charities across Britain began the work of forming committees to raise funds and to find suitable homes and accommodation for the children. Once news of Kristallnacht spread, it was clear that the situation was urgent; these children needed rescuing. An appeal for homes was broadcast on the BBC Home Service on the twenty-fifth of November.

The Central British Fund for German Jewry was established in 1933 by a number of prominent Jews including Simon Marks, the chair of Marks & Spencer, the bankers Lionel and Anthony de Rothschild, and Chaim Weizmann, who would later become the first president of Israel. Renamed the Council for German Jewry in 1936, the group were primarily responsible for establishing and co-ordinating the Kindertransport from their base at Bloomsbury House, set on one side of the London garden square close to the British Museum in the heart of Bloomsbury. As the group expanded to become the information hub and centre for an increasing range of activities - co-ordinating the Kindertransport, finding homes for the children, finding refugees work and somewhere to live, and helping refugees trace family members - it quickly ran out of space for staff and volunteers. They moved round the corner to larger premises in Woburn House and became the communication hub for many thousands of refugees and those trying to help them. Refugees reported many kindnesses from the Quakers and Jews working there. The logistics of financing and moving several thousand frightened children, who did not speak English, to their designated place to stay, whether it was to be a foster family, hostel, or orphanage, were complex. Woburn House staff continued to monitor the children's wellbeing throughout the war.

In Germany, a network of organizers had been established. These volunteers identified those children most at risk from Nazi persecution, those already in concentration camps, those whose parents were in camps, orphans, or those whose parents were too poor to feed them. Children were only accepted on the scheme if they travelled unaccompanied, without their parents. If Paula had found sending Peter to his brother in London hard, to decide to send your child to an unknown country to be cared for by strangers must have been even more frightening. Each child was only allowed to take one small suitcase, no valuables and less than ten Reichsmarks (about eight English pounds). The first train left Berlin on the first of December 1938, arriving in Harwich a day later, carrying two hundred children. Eight days later, a train with six hundred children left Vienna. As the transports only left from major cities, some parents had to arrange for their children to travel from their homes in the country, often a long journey to get to the central collection point before they could even join the Kindertransport. Parting was terrible, although parents told their children they were off on an adventure and would soon be reunited. They had no idea when or if they would ever meet again.

Ilse was fourteen when she left Vienna on a Kindertransport on fifteenth of May 1939:

I do not remember how many children were on my train. I think I blocked out the journey until we were in Holland and were fed by the lovely people there! We had many three-to-five-year-olds, who had no idea what was happening to them and only cried for their parents who had the strength to send them to a strange country – to strangers – not knowing who and if they would be cared for.

Annie was fourteen when she left a village near Augsburg, Germany on a Kindertransport:

However, the children could still get out on children's transports. My mother set it up, she only cared that my brother and I should be safe. What happened was a man in the village came to my brother, Walter, who could write English, and said, "Would you please write a letter to this lady in England whose address I am giving you. Would you please ask her whether she could do something for my two children?"

My mother said, "Sure, he will write the letter, but you have to let him write on behalf of my children as well."

So, my brother wrote the letter to this woman and he wrote it on behalf of those two little girls and cousin Rudi and me. And all four of us came out as a result of it. The whole thing took just a few months. But we didn't leave together. First, we got the news that they had a place for the girls. Rudi followed.

In my luggage, all I brought was a little bit of jewellery. It was hidden. One diamond ring, and the gold bracelet that I wear with the corals, some gold pieces and a little necklace. My mother had rolled the diamond ring into a ball of wool, the coral bracelet was in the pocket of a shirt which had zippers in the pockets, the gold pieces were put into a Nivea can, a flat round tin with silver paper on the top and she had pushed them into the cream and then put the silver paper back and the little necklace, she had taken a thread spool and taken the paper off and pushed it into the hole in the spool and stuck the paper back on. "Now that is where it is," she said. "If you are hungry, you go and you sell it."

They never found anything. But I had ten marks in my pocket when I left for England, that's all I was allowed to take, and they took that away from me at the border.

Partly, it was a big adventure for a girl of fourteen, going to a foreign country. I was a venturesome child. It never occurred to me that we would never see each other again. We never spoke about it though my mother may well have thought it. By then, we knew about Dachau, but nobody could have wildly assumed that Auschwitz would happen. How could we?

My father took me to Munich. My mother didn't come to the station with us. She stayed outside the house and waved goodbye. And in Munich, I had a little navy coat and a hat with ribbons down the back, a red ribbon, and a navy-blue dress I had made myself with red buttons (I still have the buttons). And on the platform in Munich, my father checked me in with the leader of the transport. And he put his hands on my head gently and he cried, and he kissed me goodbye, and he put me on the train. He put me on the train and that was the last I ever saw him. And there was a train full of children. And there was a platform full of parents, all weeping.

In March 1939, the German army invaded Czechoslovakia. Nicholas Winterton established a Czech organization to help children escape Nazi persecution. Some brave parents chose to send their children to safety, not knowing where they were going or if they would ever be reunited. The Czech Kindertransport saved around six hundred and sixty children. The last group of children left Berlin on the first of September 1939; the day Germany invaded Poland. Two days later, Britain and France declared war on the Nazis and all Kindertransport stopped.

Chapter 7

London: A New Life in Streatham

An anxious trip

Peter's journey from Vienna to London took three days. After his mother had seen him off at the Westbahnhof station in Vienna, the train travelled to Zurich. He had not realized how tense he was until he heard the border guard say, "Guten Tag" with a distinctive Swiss accent. He had crossed the border out of Austria into Switzerland and was safe from the Nazis. Alone, too anxious to read, he looked out of the train window and worried about those he had left behind and what he would find in London. The mountains of Switzerland gradually gave way to hills, covered in vines and valleys with pretty buildings and then flatter fields with crops and cattle as the train passed across France. After travelling for eighteen hours, the train pulled into the Gare du Nord, Paris and Peter disembarked, pleased to be able to stretch his long legs. The huge ironwork pillars that supported the glass roof soared above the platform. In many ways, this great building was similar to the station he had left in Vienna with ornate architecture and the smell of good coffee.

As he had to wait for the boat train that would take him to his half-brother in London, Peter visited the station buffet. Keen to conserve the small amount of money he had, in stilted schoolboy French, he only ordered a ham sandwich and cup of coffee. He could not help admiring the piles of croissant and patisserie displayed along the counter and, under a glass dome, a large cake made of rings of pastry, decorated with choux paste balls, frothy creams, caramel and chocolate, a Gâteau Saint Honoré. Peter promised himself that one day, he would return to Paris and have a slice of that cake. Then he washed as best he could and found a seat on the evening boat train. Peter just had to cross the Channel to reach Erich in London. Although he had messed around on boats in the Austrian lakes and been on the Adriatic when he visited Venice with his mother, this was Peter's first experience of crossing a real sea.

Every time we returned from France on a ferry as a family, we had to stand on the deck. When the white cliffs of Dover came into sight, Peter would say how, the first time he saw those cliffs, he was so grateful to the country that took him in as he realized he was arriving in a country that would make him free from antisemitism.

Erich and Karla met a very tired Peter from the boat train when it arrived at Victoria and took him to Streatham on a suburban train. Peter's first view of London was through a grubby train window. As the train rattled along viaducts, he could see houses, shops, factories and repair works jumbled together below. Peter was surprised by how small and close together all the terraces of brick houses were, built back-to-back with a small yard and, possibly, a ginnel running between rows. There was no apparent planning, streets had simply been built wherever there was space for them. He was pleased when they passed parks and gardens dotted around. Unlike the formal public spaces of Vienna, these parks had grass with borders bright with summer flowers.

The entrance to one of the blocks in 'The High', Streatham.

Arriving in Streatham for the first time was a shock for Peter, as it would be later, for Paula. In comparison with their home in Vienna, it seemed to be miles from the centre of London.

It had taken them over half an hour to travel from Victoria to Streatham. Always busy, Streatham High Road was one of the main routes out of London to the south coast. The road was lined with four and five-story blocks of flats that towered over the pavement. These blocks were mostly constructed in the 1930s with shops at pavement level on the ground floor and apartments above them. These flats began to be more popular as people fled Hitler's persecution, ending up in London. Exhaust fumes and noise bounced off the buildings. On warm days, they appeared to shimmer in a haze over the pavement.

Erich and Karla posing by the pool at 'The High'.

Erich and Karla had taken a lease on a flat in 'The High', one of the smarter buildings on Streatham High Road. In 1937, the rent on a two-room flat in 'The High' was advertised at eighty pounds per year, including utilities. Unusually for England, it offered uniformed porters, central heating, constant hot water, a residents' club and a swimming pool. The front entrance was quite imposing, with a tall, arched Art Deco front door below an ornate wrought-iron fanlight. The name of the block was picked out in black tiles on white in the exterior porch; on a fine day this reflected on the brass at the base of the front doors. The black and white checkerboard hall led to sweeping stairs with a wrought-iron balustrade. The building and flat were considered smart for a 1930s London suburb. In comparison with the opulence of Scheyvogelgasse, this flat, with its draughty metal framed Crittall windows, was small; there were only two small rooms for all three of them. Karla had a welcome meal ready for their arrival, goulash with boiled potatoes. Before they sat down to catch up on each other's lives, they telephoned Vienna to let Paula know Peter had arrived safely and her two sons were now together.

Erich sitting in the living room with a black cat on his knee.

Earlier refugees, fleeing from Russian pogroms at the turn of the century, had already left their mark on Streatham. Montague Burton, of Burton's tailors, born Meshe Osinsky in Lithuania, commissioned a spectacular Art Deco façade featuring elephants for his store at 103-105 Streatham High Road. There were even slight similarities between the Golden Domes Cinema and Palast Kino as both had a pair of domes rising above the roofline.

Peter described the Streatham flat:

Erich and Karla lived in a flat in a new block on Streatham Hill. It had a living room and a bedroom with modern, light-oak furniture. On the ground-floor was a communal billiards room, a card room, an open-air swimming pool. It was a pleasant home for a couple in their mid-twenties. I slept on a divan in the living room next to their bedroom. The rooms were small, the walls were thin. I must have been a considerable pain in their necks. They never showed it.

Peter was clearly impressed by his local 'flick':

Cinemas! The size of them, plush seats and electric organs going up and down. What first brought home to me the might of the British Empire was the Golden Domes in Streatham.

Postcard showing Peter in a striped towelling bathrobe.
Paula wrote on the back 'Peterl 1938. I have arrived in London'.

Presumably, Peter sent the photograph as a postcard to Paula. He is standing in front of the changing rooms for the swimming pool, pointing at the date on the copy of the *Daily Express* to mark his safe arrival in London.

Paula escapes too

Once Peter was safely in London, Paula began preparations for her own departure. Erich sent another affidavit. Selma, still distraught following the death of her husband, Julius, was barely functioning. Her work at the cinema was something she could hold onto. Paula's brother, Alfred, had died in 1936, leaving his widow, Laura, alone with their two sons, Fritz and Franz. Fritz was congenitally weak, epileptic and was not fit to travel. Naturally, his mother wanted to remain and care for him. As a Christian, Laura should have been safe from antisemitic persecution. Ernst and Muschi were in Brno and, like Laura, Muschi was a Christian. Despite her best efforts, Paula failed to persuade her family to join in her bid to escape from Vienna.

Paula joined the queues for the permits that would allow her to leave Austria. She had to obtain certificates showing that she had paid all government charges: income tax, inheritance tax, building charges, rental tax, welfare tax and the exit tax, before she could even apply for an exit visa. She had to queue, often for hours, outside the different offices each in a different part of the city. Occasionally, Nazi thugs amused themselves by pulling random individuals from a queue to beat them where they stood on the pavement in front of the other terrified people waiting. Offices would suddenly close and the queue sent away for the day so she had to return on another day until a certificate was granted. Individual certificates were only valid for a month; if one expired, the process had to be repeated. All personal property had to be listed and valued as it would form part of the calculation of the final exit tax which was a quarter of all assets. This was particularly difficult for Paula as her main asset was the cinema. The cinema had effectively been Aryanised. Paula and Selma were displaced as managers and two Nazi officials were instated in their place. The Nazi managers paid Paula and Selma less and less each month, until collectively, they received less than the salaries that they needed to pay their staff. Selma would also continue to need an income from the cinema once Paula had left. With each successive review, the valuation of the cinema decreased but the exit taxes increased relentlessly.

Paula was only allowed to take the contents of one room. Like so many others, she tried and failed to sell her once valuable furniture. The market was already flooded with Biedermeier furniture and Persian carpets. Paula and Seffi moved the furniture that she wanted to take to England into one room. An SS officer, accompanied by a couple of SA men, came to the flat and worked through the packing cases and boxes writing a list of what Paula would be permitted to send to England. The two frightened women watched in horror as one of the SA men shoved his rifle butt into a case of china, smashing everything. The list survives as a sad reminder of a once affluent life. Fortunately, the inspectors had failed to notice that several Persian rugs were hidden under the furniture. The permitted items were dispatched to a furniture depository in South London that Erich had contracted. They joined many similar items sent by Jews as they escaped from Austria and Germany.

Paula said a tearful farewell to Seffi, who returned to her family in the Tyrol. Then, she gave up the lease on the Scheyvogelgasse apartment and moved into a cheap hotel, Pension Cosmopolit, on Alserstrasse, a couple of streets from the Palast Kino.

Paula also needed to obtain a transit visa which would allow her to travel through countries during her journey from Vienna to London. Switzerland had closed its borders to refugees, so she would have to make a longer, more dangerous journey than the one Peter made only a few months earlier. The Nazis, keen to be rid of Jews, issued single entry visas allowing Austrians to travel across Germany to Belgium and then to the ferry terminal at the Hook of Holland.

With each week it took for Paula to get the necessary permits, the queues at the emigration offices grew, as increasingly people recognised that they needed to leave. Exit taxes became more punitive. If there was something wrong with a form, or a paper was missing, Paula would be turned away and have to queue again on another day. Sometimes, the clerks and SA turned people away for no reason other than caprice. Even with the money she managed to raise from the cinema, her dwindling investments, along with the sale of some of her jewellery and furniture was insufficient to cover the exit tax demanded.

Finally, in desperation, she telephoned Ing. Sumbul in Belgrade and explained her situation. It must have been very difficult for such an independent woman, used to providing for others, to have to ask a man for money. She had refused his many offers of marriage to retain her independence. Ing. Sumbul arranged to transfer funds to her bank in Vienna so she could finally pay the tax and obtain an exit permit. Once she had paid the exit tax, her final queue, for an entry visa, was at the British embassy. Here, officials kindly allowed the queue to stand inside the embassy, away from bullying Nazis.

Meanwhile in London, Peter also received a telephone call:

In October, we had a call from a banker. Mr Sumbul in Belgrade had instructed him to send me two hundred pounds in monthly instalments. It was a great deal of money for us.

I remembered him well. His Excellency, Herr Direktor Sumbul was tall, distinguished, a wealthy industrialist, an honorary consul, an old friend and admirer of my mother's. Her husband, too, if she hadn't said no when he asked her. Twice married was quite enough, she said. Giving up her independence in Vienna and playing second fiddle to him in Belgrade wouldn't do. He continued to take her out in style when he visited Vienna, and he was always nice to me. He never married. Two days later, we heard from mother. She had received greetings from a friend in Belgrade, she hoped we would have Christmas together.

Paula then made another round of her relatives so that she could say goodbye. She still tried, but failed, to persuade them to leave. Conditions for Jews had deteriorated markedly in the few months since Peter's departure. They all maintained the pretence that life would return to normal shortly, and they would all meet again when Paula returned to Vienna. She was particularly sad to leave her sister, Selma. They had shared so much together in setting up and running of the cinema. Selma's beloved husband, Julius, had died in a Vienna hospice a few months earlier at the end of May. Selma, numb with grief, was unable to think of moving from her routine, the familiar flat and the cinema. Paula hoped she would feel able to join her and the boys in England. Paula formally transferred her thirty per cent share in the Palast Kino to Selma in the hope that it could be restored to her once conditions improved. As she parted from Selma, her relatives and the cinema staff, some had worked there for many years and were almost like family, Paula knew she was unlikely to see some or all of them ever again.

Paula's journey to England was even more terrifying than Peter's had been as she had to cross Germany. Emigrants were only allowed to take one suitcase and about twenty pounds with them when they left. No-one saw her off at the station as it was too dangerous to be identified as a Jew. Not wanting to draw attention to herself, she wore a drab raincoat, a simple cloche hat, flat shoes and no visible jewellery. Paula looked at the ground as she walked to the platform and bore the officious examination of her papers by the SA at the station meekly. Once the train began to move through the Reich, Paula's nerves were taught, stretched almost to breaking at every station and each time uniformed men entered her compartment. Nazi guards smirked each time they inspected her papers and sneered at her meagre luggage. Finally, exhausted, she crossed the border into Belgium and freedom. In Brussels, she looked for a cheap boarding house near the station for the night and ate a frugal meal at one of the many cafes. Her only consolation was that she would soon be with both her sons in London.

Twenty new words a day
Paula was fifty-four and spoke no English when, eventually, she arrived in England. Her sons and daughter-in-law met her from the ferry when it docked at Harwich and accompanied her to Erich's small, Streatham flat. With very limited means, Karla had prepared a welcome meal with what she could manage, pork schnitzel and sauté potatoes followed by her famous chocolate hedgehog cake. The flat was cold.

Paula found London cold, grey and very damp. With the addition of Peter, the Streatham flat was already overcrowded, and her arrival did not improve the situation. Erich took any work he could find but there was little he was suitable for, so there was not always enough money to buy more than basic food.

Erich and Karla had not wanted to worry Paula with their problems while she was trying to escape from Vienna.

Following the Anschluss, Germans had taken over the engineering company which had employed Erich as a sales representative. Once the company was given over to arms manufacturing, their requirement for a sales representative in England had ceased and Erich had been made redundant.

Paula spent a great deal of time in public libraries, using the small dictionary she'd given Peter when he started English classes back in Vienna, to translate the front page of the *Daily Express*. She wrote a list of twenty new words to learn each day, and her boys tested her pronunciation.

Money was short but the family still needed to pay for food, rent and for Peter to study. Ing. Sumbul arranged another payment to a bank in London although he was also beginning to experience problems as living conditions deteriorated in Belgrade. Woburn House in Bloomsbury was a centre for refugees, an information hub for missing persons, for jobs and for co-ordinating the placement of Kindertransport children. Recognising she was an additional strain on Erich and Karla's limited finances, Paula applied to Woburn House for work; she was prepared to do anything. Her registration document shows that she spent a month at 3 Hunter Street, WC1, probably a cheap guest house close to Woburn House, before moving briefly to spend a couple of weeks with a doctor and, presumably, his family, in SW1. She may have been employed as a domestic help for the family. Paula's domestic skills were limited, her parents had a girl from the country for heavy work and Seffi had looked after the family in Vienna. She didn't know how to clean a grate or lay a fire. Permanently cold, Paula missed the stoves she was used to in Vienna. Her clothes were entirely unsuitable for damp England, too smart, too cosmopolitan and too expensive. However, she was extremely glad that she had sewn her fur coat inside the old raincoat she had worn for the journey to England as it made a welcome extra layer on her bed as the nights were cold.

Chapter 8

Tynemouth: The Hostel is Created

The Jewish Community in Sunderland

At the beginning of the eighteenth-century, Memel was an important trading centre. Its location at both the most northern and most eastern points of Prussia, plus an excellent natural harbour, that gave easy access the bay to the major port at Gdańsk and then to the ports of northern Europe, were all major assets that formed the city. Today, it is Lithuania's third largest city, Klaipėda. With one of the strongest fortresses in the country, Memel became a major port primarily exporting timber to England for use in shipbuilding. Sawmills and furniture-making businesses developed in the area. In 1795, a small town twenty-five kilometres north of Memel, Kretinga, was occupied by Russia. As it was positioned so close to the German border, Kretinga became a centre for international trade. From the middle of the eighteenth-century, Jews began to settle in Memel, earning their living chiefly from trade. Some ran shops, others worked in the lucrative amber trade, selling their products in Russia or at the tourist shops in the nearby coastal resort Palanga. As in Boskovice, the ghetto outside Brno, the population was stable with the same extended families living side-by-side for several generations.

By the middle of the nineteenth century, although industrialisation had spread across Europe, Memel was a backwater, still dependent on timber and hand-crafted furniture making. Russia needed coal to fuel its own industrial revolution. Timber was no longer required in England, instead, coal from the mines in the North East of England was exported via Sunderland to Memel. Under Russian rule, living conditions deteriorated and Kretinga was no exception. Jews began the journey to Sunderland, both as economic migrants hoping to improve their lives as well as to avoid being conscripted into the Russian Army. English ships would normally return to Sunderland empty; the industrial revolution in Britain meant there was now no longer any need to import timber. Rather than travelling empty ships' captains were pleased to take Russian and Polish Jews as passengers for modest sums. Most passengers intended to travel further to the major ports at Southampton and Liverpool on their way to America or to make a living in London. A few stayed in Sunderland and a community developed. Some of the families who had been neighbours in Kretinga became neighbours again in Sunderland.

Israel Jacobs was one of many who travelled from Kretinga to Sunderland. Instead of continuing his journey, he remained there. In 1876, he married Augusta Asher and became a naturalised British citizen ten years later, on the fourteenth of May 1886. Israel and Augusta had eleven children, seven boys and four girls. Five years later, the 1891 census showed the family were living at 11 Nicholson Street, Sunderland and Israel worked as a pawnbroker. The 1901 census shows Israel was dealing in furniture and was also a shopkeeper, and the family had moved to Thornhill Park in Bishopwearmouth. Clearly, the family furniture business did well as according to the 1911 census, they were living in a house with ten rooms and had a servant. Israel prospered in Sunderland, yet he retained ties with the community in Kretinga and was one of the key members of the Crottingen Relief Fund, a group established to raise funds to help rebuild the synagogue and homes damaged by fire in 1889.

At the outbreak of the Great War, the Jacobs' boys volunteered. George, a mining engineer, was one of the first to enlist in 1914. He was awarded the Distinguished Conduct Medal for bravery, while driving field ambulances and had just been recommended for a commission when he was killed near Martinpuich on the tenth of October 1916. His only son was to die in the next war. His brother Cyril was the medical officer for the Lincolnshire regiment and was awarded the Military Cross and bar for evacuating wounded soldiers from the battlefield and then for evacuating the wounded from his dressing station after it had been hit by heavy fire. Cyril survived the war and went on to become an ophthalmic surgeon practising in Manchester and Crewe. Harold also survived the war as a mechanic with the Royal Flying Corps. No doubt their four sisters: Bertha, Grace, Rita and Flora did much to support the war effort.

Dr Alec Freedman was posted to the Russian front as an army doctor in the Great War on the assumption that, being of Russian extraction, he spoke Russian. He did not but survived the war with honour. Returning to Sunderland and the Russian expatriate community, he met and was entranced by Rita Jacobs, Israel and Adele's penultimate child. They married, establishing themselves in Roseworth Tower, the Grove, Gosforth, and had two sons, Roland and Huntley.

Jewish Boards of Guardians

Large numbers of immigrants from Russia and Poland began to arrive in London and other major cities in the nineteenth century looking for a better life. Some found work quickly or started businesses; others took time to establish themselves, and some fell on hard times through bad luck, sickness or bereavement. In the last category, many were widows with children or orphans with no way of supporting themselves. In 1859, the Jewish Board of Guardians was established by a consortium of synagogues in the East End of London to alleviate the growing poverty and distress within the immigrant community. Funded by donations from affluent members of the community, individuals could apply for aid once they had been in the country for at least six months. Following this model, Boards of Guardians were then rapidly established in cities throughout the country and remain active today.

The Newcastle Committee

In the 1930s, Newcastle was a major industrial city in the Northeast of England. Built along the River Tyne, the shipyards and the heavy industry that supported the city were becoming increasingly uncompetitive in the global market. When the main shipyard, Palmer's, closed in 1934, there was no alternative employer in the area to replace them. Unemployment was high, and families had to rely on food handed out by Salvation Army soup kitchens. In 1936, two hundred men walked from Jarrow to London to petition Parliament. Known as the Jarrow March, it lasted from the fifth to the thirty-first of October highlighting poverty in the North East.

In response to the publicity surrounding the Kindertransport, a committee was formed under the auspices of the Newcastle Board of Guardians to establish and run a hostel for children who had escaped from the Nazis. David Summerfield, a well-respected jeweller with a shop in one of the premier shopping streets in Newcastle, was elected as the chairman and became responsible for raising funds for the hostel. Although the Jewish community in Newcastle was small in comparison with London or Manchester, there were fifteen synagogues in the city and surrounding communities including Gosforth, Jesmond, North and South Shields, and Sunderland. At each synagogue, the rabbis appealed for donations of money and goods to set-up the hostel saying, "if it isn't good enough for your children, it isn't good enough for these girls!" Some communities, like the Whitley Bay Hebrew Congregation, undertook to raise monthly subscriptions. The expectation was that the hostel would be temporary, caring for about twenty to thirty children until things had settled down and their parents were able to collect them.

Roseworth Tower, the home of Dr and Mrs Freedman, was the hub of the operation. The imposing Victorian building was both their home and Alec's clinical practice, with consulting and waiting rooms and as was usual in those days, a dispensary. The house and practice operated apparently effortlessly. Rita Freedman, known as 'Mrs' or 'The Mrs' to Alec's 'Dr', was so unobtrusively efficient that things just worked. She would create and serve a complex meal whilst apparently just chatting in her kitchen, immaculately turned out with a silk scarf elegantly draped around her neck. They were established members of the community. Dr Freedman was the police surgeon, chairman of the local Rotary Club and played both tennis and bridge at tournament standard. They were popular, well known and enjoyed a brisk social life with regular trips to the races. They were a generous and powerful couple who would, much later, become my Auntie Rita and Uncle Alec.

My first appearance on cine film, aged around six months, was in the garden at Roseworth Tower, posed for the camera in a pretty white dress and cardigan resolutely unsmiling. 'Dr', immaculate in a dark suit, white shirt, with impeccable cuffs fixed with gold links, and broad pale blue tie. 'Mrs', elegant in a white turn-back dress with an abstract black pattern, jiggled me in her arms coaxing a smile. 'Dr' held out a bunch of flowers, picked from the rich herbaceous border surrounding the very green lawn. I snatch at them. Then, he held up his black Scottie dog for me to stroke. Adult hands curb my enthusiasm. Even in a short, slightly out of focus cine film, it is clear that the Freedmans were kindly supporting my parents who were still not entirely comfortable with their infant.

Rita, always generous with her time and sympathy, enrolled other members of her family, the Jacobs, on the hostel committee. Colonel and Mrs Jackson, a jolly pair who had travelled extensively in the Far East, became active members along with Mr and Mrs Wilkes. At the time, housing boys and girls together could not be countenanced. Following a fierce debate amongst the committee, it was decided to offer places to girls as they were considered to be even more vulnerable than boys.

Whilst David Summerfield concentrated on fund raising, the remainder of the committee, no doubt led by Rita Freedman, embarked on the task of finding and equipping a suitable house and recruiting matrons to care for the children. They wrote to Woburn House asking for recommendations of suitable German speaking refugees to fill these posts. With her culinary expertise, Alice Urbach was an obvious choice for cook. Rita Jackson travelled to London to interview her. Fortunately, the two straightforward women formed an instant rapport as they shared a forthright manner and no-nonsense approach. Alice, in turn, recommended her good friend Paula for the matron's job. Aside from motherhood, neither woman had worked with children; their expertise lay in running cinemas and cookery schools. Both had boys, so neither had any experience of girls as children or teenagers.

The Tynemouth Hostel

In January 1939, the committee found a suitable property to use as the hostel; the house was loaned to the committee by the kind person who had just inherited it. 55 Percy Park, Tynemouth was a very large, three-storey, late-Victorian, terraced house that had been built to last. It overlooks Seafield Green, the Grand Hotel, Longsands Beach and the North Sea. With eight rooms and a huge kitchen it seemed perfect. Less than half a mile from the station, it could easily be reached by a local train from Newcastle.

Built by the Duke of Northumberland in the 1860s, Percy Park is a street of brick-built, tall, terraced houses facing the green and at right angles to the beach. The houses were built to withstand storms. Like most Victorian houses, it has a stone-faced bay on the ground floor. There is a small lobby between the wooden front door and an inner door with a stained-glass panel, the inner door is framed by coloured glass panels made of simple disks of yellow and orange glass set into lead. Colours from these panels reflect along the hall when the outer door is open and the sun is shining. The newel post and nicely turned spindles are wood and the sides of the stairs themselves are finished with sweeping Art Deco swirls. The rooms are large and square, finished with ornamental mouldings around the ceiling and central roses. No doubt, the sash windows encouraged drafts and a considerable amount of effort was required to maintain the open fires, particularly in the carrying of coal upstairs to the top floor.

The *Shields Daily News* ran regular articles about the hostel reporting on ninth of January 1939 that members of the committee had completed an inspection to see what needed to be done to open the hostel for twenty young women. All the approvals necessary for the project and the costs, which the Newcastle committee had to fund, were mentioned in the article which also noted an affiliated committee set up in Whitley Bay.

The committee succeeded in persuading many in Newcastle to contribute the money, time, furnishings and supplies needed to establish the hostel. The community gave what they could and were very generous. Local builders and tradesmen helped to get the house into order, decorating, repairing the sash windows and shutters, cleaning chimneys and servicing the ancient stove. Shops donated wood and coal needed to heat the house; others donated curtains, carpet and bedding and food. Some lent vans to deliver items to Percy Park. Committee members Rita Freedman and Nolly Collins remade the curtains to make them fit the ground floor bay window, as well as each of the imposing rows of three, tall sash-windows on the first and second floors. The committee managed to acquire enough to furnish the house from the kitchen with two sets of everything to meet kosher dietary requirements to tables, chairs, beds, cots to bedding. They needed a constant supply of food, and fuel while the hostel was operating. Alice and Paula worked hard to organise the house. It took less than three months from the committee's decision to set up a hostel to welcoming its first children.

The first groups of girls arrived early in 1939 to a house that would become home to over forty girls during the time it was open. Although the original intention was that the hostel should only be a temporary refuge, the Newcastle committee would eventually end up supporting the girls until they were able to move on to other things, many not until after the war had ended in 1945.

On Friday the seventeenth of February, the *Shields Daily News* published another article, a long one this time. The article noted the involvement of Paula and Alice as taking on lead roles in running the hostel where they would be responsible for the cooking and housework but not the teaching of the girls, which would be carried out by teachers. The article provided details of Paul and Alice's backgrounds in Vienna and also details about their children. Paula and Alice were quoted as being excited about the task ahead especially the visit of the King and Queen when they were planned to visit the borough the following Tuesday.

The children arrive

The first children to arrive at the hostel came on a Kindertransport ship that docked at Southampton and they were taken initially to Dovercourt, a hastily repurposed Butlins holiday camp. Given the need to find accommodation for the children during their transition to more permanent arrangements of foster families or hostels, a holiday camp met most requirements. Empty in January, the Butlins camp already had kitchens equipped to feed large numbers of people, ample sleeping accommodation, and spaces for recreational and group activities so it was a simple way of meeting these needs quickly. Although the charities managed the children, Butlins retained the catering contract.

Papers from the national archives show that the Women's Voluntary service sent Lady Marian Philipps and N. de Selincourt to inspect Dovercourt who concluded on the twelfth of September 1939:

The camp leaders were very keen, full of human kindness, vitality and emanating a cheerful atmosphere. Great efforts are made to stress the future hope of the children and so help them to forget the past. They seemed wonderfully happy, considering all they had been through. The arrangements for heating, clothing, sanitation and health were good, and the occupation of time as regards leisure seemed fairly satisfactory for an emergency measure. Better organisation for lessons and more variety in games would no doubt be possible over longer periods and in camps for boys or girls only. The one glaring defect appears to be the profiteering on catering which should be remedied. The excuse for this would seem to be the difficulty of finding suitable accommodation in a short time, which necessitated using the easiest available.

N. de Selincourt

The majority of children arrived at Dovercourt straight from Harwich; a few were sent to Liverpool Street to travel on to their future homes; and a few had to return to Dovercourt from Liverpool Street and wait for their accommodation to be arranged. For some of the children, it was the first time they had been separated from their parents and siblings. All were unhappy having to leave their homes and come to a strange country. They had been travelling for several days and were tired, scared and hungry when they finally arrived at Dovercourt. Very few of them spoke any English. Recognizing the trauma these children had experienced and how difficult their present circumstances must be for them, the camp leaders worked hard to produce a cheerful environment by organizing games, music and English lessons. A few undergraduate volunteers organized tutorials and group activities. Unfortunately, some of the girls destined for Tynemouth were delayed when an outbreak of measles at Dovercourt meant that they were then quarantined.

Some reported their shock at English catering. Paula was fifteen when she arrived from Vienna.

In 2018, she recalled:

They made us eat raw cabbage and uncooked tomato! I'd never had an uncooked tomato before.

They gave us this strange drink they called tea. It wasn't like any tea I'd had before, it was thick, with milk in it.

Others came via Liverpool Street where they were met by Woburn House representatives, organised into groups, and sent onto their temporary homes unaccompanied unless there was an older child available to look after them. Seeing signs to Liverpool Street Station, some of the children thought they had been taken to Liverpool not London. It was very noisy and smelt very differently from Vienna; there was no smell of coffee. London smelt damp and sooty, even the cigarette smoke was different. The huge concourse was full of adults in strange, grey clothes, rushing around. There were lots of small children with small suitcases and labels round their necks. Men and women with clipboards were trying to organise the children into lines; others offered drinks and sandwiches with unfamiliar fillings. Even the bread was different and everything tasted of salt. Then, they were faced with another long journey, without any idea of where they were going. None had any idea of England's geography, even the fields looked different from home and there were few mountains. Nor did they know what to expect when they finally arrived at their destination.

They were met at Newcastle by one of the matrons and taken to the hostel. Annie's story below shows how frightening this experience must have been. The children had been separated from their parents for less than a week, had travelled on strange trains and made the ferry crossing across the sea; the Channel was often rough, alone with unfamiliar companions who were also alone and scared. They were tired, cold, hungry, frightened and they could not understand English.

Annie was fourteen when she arrived from Germany in May 1939:

I remember little about the trip or about my arrival in England. A musty ship's cabin, arrival in London, name tag round my neck. A slim woman found me, handed me a little gift-wrapped package, a train journey, tea with milk, juck. I opened my gift, a tiny volume of Pride and Prejudice, leather bound, gold trim, couldn't read it then but have loved it ever since. Still by my bed. I ended up in a children's hostel, don't remember arriving there either. We were about twenty Jewish girls from about four to fifteen. We were well taken care of, the only hardship being unloved. It was before the war. The Jewish community of Newcastle was well to do and generous.

Ilse left Vienna on a Kindertransport on the fifteenth of May 1939. She was fourteen years-of-age and recalled:

After the two days (with my Mother in London), I was put on a train going to Tynemouth where a Jewish committee from Newcastle had rented a house for twenty children. The committee was informal with no meeting records kept. They were chaired by a well-known Jewish jeweller who was the spokesman and fundraiser in the community and very popular with us.

The group consisted of several couples, all living close to each other and not too far from our house at 55 Percy Park. It was within sight of the sea. They provided everything we needed – clothing, food, beds, curtains, carpets, coal, firewood and cleaning materials. Everything had to be marked milchig and fleischi – it was to be a kosher home.

A matron was hired, Mrs Urbach, who had been my mother's teacher in her cookery school in Vienna. She, in turn, brought in Mrs Sieber, her friend who had owned a movie house in Vienna. Both ladies, refugees themselves, had sons.

The children started to arrive in twos and threes and were separated into three groups: 'little ones', 'middle ones' and 'big ones', according to age. We big ones had to look after the younger ones and help with the housekeeping. It was very hard for some of the children who kept crying for their parents and who did not know if they would ever see them again. Of course, we did not speak English and one of the girls who came from Czechoslovakia did not speak English or German.

The matrons were kindly but also imposed rules and regulations which some children found hard and resented. Luckily, for some children, their parents came and picked them up. Some parents got jobs near the hostel to be close to their children.

The patrons of the hostel insisted that the food served met the requirements of a kosher diet which prohibits some foods altogether, for example pork. Mixing milk and meat is forbidden and households keep separate cutlery marked milchig (milk) and fleischig (meat) to avoid cross contamination. Kosher meat requires animals to be slaughtered and butchered in specific ways.

Dasha was seven years old when she arrived from Prague in 1939:

> It must have been early in 1939, all kinds of preparations were being made. The next thing I remember is going to the station where a ticket with a number was tied around my neck. My brother and two other girls who were friends shared our compartment. My mother was crying bitterly and for me the feeling of being abandoned was the most horrific experience of my life. At this stage, I did not understand the implications of our parting. Now that I myself am a mother, I well know the utter despair and helplessness that my parents would have felt, seeing their only two children leaving in a children's transport to an unknown destination in England. They chose this way for us as the shadows of war were upon them and they feared for our safety and hoped to follow shortly.

> The train pulled out of the station and we were excited with the anticipation of the journey ahead. Frightened at being torn away from my family, I was lucky to have the company of my brother who was five years older. The stability of being with my brother did not last – we were parted on arrival in England. I have no recollection of my arrival at the hostel in Tynemouth. Fortunately, the two friends who travelled with me in the same compartment stayed at the hostel for three months and I could communicate with them in Czech. All the other girls spoke German. At school, English was spoken which meant that I had to learn English and German at the same time.

Lisl arrived in London in August 1939 on one of the last Kindertransports. Her father was in England, whilst her mother remained in Vienna and was later sent to one of the camps:

> My father, after being in England for five months, managed to find a place for me and I left Vienna with the last Kindertransport on 22nd August 1938, leaving my mother alone

in Vienna. I was sent to the Tynemouth Hostel having gone through a traumatic journey getting there. We were twenty girls, the youngest was three, the oldest twelve. World War II broke out on my tenth birthday. Our committee consisted of very good Jewish people from Newcastle, and two Jewish refugee ladies were our caretakers.

Nobody came to pick me up. I was looking for my dad. I was told by a man from the Jewish agency, "You have to go to Newcastle." He bought me a banana and put me on a train but I did not know where to get off. My mother had given me a dictionary English German so the man who sat opposite me on the train went down the whole train and asked everyone "can you speak German?" And to this day, I feel bad that I never thanked him for it. I could not speak the language and did not know how to thank him. He found an old lady and a priest and they said to the man why are you shouting for someone who speaks German? And he said, this little girl is sitting here crying all the time and needs to speak German. And the lady understood me. And I asked: "What is Newcastle? I have to get off at Newcastle but the train does not stop." And she said, "you got on the train in London and Newcastle will come up in an hour." They were very nice and they were heading to Edinburgh but they got off at Newcastle just for me and found the people who were to pick me up.

The lady waiting for me said, "We have nineteen girls and you are number twenty." She spoke German but was from Czechoslovakia. I was in the taxi and came to a street and it was all dark. I was shivering and scared, I thought they might just have invented this hostel and kill me and throw me in the river. But all the girls were standing at the entrance, greeting me.

Although Alice and Paula did their best, greeting new arrivals with hot soup and cake, it took time for the girls to settle and form a community. Some children never settled, finding the regime harsh, lacking the individual love and care they found in the families they had left. Later, some would be angry at the limited opportunities offered by the strict regime. Others made the best of what was on offer. All hoped their parents would come and collect them soon.

Institutional life in the hostel was very different from the loving families the girls had been forced to leave. Some were disappointed not to have been allocated to foster families but realized later that there may have been advantages of being one of a group. Girls in the hostel were able to support one another and were sensitive to each other's needs, especially within their particular age group.

(Left to Right) Alice Urbach, Mrs Wilkes, Paula Sieber, Lisl and local help. 55 Percy Park, 1939.

As Elfie recalled:

Well, we were all in the same boat. I came to England with a friend, with Greta and she went to a family in London. We didn't know where we were going but she went to this family in London.

I came to the hostel and I used to think, "Oh Greta is so lucky to be with a family." But in fact, I learned many years later from her that they treated her like a maid. Oh. You know she was very unhappy there. Except they had another young woman staying at her home with them and I always assumed it was their daughter but they adopted this girl and she was oh, I think she was in maybe eighteen and Greta said to me after many years: if it hadn't been for her, I think that I would have run away so in the hostel, we were at least all in the same boat you know, coming from different countries. There were four girls there who came from Czechoslovakia. The majority came from Germany and I think there were just six of us who came from Austria.

Annie also remembered:

I don't remember my arrival finally in the hostel in Newcastle. We were about twenty Jewish girls of all ages, from about four to fifteen, and there were eight of us who were thirteen or fourteen. We were well taken care of. I did not suffer any hardship. There was plenty of money. There was a big house and we were excellently fed. It was before the war; there were no shortages. We were a block from the beach and it was summer, and so we went to the beach every day.

Thanks to Elfie for this picture of the girls on
Tynemouth beach. July, 1939.

We were still able to write to our parents – all the time – and I was able to tell them that I had arrived. Mail was very fast – German mail was very efficient – and there was nothing to say that was forbidden. There was a street photographer and for two pennies, you could have your picture taken. And we were constantly having our pictures taken and sending them home to our parents. That's when I learned to swim. One bank holiday, we even made it to the local paper, eight teenage girls in bathing suits. We had free access to the pool because we were refugee children and we were allowed to go to the movies once a week, free, which was good for our English. It was a beautiful summer in '39. There was no war yet.

All the children were troubled, missed their parents and families, letters were infrequent and often abruptly stopped altogether.

The children attended local schools and so they all had to learn English before they could learn anything.

Dasha explained how she needed to learn English and German at the same time before she could either learn anything at school or talk to her companions:

The difficult task of running a home in such hard times where both the matrons and the children were from all types and backgrounds were wounded by the traumatic events in their lives at that time.

After coming from a loving family home, I had to adapt to community life which was devoid of any personalised attention. To a seven-year-old child who could not make herself understood it was very traumatic, and I was miserable. I cried at the least provocation. The boredom at school was unending. Added to this, the bombing started. The shrill sounds of sirens became a nightly routine. We were woken at all hours of the night and herded into underground air-raid shelters for hours on end. During the days at school, there was continuous drill learning how to put on the claustrophobic rubber gas masks.

Running a home with twenty or so children involved a lot of menial, physical work. With only Alice and Paula to run the house, all the children had to carry out some of the routine tasks: cleaning, laundry, setting and cleaning fireplaces, cooking. Central heating, washing machines and dishwashers were things of the future. The girls were grouped by age, they shared bedrooms: younger, middle and older. The older girls were expected to look after younger girls, check that they did their homework, cleaned their teeth and brushed their hair properly. In turn, middle girls were expected to look after the little ones. The children, sensitive to the horrors their companions faced, comforted one another finding support from others in a similar position. Letters from parents arrived relatively regularly at first;

their flow diminished as conditions in Europe deteriorated. Understandably, these letters were prized possessions which, along with photographs of their families, were often kept under the girls' pillows.

The locals at Tynemouth welcomed these strange children treating them with generosity. News of this novelty spread quickly. They even appeared in the local paper.

Lisl remembered:

Two days I had been there and then the matrons said I have to go to school. I said I am not going. All the other girls had already gone to school, I was the last one, number twenty. I went with them on Monday. I did not know one word of English. The first lesson was geometry, I did not understand anything. The teacher comes to my desk, I had not written anything. The teacher pulls me up by my ear and puts me in front of the class. She has a cane and says give me your hand. But a girl gets up and says to the teacher, "She came with the people from the home" and the teacher puts down her cane. And she said: Your address? I say: 55 Percy Park. She embraced me and later helped me with my lessons.

The children suffered from all the normal childhood ailments. The matrons insisted all should have their hair cut following an outbreak of lice and enforced regular combing which greatly upset Ruth as dragging a comb through her curly hair must have snagged.

The local newspaper reported an outbreak of scarlet fever but that only affected one child. An undetected carrier for diphtheria infected most of the others; that necessitated the district nurse visiting to take throat swabs daily, as well as a trip to the isolation ward for many. None of the girls could go to school.

As Elfie recalled:

One girl, Ruth, she had both scarlet fever and diphtheria. The eldest girl, Margo, had a bad throat and the doctor diagnosed her as having just a bad throat and that's what we were told. It turned out that she was a carrier for diphtheria. So, every day, a doctor and a nurse came and swabbed everybody. And usually, one or two of us were carted off in an ambulance to the local hospital. And Ruth had both scarlet fever and diphtheria. So, she was on her own and I think she was in the hospital for quite a long time.

1939 was a hot summer. The older girls lived in rooms at the top of the house with sloping ceilings, straight under the roof, which must have been very hot in summer and very cold in winter. Sash windows are draughty in winter and can only be partly opened in summer. A house full of hot fractious girls, quarantined together for ten days, must have been difficult for everyone.

Ruth and Elfie, inscribed on the back, 'A reminder with love and thanks. Elfie'. 55 Percy Park, May, 1939.

Once quarantine was over, as the weather was warm and dry, the matrons sent the children out to the beach with packed lunches.

Elfie confirmed:

And 1939 was a beautiful summer. The hostel was just up the road from the beach. So, they sent us with sandwiches and things down on the beach during the summer holidays and we spent the days on the beach. Very nice. Next to the beach was a swimming pool. So, from school, we used to go to the swimming pool and I remember, I could swim because when I was much younger, my parents sent me with a party of people to Italy and I learned to swim there on the beach in the water so I could swim but I couldn't jump in and swim. I always lost my breath if I jumped in. And I always remember to get your certificate you had to swim from the deep end into the shallow end and the teacher said you go down the steps and then swim. But that was right next to the beach. During the summer holidays, we spent all the time on the beach.

In July, there was a long article in the *Shields Daily News* about the girls' experiences of the Priory School, Tynemouth. The reporter acknowledged the difficulties posed by teaching children who could not speak English and the importance of teachers addressing this problem. Mr Russell, the headmaster, explained his approach was to only allow the girls to speak English, and that by mixing in small groups, they learnt to understand speech quickly but were slower to speak or write English. The girls attended normal lessons and were generally good at arithmetic.

The article reported Mr Russell saying:

"Helene came here on March 15th and two months later wrote an essay. It's covered one and a half pages of foolscap paper, and while it is not perfect English, it is understandable. The other children have taken to them very kindly and the refugees have had several girls to tea at the hostel."

With regard to games, the headmaster said the children were clumsy at first with English games but were picking them up splendidly. When questioned, Frieda, Elfie, Lottie, Lisle and Helga were all positive about school and they were particularly pleased to have got their sums right! They enjoyed swimming but they had not played ball games before in Germany and Austria.

The girls. Tynemouth, 1939. (Left to Right) Back row: Hedy, Ruth, Sophy, Lisl, Ruth. Middle row: Lore, Hilde, Elfie, ?, Dasha. Front row: Frieda, Lea, Inge.

Teachers

The generosity of schoolteachers in helping these girls to adjust to a very different education system in an unfamiliar language both in Tynemouth and, after the hostel moved to Windermere, is mentioned by several of the women who were in the hostel. It is difficult for us to understand now how different the school systems were in the 1930s. Clearly, teachers in Tynemouth were impressed by the girls' numeracy and their ability to structure essays despite their limited exposure to English.

As Elfie recalled:

So, I went to secondary modern and we had to write an essay. And I wrote an essay and I can't remember what they said was about and we had to hand it in and then the teacher handed the essay back to us. And I was very shy in those days. And the teacher said you've all had your essays but I do not understand. I can see her now standing there on the podium. And she said here is a girl who can't speak English who's just learned English. She can write a good essay in beautiful handwriting.

Why can't you all do the same? And I felt, Oh, I wished the ground would open. But that must've been the schooling in

Austria which I think must've been better than schooling here. I think education was very strict in Austria.

King's College Durham

When a group of English scientists, led by William Beveridge and Lionel Robbins of the LSE, learnt of deteriorating conditions for Jewish scientists in Germany and Austria early in the 1930s, they set up a fund to help academics fleeing from Nazi persecution. Led by Lord Rutherford, in 1936, this grew into the 'Society for the Protection of Science and Learning'.

The society rescued six hundred scientists by finding them work in Britain and the US. Already part of the scheme, the University of Durham employed several refugees as academics. In 1937, King's College opened in Newcastle. It was formed by the merger of Newcastle College of Medicine and Durham's Armstrong College. The first rector, Lord Eustace Percy, persuaded the college council to endow ten places for refugees. On Tuesday, twenty-fourth of January 1939, the *Newcastle Evening Chronicle* reported that a maximum of ten refugees would be exempt for fees from King's College.

There were ten places, and entry requirements would be individual for each student. Rita Freedman, knowing that Paula was unhappy to be so far from her younger son, who was still in London with Erich, suggested that Peter should apply for the scheme. Peter was offered a place on the condition he passed the matriculation ('matric') examinations within a year of his arrival in England; this gave him around eight months to prepare.

He remembered:

> We had to pass five subjects. Since German was one, I had to worry only about four, but everything was unexpected. I took maths, for engineering. I'd done geometry, presumably the same geometry, but I'd never heard of Euclid. I opted for the history of the French revolution and the Napoleonic wars because I'd recently done this bit in Vienna.

> Everybody knows the battle of Waterloo was won by Blücher. It was news to me that the venue was a London railway station and the battle had been won by Wellington. Everybody should learn history in two countries at least, it gives one a better perspective. The only episode that was the same in the

Viennese history class and in London was that Marat had been stabbed in the bath by his mistress. That is universal.

The hardest by far was English. No allowance could be made, quite rightly so. I had to get through on the same terms as the natives. I passed. I'd been a poor pupil in Vienna, I was no cleverer in London. The difference was only that here it was essential for me to get through.

Mother gave me five pounds. I got a third-hand bicycle and a new slide-rule and had a little left over. I was enrolled as a student of electrical engineering in the faculty of Applied Science at King's College in the University of Durham.

Peter became an undergraduate in autumn 1939, studying electrical engineering. He'd moved to Newcastle earlier in the year. Paula hoped to find him a cheap room but Rita Freedman said, "He can stay with us at Roseworth Tower for a few weeks until you find somewhere for him."

Peter recalled his arrival and time there, fuelled with tea:

I arrived at Roseworth Tower, in Gosforth, in the spring of 1939. I was to stay a few weeks. The weeks became years. In a way, in my mind, I never left. So, I met Alec Freedman and Rita Freedman and their two sons, Roland and Huntly.

I worked mainly at the scrubbed table in the kitchen, at night. It was comfortable by the open grate, and silent, and I had a constant pot of strong tea.

The remaining refugee students were supported by the wider community. Some were given temporary accommodation by a parson in Whitley Bay, and with the Dodds sisters, Quakers in Low Fell, Gateshead until they could find rooms. Hans Kronberger was one of this group who remembered receiving a pound a week from the Society of Friends (Quakers) which enabled him to pay rent and buy food. He also used some of his money to buy books and a bicycle.

Section 2

1938 – 1945:
World War II

Chapter 9

Windermere: War Starts

The world changes

On the first of September 1939, Germany invaded Poland. Two days later, Britain and France declared war and everything changed. There would be no more Kindertransport, and no more parents would arrive to collect their daughters. Letters and other news were censored and increasingly infrequent. The hostel, intended only to provide temporary refuge for girls until their parents could fetch them, now had to care for them for however long the war lasted.

Overnight, Paula, Peter and the children in the hostel became enemy aliens. The terrified matrons instructed the girls not to speak German outside the hostel and to destroy all the letters they had received from their families in case they should be identified as German speaking. Most of the girls disobeyed this instruction; letters from home were their last vestigial connections with their parents. In any case, their broken English and strange accents would have identified them had an invasion happened.

Paula's female exemption from internment enemy alien certificate. Sixth of November. Occupation – second matron.
(The National Archives)

Peter was told to report to his local police station where he was instructed not to be away from home between ten thirty at night and six o'clock in the morning without a permit, nor leave the district without permission:

"You understand, dinna, lad," he said when he had finished the official business. Of course, I understood, that he meant me no harm, that he didn't think I was Hitler's agent, that he was sorry about it all. Of course, I understood, perfectly. The prohibition itself was no great hardship. I wasn't having a lot of riotous late nights on my pound a week. Mother gave it to me. She had three pounds a week, all found.

Term started. We had lectures in the mornings and labs in the afternoons. In the first year, all the engineers and the medics were together for physics and chemistry. Medics had stethoscopes dangling from their pockets to denote their status. We had slide-rules sticking out of ours. Enemy alien or not, nobody ever said a nasty word to me.

Before the National Health Service was founded by Nye Bevan in 1948, medicine was privately funded. Patients only received care if they could afford it. Although Lloyd George introduced his National Insurance scheme in 1911 for working men earning less than one hundred and sixty pounds a year, it did not cover their families. Alec Freedman ran his own scheme which provided health care for an entire family for six pence a week. At this time, a typical house call would then have cost around ten shillings and sixpence (equivalent to about twenty pounds in 2017), about the same as a man was paying to cover his entire family for six months. The dispenser, Jimmy Foster, would bicycle round the mining villages north of Newcastle, collecting subscriptions. Once war was declared, Jimmy Foster signed-up in the armed forces and was replaced by a woman with a wooden leg, who was unable to ride a bike and so was unable to collect the subscriptions.

Peter, eager to do anything to help and begin to repay the Freedman's hospitality, took over the round:

In Newcastle, if you come from Sunderland, you're a stranger. I might have come from the moon. Why, man, I couldna even speak it.

At first, they called me doctor, or mister, or Lloyd-George-man. After a few weeks, here and there, they started to say "Comin ya bugger an-have-a-cupatea."

In Coxlodge, a village a mile and a half north of Gosforth, I learned over thick, sweet tea that the Co-op, the only shop in the village, never stocked butter. There was no call for it. The shop never had prime cuts of meat; it got the poor cuts from the butchers in places like Gosforth. It was the same in all the mining villages.

I learned about hip baths and poverty, about the solidarity between these families, and met an old arthritic miner who recited Shakespeare.

Three weeks to move

During the 1930s, the French, eager to avoid repeating the horror of trench warfare that dominated the Great War, built the Maginot Line, a concrete wall along their border with Germany designed to prevent German troops marching into France. This section of the Maginot Line was mostly concrete, with complex underground bunkers, and multiple defensive layers. On the assumption that the Low Countries, Belgium and Holland, would resist an attack, the section they built along the Belgian border was much weaker. The German offensive began with an ambitious surprise attack on Holland and Belgium on the tenth of May 1940 with air raids, followed by parachute drops accompanied by attacks from tanks and ground forces, a blitzkrieg. Instead of acting as a buffer, defending France, the Low Countries were rapidly conquered. The Dutch surrendered after four days and German forces continued to push northwards relentlessly. Germany had effectively walked round the Maginot Line and attacked via the much weaker front. The Allied Forces, France and Britain, attempted to stop the advance but failed as German tanks, aided by aircraft, cut through the Allied supply lines as they raced towards the Channel coast. On the twenty-third of May, the British Expeditionary Force, encircled by

German tanks, abandoned the planned Allied counterattack and hastily arranged evacuation which happened at Dunkirk - the famous sea rescue by a wide range of small and large vessels.

As France fell, the invasion of Britain, especially the South Coast, appeared imminent and government introduced a range of precautionary measures. The internment of male enemy aliens began in May as those aged between sixteen and sixty- years-old were arrested and taken to holding camps, chiefly on the Isle of Man. All enemy aliens were barred from coastal areas which were designated Defence Zones. German aircraft began sustained bombing raids on major ports, shipbuilding and industrial centres along the coast and London. The first major bombing raid on Tynemouth was on the twenty-second of June 1940. Several of the girls recorded their fear of the warning sirens and of being taken down to the air raid shelter at night. Although the hostel was home to only children and the two female matrons, as enemy aliens, they were perceived as a possible threat of being fifth columnists. They could not remain inside the coast Defence Zone. Nor was it safe for them to remain close to the coastal bombardment. The occupants and committee were given notice to leave. As a concession, they were given three weeks to find another property away from the coast and to arrange the move. Although it had taken three months to initially set-up the hostel, they had to complete the move in just three weeks. Finding a suitable house and organising the transport of their furniture and possessions, twenty-plus girls, and the two matrons, seemed unimaginable.

South Wood

Some of the girls remembered the uncertain time.

Annie recalled:

> And then came the law that all aliens over sixteen had to leave restricted districts in case of spy activity, and the coasts were obviously restricted districts. In fact, we were still German citizens, the fact that we were refugees didn't really count. Our passports were German rather than Jews and in a country that doesn't officially discriminate, being Jewish was no different from being Christian. Officially, we were just German.

Mrs Sieber and Mrs Urbach, the two ladies who took care of us were obviously over sixteen and they had to leave. And it was obvious that in due course, we would all turn sixteen because it was now self-evident that we were not going to join our parents in the near future. So, they had to do something, and the committee got busy, and they found us a house in Windermere, in the Lake District and it was absolutely the most enchanting place in the world. Hills, I do not know how to describe it and one lake after another. Wherever you looked, there were lakes, and wooded, green hills with a profusion of flowers all growing wild. In Windermere, you literally do see meadows covered with daffodils, graveyards that in spring are a sea of bluebells. All you see is blue. Covered in blossoms. And Rhododendrons growing in such profusion that you cannot begin to believe and not just in the beigey pink but in dark reds, purples, and lavenders – great hedges of it and they bloom and bloom.

The Wood estate is a mile from Windermere station down Ambleside Road. The original estate included a pretty Georgian villa with curved walls and delicate metalwork awnings, along with rambling collection of cottages, coach houses, a walled garden and glasshouses. Jane Yates lived at the Wood between 1806 and 1862 and was a local benefactress. Amongst other things, she founded the school at St Mary's Church with its steep roofs of curiously shaped tiles. She was replaced by the Crewdsons, members of a large Quaker family who had made their money in the wool trade, founded the first bank in Westmoreland and diversified into local ironworks. For several generations, members of the family were pillars of society, mayors, civic dignitaries and they were also closely involved with the Quaker movement. The Crewdsons left the Wood around 1880 and were succeeded by Colonel Howarth followed by a Miss Wrigley and then Clara Constance Carus.

At some point, a large porch was added and the front of the house was remodelled to make it appear rectangular. A cedar was planted in the lawn in front of the house, possibly in the early nineteenth century, which grew into a magnificent tree. The huge house was then divided to create three separate homes. The smart, light-filled rooms that faced the garden that had been used by the family, created South Wood. The smaller, darker rooms at the back that had previously been used by servants were split to form two smaller properties, East Wood and West Wood.

South Wood, viewed from the front in 2013, showing
the additional buildings nestled behind.

In 1938, Clara Constance Carus sold the Wood Estate to her son John, a young Liverpool–based barrister, because she wanted to move to a more remote part of the Lake District. By 1940, John was serving in the Fleet Air Arm and looking for a tenant for the main building, South Wood. Somehow, the Newcastle committee learnt it was available and more importantly, suitable to house the girls and the move from Tynemouth to the Lake District was arranged. Paula's registration book shows that she spent three nights in Durham, one night in Castle Rydding, Windermere, before moving to South Wood on the twenty-eighth of June 1940. Members of the committee came to help prepare the house. Alice and the children followed.

Ilse remembers helping to make and hang blackout curtains over the massive windows:

The committee was given three weeks to find another home for us and moved us, with all our household goods, to a Quaker house in Windermere in the Lake District. It was a lovely old house with a garden, which we first had to clean. Now, we were removed from the committee's help. Keeping kosher was also a challenge. Meat had to be sent to us from Newcastle. All the school personnel were very helpful and placed children as best as they could. The older ones had to find jobs and still do the housework.

Lisl also recalls the important tasks that the girls had to perform:

Downstairs was the dining and living room where we did our homework. Upstairs were the bedrooms. We had a big porch. There was no outside help all those years. Each one of us did all the cleaning and washing and taking care of everything in the house. One of my jobs was when the war started, there were curtains with rings and there were blackout and I had to stand on the ladder and sew the rings on. Maybe that made me a dressmaker. And I was scared to fall off, someone held me by the legs. Each one of us had a job.

Alice Urbach (left) and Paula Sieber in the porch at South Wood.
United States Holocaust Memorial Museum,
courtesy of Alisa Tennenbaum.

Behind the trellised, Edwardian porch, the original front doors to the house were imposing. The huge domed doors had curved tops and were inset by panels of hand-painted leaded glass lights with images of a range of drawings of single flowers.

Light streaming through the glass panels cast coloured shadows on the hall floor. The hall beyond was huge, at the back there were two separate staircases, one to each side of the building. Arched stone doorways facing one another on either side of the hall led to the two large front rooms that would become the dining and sitting rooms for the girls. The smaller darker rooms behind these reception rooms were the kitchen and Paula's office where she must have maintained her ledgers and kept the huge Singer sewing machine on its ornate cast-iron treadle. Upstairs, the pattern was the same, the two big front bedrooms each had six of the middle and older girls while the little ones were in one of the smaller rooms at the back. Alice's bedroom was the room over the balcony in the centre front of the building whilst Paula had a small bedroom behind the stairs. The bathroom was modified to accommodate two baths, two lavatories and three basins, separated by flimsy hardboard partitions; hardly lavish for twenty to twenty-five people.

Although South Wood is a large house by domestic standards, the rooms are not huge. The kitchen, where Alice produced three meals, every day for five years, was a small room (4.8 x 3.5 metres) whilst the front bedroom with beds for the six older girls was a bit bigger (8.5 x 6.7 metres). It must have been crowded, with the beds being so very close together there was very little personal space. Routine was re-established rapidly. The girls went to the local school, and each child had their allotted after school chores. The girls' duties in the kitchen meant that Alice was able to pass on her culinary skills to them.

Elfie remembers having to roll strudel pastry as thin as possible:

We had a big kitchen table in the kitchen, a huge table and she used to make an apple strudel on this table and she always said you know you have to pull out the dough. And she said it must be so thin that you could read a newspaper through it. Really. Yes. And I always helped in the kitchen.

Lisl used Alice's recipes long afterwards:

In the kitchen, my turn to help was every fourth Thursday. One of the reasons I am still making yeast cake every Thursday, we did that in the hostel every Thursday. I beat the dough.

Elfie remembers bicycling to Windermere station every week to collect the parcel of kosher meat sent from Newcastle. Peddling up the steep hill into Windermere must have been hard work. In the holidays, parties were sent outdoors to collect firewood, apples, nettles and blackberries. Some remember enjoying the freedom of being outside whilst others hated it. The locals were generous, donating apples and other produce to the hostel. Alice used the large cellars in the basement to dry fruit and store the preserves she made during the season. All the girls commented on the excellent cooking, remembering the innovative food Alice made for them, cakes made with vegetables, muesli and nettle soup; their diet was both healthy and satisfying. Food rationing was introduced in January 1940 when bacon, butter and sugar were rationed to ensure that the distribution of food was fair. Later, meat, tea, jam, cheese, eggs and other items, were added to the list of controlled food. Individuals were issued with a ration book containing coupons that were swapped at a shop of their choice for the designated items. People were encouraged to grow vegetables which, along with many other foodstuffs, were not rationed. From the girls' descriptions both of being sent out to forage, and of the meals Alice cooked for them, it is likely that she used both ingredients that were not rationed and foraging to create nutritious and varied food. Alice may well have learnt to cook frugally, turning vegetables and foraged plants into appetising meals in Vienna after the Great War as, for a number of years, food was in extremely short supply.

Of course, there were times when the girls were naughty; they were children. Some of their antics have become cherished stories: one of the girls left South Wood to join her mother who lived locally and could afford to send her to Kendal High School. As she was still relatively close, some of the girls took to hiding notes for her between the stones in the dry-stone wall along the road.

Worried by what she saw, a neighbour informed the local police as Elfie confirmed:

If you walked out from the hostel there was the road up to Troutbeck with old stone walls. We thought we'd write a little note put it in the wall. And then she could pick it up and read it and take it to her mother. I mean I don't know how long for.

And this old lady had watched us and reported us to the police. We must be spies. And I remember being called before both matrons and being told off about it. And we said you know we just wrote silly things the notes but we shouldn't do it at all. Because people were so frightened in those days. I mean one heard of somebody being on the bus dressed as a nun and somebody noticed that they had like men's shoes on. It wasn't really a nun. It was a German spy. Whether it was true or not I don't know.

Dr and Mrs Freedman had taken a lease on West Wood, at the back of the complex, which they used for holidays and to escape the Newcastle bombing. As a medical practitioner, Alec must have had petrol coupons as he regularly transported his family, and sometimes Peter, who was still living with them, together with donations collected by the committee for the hostel, across the Pennines. Home from boarding school, their two sons, Roland and Huntley, who were about the same age as the older girls, were popular visitors.

Clothing and fabric rationing was introduced in June 1941. New civilian clothes were in increasingly short supply as the war progressed as manufacture concentrated on producing uniforms for the services. Coupons were required to buy either clothing or most fabrics along with payment for the item. The government promoted 'make do and mend', an initiative to repair and remodel clothing to make it last longer.

Recycling clothes for twenty plus growing girls must have been a lot of work. Donated clothes were adapted to fit; as one girl grew out of something, it was remodelled to fit another. Some girls, to this day, resent having to wear dreary second-hand clothes; another appreciated the quality of these clothes, recognizing how difficult it would have been to find clothing during a time of rationing.

The girls at Windermere. Summer, 1939.
(Left to Right) Back row: Edith, Hanna, Elfie, Stella, Lore, Dasha, Helga, Annie (with visiting cousins), Ruth, Marion. Front row: Margot, Lore, Lisl, Ilsa, Eva.

Each child came to the hostel from a different background and family history. Most came from close, loving families prepared to sacrifice contact with their own child in exchange for their safety. When they arrived, the girls ranged from very young children to teenagers who had already experienced family life and, to some extent, had already formed characters. The older girls appear to have found adjusting to the strict regimen hardest and are more critical when they reflect on their time at the hostel, whilst the younger ones remembered little of the time they had spent with their parents.

Hostel Days
Lore wrote a summary of her story:

55 Percy Park, Tynemouth. That is where it all began. It had been established some months before my arrival by a group of Jewish philanthropists to provide a temporary home for Jewish refugee children until such a time that they could be reunited with their families. Unfortunately, as war progressed and the persecution of Jews spread across Europe, the role of the hostel gradually turned into that of an orphanage.

In 1940, the hostel was evacuated to Windermere, in the Lake District, where it continued to operate in a safer and more attractive environment until the war ended.

I was the third youngest of twenty to twenty-four girls aged between four and eighteen. We were divided into three groups – the big ones, middle ones and little ones. Two matrons were in charge of us for the entire seven years. There was Mrs U, a stocky grey haired green eyed Viennese woman in her fifties, who ruled the hostel with an iron thumb. Can we ever forget her draconian ways and her fiery temper … She was assisted by Mrs S, a dark-haired, middle-aged woman from Prague, quieter in nature and rather self-centred, perhaps like a fading Prima Donna.

At a fiftieth reunion of the Hostel Girls in 1989, it was surmised, and I well believe, that Mrs U and Mrs S were appointed to their positions on the basis that one could cook and the other could sew. They were both widows with grown sons and seemed to have no experience with little girls. However, they both worked hard under difficult circumstances and limited funding to provide a Spartan existence for us. Order, silence (especially after lunch when the matrons took a nap), obedience and cleanliness were maintained at all costs.

Mrs U, we were told, had indeed owned a cooking school in Vienna and had written an impressive cookbook. By adapting her recipes to British war time ingredients and restrictions imposed by ration cards, she managed to provide basic hearty meals. Never mind if the cocoa was lumpy, or the cheese dry and crumbly, there was always plenty of food. And we had to eat all we were served …

Birthdays provided Mrs U with a special challenge. About twenty-six times a year, she would rise to the occasion with a beautifully decorated cake and was justifiably proud of making each cake an original one.

Mrs S, as I recall, always seemed most contented at her large old Singer sewing machine where she spent a lot of time repairing clothes and linen, or creating things, even a fancy-dress costume on one occasion. However, there was one time when her creativity was not appreciated. I needed a suspender belt. Such items were costly in money and clothing coupons. "I'll make one for you," she said pulling out several pieces of colourful leftover cloth, which when sewn together and attached to suspenders, was perfectly adequate. How my classmates at school teased me when they spied this odd apparition round my waist, when I changed for gym. For me, this was one of the many times I was DIFFERENT. It seemed that from the time I left home I felt different. How I longed for normality and belonging.

Coming from a warm loving home to a harsh, impersonalized institution was indeed a traumatic experience for me as a six-year-old. I felt alone, afraid and always cold.

I have clear recollections of having frequent temper tantrums and being sent to bed where I would cry at the slightest provocation. At times, I would find solace by withdrawing into my private play world with my favourite doll.

The first three months seems interminable. Imagine my joy when I was told that my brother was on his way to England. It seemed like a miracle. He was to live with a family in Newcastle. Whereas we did see each other periodically throughout the war, I do not remember our first meeting.

My only contact with my parents was in the first couple of years or so by means of twenty-four-word Red Cross letters. One of the matrons would read these with the little ones. Naturally, the gist of these letters was very superficial, stating we were well and happy, but at least they reassured me that my parents were alive and well. One day, I learned that my father, a lawyer, was going to work for the Nazis, repairing shoes. This puzzled me. I did not begin to understand the implications of this move.

In the daily hostel routine, the older girls were all assigned to domestic duties to be done before and after school. The matrons set very high standards and the girls would be severely punished for the slightest misdemeanour.

A crumb left on the table would be enough to trigger off a ROW, one of the first words in my English vocabulary. It was usually Mrs U's booming voice echoing throughout the house, delivering a slap on the face against indignant cries of the poor victim. Yes, discipline WAS harsh. Threats were common. The threat of having a birthday ignored, was in my mind a fate worse than death. And there were face slaps and sometimes beatings. I did not escape Mrs U's wrath. Could I ever forget the pounding of her hands on my bare bottom when my std. 3 school report showed only eight or nine marks out of ten for conduct. "Not everybody can be top of the class," she yelled, "but there is no excuse for not getting ten out of ten for conduct." I was incensed. I screamed and kicked her in retaliation. She probably hurt my pride more than my hide …

For the most part, school was a welcome escape. We attended St. Mary's School for Girls, tucked away behind a beautiful, historic, twelfth century church. As this tiny school already accommodated schoolgirls and teachers evacuated from South Shields, the classrooms were bursting at the seams when approximately a dozen of us arrived on the scene. The teachers were usually pleasant. I particularly liked my S1/2 teacher, stern but kind with a real gift for storytelling.

The middle ones were usually required to supervise dressing, washing etc. of the little ones. Hair-washing day, I believe came round about once a fortnight. I used to look forward to that day. Aside from the pleasure of having clean, shiny hair, mine was the most popular to wash because I had a long supple neck which eased well down into the sink, making the job fast and easy for the hair-washer.

In the course of time, I befriended some of the hostel girls. In the absence of family, we learned to turn to each other for companionship, support and trust. In addition, I found role-models among them. These bonds became invaluable especially with the traumas of war which followed.

Four girls pose in front of a car. Windermere, 1942.

School

The younger girls were sent to the small local elementary school, St Mary's, a neo-gothic building by the church that was only half a mile from South Wood, a ten-minute walk along Ambleside Road, less on a bicycle. Once girls reached ten, they were faced with a bus journey to the secondary school in Ambleside.

At fourteen, the school leaving age at that time, they were expected to either find work locally or go onto further training. The chairman of the Newcastle committee, Mr Summerfield, interviewed each child to see what they hoped to do. Some found jobs in Windermere as hairdressers, dressmakers, and as shop assistants. They continued to live in the hostel and were still expected to help with their share of the chores when they returned from work. The matrons persuaded a London-based relative of Ruth's to pay the fees that would allow her to continue her education at a nearby private school. Without access to funds, other girls had to leave school. Eva moved to the local cottage hospital to train as a nurse; others had to move further afield.

Mr Summerfield, chairman of the Newcastle committee, with his
wife (left) and Alice Urbach, in the garden of South Wood.

Again, teachers were incredibly generous with their own
time, helping the girls out of school hours, as reported by Elfie:

*Yes, I remember when we left school at fourteen, I said I would
like to work in the local bank. There was only one bank in
Windermere. And so, I went to the bank and I said, "I'd like to
have a job here."*

*And they said, "Have you got … I don't know whether it was
called School Certificate or matric or what?" And I said, "No I
haven't. I'm sorry."*

"We can't employ you."

*And I remember, I went back in tears and I said, oh I'll never be
able to get a job. I'm just going to be a cleaner somewhere*

because I haven't got my matric or my school certificate. I don't know what you're left with. I suppose nothing at the age of fourteen. You had to go to a higher school, the grammar school and I went to my headmistress who had been teaching my class and I said to her, I'll never be able to do anything. I haven't got my school certificate.

And she said, "Leave it with me."

And she found various teachers who were prepared to teach me. She did English with me.

She said, "One evening a week. You come to my house and we do Shakespeare together."

And she found another teacher who taught at Kendal at the girl's grammar school; I forget what she did. I think English, genuine English. Another teacher who did history. And another one who did geography. He was a useless geography teacher; I didn't understand anything. In reality, it didn't mean anything to me and then he left the school, so I was looking for another geography teacher. And in Windermere there, very near the hostel, was a geography teacher. I remember going to him and after the first lesson he said.

"Goodness girl, you don't know anything."

I said, "I know. I didn't like my teacher and never learned anything from him."

"Well, we'll have to get on!"

And he was brilliant. And he'd written a book on geography and he made me a present of the book after work you know. But I managed to get a credit in geography because he was such a lovely chap. Anyway, I had enough teachers to do the subjects that I needed for my chance to train. So, every night was occupied.

When I think of it now, these teachers had a day's teaching. Came home, perhaps had their tea, and then gave an hour for nothing when they must have been tired. It was really wonderful, wasn't it? Yes, wonderful and so all these teachers did one evening a week for me."

Some of the girls deeply resented the limited education available to them; but no provision had been made to fund their continued education, not least because when the hostel was initially founded it was only expected to be temporary. Further and Higher education were not free in the 1940s, so the committee would have had to find funds to cover the tuition fees and living costs for multiple individuals.

Ruth David is very critical of her unhappy experience in the hostel in her book *Child of Our Time*, describing the matrons as draconian. However, three former hostel girls responded to Dorit Bader-Whiteman's survey, each with a different attitude to Alice Urbach.

Beginning with Marion:

"We had two matrons who looked after us. I did not like either one. The cook was round and chubby, the other one very severe. Neither one ever had time to listen to my feelings or my confusion."

Paula's view was somewhere in the middle, taking a neutral tone:

"We had two Viennese teachers. They were OK but not the confiding kind."

Ilse talked about Alice Urbach:

"One of the matrons, a former cooking teacher in Vienna, a very famous personality, an author of a cookbook, had feelings for me. I was extremely fond of her. I stayed in touch with her till she died. My husband and I visited her in 1979 in California. I have her book "So Kocht Man in Wien" [That's How One Cooks in Vienna]. It is one of my treasures, as are the last letters she wrote to me."

Bader-Whiteman's conclusion is sensible:

… It could, of course, be that all three descriptions of Alice by the Kinder are correct. Perhaps her bouncy manner did not

suit every personality. Perhaps she formed better rapport with one type of child than another. Perhaps she did not know how to respond to one child's particular problem. The different descriptions of her are illustrative of the different impact the same person may have on different personalities."

It is true that we do all react differently, and we connect with some people but not with others. Neither Paula nor Alice had any experience of raising girls, let alone children separated from their parents under tragic circumstances. A lucky few had relatives in the UK who were able to visit, however infrequently. Most had no news of their parents. The matrons, separated from their own children and scared for their families left behind in Europe, did their best in difficult circumstances. It should also be remembered that expectations were very different in the early 1940s from today's hopes and aspirations. We treat our children very differently in the twenty-first century than was customary during the war, more than sixty years ago. Discipline was much stricter in my childhood than it is today. Back in the 1940s, slapping, spanking and caning were routine both at home and in school. Alice used corporal punishment, as was then usual. Today, we would not appoint two women with no training in childcare or psychology to take care of a group of vulnerable, traumatised girls.

Several of the girls commented on the Freedman's kindness. Elfie remembered being taken to the races by them, when Mrs Freedman gave her the money, helped her to place her first bet and explained how she should collect her winnings!

Annie described the Freedmans at length:

In one wing of the house, there was a family with children whom we didn't have anything to do with and the other wing, in due course, was bought by our patroness, one of the driving forces of the organisation that took care of us. Her name was Mrs Freedman. She was the wife of a doctor in Newcastle. I was very fortunate to have caught her eye and she took a great interest in me. She had two sons and she had always wanted a daughter and she had already taken in a refugee girl and she also had the son of Mrs Sieber living with her as well. So, she had really been doing her part. Then she kind of took a fancy to me and singled me out in all kinds of ways to spend extra time with me. She would sometimes find extra clothes of hers for me to wear and this benevolent interest in me was frowned upon by the two ladies – Mrs Urbach and Mrs Sieber. It was interpreted as 'one must not bother Mrs Freedman because she is an angel of mercy and one must not take advantage of her'. The fact remains that Mrs Freedman was the bright spot in my life.

The Donkeys
Chanukah is the Jewish winter festival of lights where one candle is lit each night until all seven on the menorah, a boat-shaped candle stand, are alight. Another tradition that accompanies the festival is that children are given money or chocolate money. Today, gifts often substitute for money. Both money and chocolate were in short supply at the hostel and sweets were rationed. Paula's donkey business may have started as a way of making a Chanukah gift for each child. Because of the war, there were few toys in the shops, nor was there any money to buy them. Modelled on the traditional Czech stuffed fabric donkeys from her childhood, Paula used fabric scraps to make these small models in the evenings, once the children were sleeping.

I remember the donkeys from my childhood, about twelve centimetres high, often in rough wool left over from her dressmaking, their manes and tails sewn on with co-ordinating wool attached to the body so that, like hair, it hung down.

What started as a kindness, morphed into a cottage industry when Paula found that she could sell her creations in one of the Windermere shops. Her range expanded to include large fabric bags with round wooden handles that could be used to support the bag open on a table, with lots of pockets, they made excellent sewing bags; and there were fabric-covered coat hangers with strange triangular fabric pouches hanging from the body of the hanger. She must have worked hard, swapping her personal fabric coupons for remnants from a local dressmaker, persuading a local carpenter to make handles for her bags cheaply, buying cheap cotton waste by the sack, from a mattress manufacturer in Bowness, which she then used to stuff the toys, as well as spending hours at night sewing. With the money she made, Paula first bought gifts for Peter and Alice before opening a savings account at her local post office and beginning to save.

Chapter 10

Isle of Man, Canada: Internment

Enemy aliens

Once war with Germany had been declared, any German or Austrian national in Britain automatically became an enemy alien. This posed a problem for the government as there were around eighty thousand aliens in Britain. Of these, fifty-five thousand were refugees from Nazi oppression who were unlikely to be spies or to want to assist Germany in any way, like Peter and Paula. A further thousand or so were not considered a threat, whilst six thousand five hundred were kept under observation. Of these, only six hundred were considered to be dangerous and had already been incarcerated. As enemy aliens, Peter, Erich and Paula were issued with aliens' registration cards which they had to show at their local police station once a week.

The situation changed in 1940 when Germany invaded France and Holland. German troops were then just across the Channel and the threat of invasion via Southern England became real. At the end of May, the hasty evacuation of the army by a flotilla of small boats sailed across the Channel to Dunkirk to rescue soldiers stranded in Northern France by the German advance. As fear of invasion increased, so did the public's perception that enemy aliens were dangerous. After Dunkirk, the press, in particular the *Daily Mail*, stoked fear amongst the population; all enemy aliens were spies and Nazi infiltrators. In response, Churchill issued an order to 'collar the lot' and the Home Secretary, Sir John Anderson, ordered the mass internment of all male enemy aliens: twenty-seven thousand males (aged between sixteen and sixty years-of-age), and five thousand women.

Arrangements to house the internees were needed rapidly and were based on those used during the Great War. Just as Butlins Dovercourt holiday camp had quickly been repurposed to accommodate children arriving in Harwich via the Kindertransport scheme, holiday accommodation, chiefly on the Isle of Man, already provided the basic requirements necessary to house internees. Huyton, an unfinished housing estate outside

Liverpool, was used as a staging post for internees destined for the Isle of Man. About fourteen thousand men, of whom approximately eighty per cent were Jewish refugees, along with a few German Nazi sympathisers, were housed on the island. Internees were guarded by a mixture of local police and army and they were housed in a few camps in Douglas, Ramsay and Peel. Once it became clear that the refugees posed little threat to the country, they were allowed to use local shops, swim in the sea and work locally. Most of the detainees were young, many were academics and students who rapidly established debates, lectures, and concerts (the original members of the Amadeus String Quartet met on the Isle of Man). An Austrian baker ran a café in a laundry room, tailors and shoemakers offered their services whilst those with medical training helped in the sick room. Each camp was autonomous.

Peter was a first year undergraduate when he was interned. Like all science undergraduates, he was being taught to record his experiments during the practical classes he attended in a laboratory notebook. Rather like a lab book, he kept detailed notes throughout his internment.

Isle of Man
The following entries, taken from this journal and correspondence with his mother, are his record of events as they happened to Peter but they also show the ad hoc way that internment was implemented:

> On Thursday, two men in raincoats arrived early in the morning at Roseworth Tower and told Dr Freedman they had to take me away, with their regrets, mind.
>
> I was allowed to take - you've guessed - one suitcase. We walked solemnly through the nearly empty high street, observed only by the milkman who no doubt then distributed, together with the milk, the news that a dangerous spy had been apprehended in the Grove.
>
> We walked to the police station. My friendly sergeant shrugged his shoulders as if to say don't blame me, lad, who knows what they get up to in Whitehall. I was told to wait as other enemies of the state were brought in by plain-clothes policemen. When there was a truck full of us, we were taken

to the drill-hall of the Royal Northumberland Fusiliers where we were guarded by fusiliers complete with steel helmets, gasmasks (in the canvas pouches vouchsafed to service personnel) and rifles. All through the day, the hall filled up with prisoners.

The soldiers were friendly and gave us cigarettes. Their officer, a second lieutenant, was embarrassed and confused and chatty. That's how he found out that one of us villains was doing a master's at King's on Hazlitt. So, in this small world, had the second lieutenant, in Oxford, before joining up. The second lieutenant settled down on the floor next to his prisoner and stayed there discussing the finer points of Hazlitt, interrupted only occasionally by the sergeant with trivial questions about how to feed a drill-hall full of spies and the corollary problem of a shortage of latrines. For the night, we were given blankets and pillows. There was no call to complain, was there, with plenty of room for us all on the floor.

After two days in the barracks, we were taken in army trucks to Huyton near Liverpool, where a housing estate had been nearly completed and was not yet occupied. Things were a bit rough there - straw sacks, atrocious food, no medicines and not a penny for things like soap.

We weren't long at Huyton. In the second week of June, we were taken by train and boat to Douglas on the Isle of Man. It was a bit awkward being watched by other passengers as we were herded along by guards with fixed bayonets. On the way, we heard that Italy, expecting easy pickings, had attacked France in the back; the French army was in a desperate situation.

At Douglas, a compound was marked off for us, surrounded by barbed wire and guarded by armed sentries on watchtowers.

We lived in typical English sea-side boarding houses, two to four in a room depending on its size, and many of us had beds. The houses were the traditional stone's throw from the sea. The windows faced the ocean. To prevent us from signalling to our friends in the U-boats, the windows were painted blue. It was like living in a fishbowl.

We were given provisions and meals were prepared in the different houses. Internees who could cook were stars. We got a shilling a week for necessities. We became familiar with the patterns of that peculiar form of imprisonment, the internees. Similar to the prisoner-of-war (POW) in that we were allied by a common history. Greatly different from the POW because we did not have the structure of military rank and discipline, and we thought of the troops that guarded us not as our enemies but as our friends.

There was no physical suffering in the camp. The deprivation was in the fact of imprisonment, of isolation from the real world - much greater for the men with dependent wives and children. The hardship lay in negatives, being shut out of our usual lives, excluded from all that was going on that hectic summer, with no work to do. We were allowed to write letters. They were censored by the officers. An order was put up: we were to write in German, the censors couldn't understand our English.

The days were long. We started to fill them. We were lucky, we had internees of a great variety of age, occupation and experience. We had some interesting people with more time on their hands, more approachable than we were ever likely to find them anywhere else. They were happy to talk, to teach, to hold court.

We had painters and musicians. Some had come with their instruments. The major in charge of the camp was no philistine and well-disposed to us. Somehow, he procured what we lacked. We had chamber music, concerts, poetry readings, live painting classes, a chess club, a bridge club. We had physical training instructors, runners, football teams. It was a hot summer. One of the beaches was cordoned off and we were allowed to swim from it. One internee swam out of our camp and into the next one along the coast. He said he was short-sighted. It played hell with the roll calls.

Associations were formed, friendships with the false intensity of holiday encounters, with deceptive depth and no durability, valuable nevertheless at the time. And for the exception to prove the rule, it was the unlikely birthplace of the Amadeus Quartet.

Peter was only allowed to write two letters a week from the Isle of Man that were then censored.

His letters to Paula were clearly intended to reassure:

> I received another of the very nice food parcels (date 15) and thank you very much for it, but please don't spend so much money on it; we don't starve. Don't send money, we don't get it through easily and I am still all right.

> Life here is quite nice and we are all in good spirit, although it is very trying to be cut off from news entirely. What we do get are wild and contradictory rumours and we do not know what is happening outside. We live in nice houses, have lectures, walks, swimming and quite good food.

> Don't worry about me. The only thing that is wrong here is the anxiety about you and our friends outside.

Canada

As more people were interned, space ran out in internment camps. Many internees were sent by ship to Canada and Australia in convoys, guarded against German ships and submarines by destroyers, their 'sheepdogs'. These transports contained a mixture of Italian, Austrian and German internees: although some were high-risk Nazi prisoners-of-war, the majority were low-risk Jewish refugees. All were guarded by army and navy personnel.

Peter described how the process began:

> On a bright summer's day early in July, a list of internees was put up. Those on it were to be ready in the morning with their suitcases to go to other camps. Nobody would tell us where. If there was a rationale in who was on the list and who was not, we never discovered it. My name was included.

> We went by boat to Liverpool, and from there onto one of several passenger liners lying along the quay. She was the 'SS. Sobieski', Polish registered, built in Newcastle-upon-Tyne and now carrying refugees from Germany and Austria and British guards. Once on board, we were told we were going to Canada.

During his time on board the *SS Sobieski* and throughout his time in Canada, Peter kept a daily journal where he recorded his thoughts, activities and expenditure. Of the sea crossing, he recorded that he was seasick, that when the convoy became stuck in fog and his ship, the *SS Sobieski*, was separated from the main convoy, protected only by their 'sheepdog'. As the internees had little access to information on how the war was progressing, rumours circulated. Peter was upset by the tensions between Jewish refugees and Nazi prisoners of war.

He described how he met up with some like-minded fellow internees:

> "Let us go," said a small chap standing next to me, "quietly and calmly, and take tea. I'm Goldschmidt by the way." He was short and thickset, with a chubby face dominated by darting eyes that didn't miss much, and he liked to pretend that he was bone idle. He was the best man I met at finding shortcuts. A sumptuous tea was laid on in the first-class dining room, and only a handful of internees were there. Not many knew about it. Goldschmidt would be one of them, naturally.

> He was in his second year of law at Oxford, he told me. "There are a few of us here from Oxford; you must meet them." There was only one other from Newcastle on board the ship, Friedrich Mautner, a mathematician, in his way, infinitely the cleverest of us all. He lived in a world of equations: he wrote them in notebooks, on loose sheets of paper, and on the backs of old letters. Over the next day or two, I met others from Oxford, and through them students from other universities.

> There were radios in the public rooms and we crowded around them to hear the news. At every bulletin, we were afraid to hear that the invasion of Britain had started. The whole country, it seemed, was holding its breath.

The *SS Sobieski* docked at Québec City on the fifteenth of July 1940. Peter's detailed diary continues throughout his time in Canada. The internees were first were taken to Trois-Rivières, a riverside town, one hundred and thirty kilometres southwest of Québec, by train.

Peter described the internees moving from their ship to the train for their journey to Trois-Rivières:

On the dockside, our lieutenant and his men handed us over to Canadian guards. The captain and his sergeant looked at us in disbelief: soldiers they understood. Prisoners-of-war were foreigners and spoke strange languages. Still, they were soldiers of a kind.

The captain and the sergeant weren't prepared for our dishevelled bunch standing about in untidy groups surrounded by suitcases, holdalls, rucksacks, paper parcels, chessboards and musical instruments. Many of us were smoking cigarettes. A group of very Orthodox Jews wore black overcoats and fur-trimmed black hats - all the rage in Poland in the nineteenth century.

The captain shook his head, said: "Get them to the train, sergeant," and walked ahead.

The sergeant was even more discouraged. He shrugged his shoulders and gave up any idea of the "AttenTION" type of military commands he relished. "Does anybody here speak English?" he asked. "We all do," we assured him.

"Okay, let's go," he said. We could tell that this civilian colloquialism went against his grain.

We took up our parcels and shambled after the departing captain. The soldiers walked beside our long column pretending they weren't with us. This wasn't convincing as we took up the whole street and stopped the traffic, with many passing citizens watching us. The sergeant followed behind making sure nobody got lost. It wasn't far to go to the station and we saw next to nothing of the town.

An empty train was waiting for us. Without any spoken intention, seemingly by some automated chromatography, students gravitated to the same carriage, and other homogeneous parts of the mix sorted themselves into other compartments. Our groups were forming, and we never knew how it happened. Counting along the compartments, mine was number eight.

They were taken by train to Trois-Rivières. The Canadian commander in charge of the group quickly realized that housing German Nazi POWs alongside those fleeing from their persecution was inappropriate and arranged for the POWs to be moved to another camp.

We stopped at a large newly built and not yet completed sports centre and exhibition hall at the outskirts of the town. We would be there, we were told, only until our 'proper' camp was finished.

Barbed wire on top of the boundary wall and a machine gun on a wooden tower instantly made us feel at home.

Over six hundred of us were put into a huge hall. It was dark and dusty and all there was for us to sleep on were straw paillasses so close together that there was hardly a passageway between them.

Man is a fast learner. We were getting to be advanced internees; we knew how to settle down in a new place. We picked our spots, by and large, staying in the same groups, put down our gear and were in the dining hall inside ten minutes. The food was good and ample and the crockery was new.

Far more serious than the makeshift accommodation, there were German Army Prisoners-of-War in the same complex. Watching us as we arrived, they welcomed us by breaking out into a popular German ditty *The Horst Wessel Song* with the words 'When Jewish blood drips off the knife'.

The main thing about our posting is that the commander thought we shouldn't be together with the German Prisoners-of-War; they would be moved somewhere else. We should not be here at all, a point where I fully agree. He said that Canada expected wild POW and we are harmless refugees. (He is fortunately on our side and has sent a note to London to clarify our position).

Thursday 18th July

We told the captain how worrying it was for us not to know the war was going and what was happening at home, in England. From then on, officers gave us brief news summaries every morning and soon we got daily papers as well. At least, we knew Hitler hadn't yet tried to invade Britain.

Many of us carried a book or two. We arranged a primitive 'circulating' library to borrow books from each other. We were surprised how many there were. It was sunny and hot. We sun-bathed and read and played handball in the yard and some played bridge. We talked. There was a lot of talk.

After a month at Trois-Rivières, the internees were again put on a train and moved to Fredericton, New Brunswick, deep in Canadian woodlands:

> We got off the train nowhere in particular, at a little clearing in thick pine woods and were greeted by Canadian mounted police. They were very smart, very correct, and also very kind, waiting and helping. A two-hour walk through more interminable forest took us to the camp.
>
> It was a rectangle cut out of the trees. Here, I couldn't help thinking, one could easily be forgotten, overlooked, mislaid. It was a dismal, God-forsaken place to be marooned in while Europe stood on a knife-edge and anything might be happening to England and to our people there.
>
> We found ourselves in a brand-new POW camp. Deep, barbed-wire fences and guard-towers with machine guns, old familiars. Wooden huts to make our living quarters lined both the longer sides. The entrance gates, guardhouse and stores took up one of the narrow sides. The other held a large community-cum-dining room and a small sick-bay.
>
> Our sorting process that had started on the ship and been refined on the train and in the last camp, now reached its final, solid state in the occupancy of the different huts. We had pet names for them: the 'Berliners' and the 'Viennese'. The Orthodox 'Worshippers' with their extra problem: the Canadians made no allowance at all for their dietary need and there wasn't much our cooks could do about it. We had the 'Red-Reds' clinging to Marx in spite of the Hitler-Stalin pact, the 'it-never-was-true-communism', 'Lesser-Reds', and a hut full of 'Pinks'. Ours, the 'Students'.
>
> Two huts formed an 'H'. We slept in two-tier bunks, twenty-five of them in each wing of the 'H'. There was about six feet between one bunk and the next. In the middle of each wing

were fifteen-foot cylindrical metal stoves large enough to take a whole tree-trunk. Between the huts, there were very adequate washrooms, showers, a reading room and a small oratory for prayer meetings. It was well-planned.

Many in our Group No. 8 were from universities, by no means all: we had five schoolboys, eighteen students, seven university staff including four doctorial researchers, a lecturer and a professor, and also a leatherworker, a farmer, a gardener, a toolmaker, a foreman and a tailoring manager, a merchant and a businessman.

My bunk was above Goldschmidt's because I was the taller, next to him in the lower bunk was George Schindler, also studying law at Oxford and something of a theatre buff at heart. Above George was Friedrich Mautner, the mathematician from Newcastle. He did his equations and hardly spoke a word to anyone all the time we were there. He was with us only in body, not in spirit. We had to tell him when to wash, when to go to eat, when to turn in. Eventually, he returned to England, took a first and before very long, he was back in America at Princeton under Einstein.

We dropped our things and went to the eating hall. There was a year's English ration of corned beef and super, tinned ham waiting for each of us, and a heavy plum pudding. There were sugar mountains and thick Carnation condensed milk lakes. We weren't likely to starve.

Peter's journal lists the following staff member names:

Spokesman	Dr H.L. Oettinger
Deputy	A.J. Frisch
Labour	Dr Wieneris
Lord Privy Keeper of the Rolls	Dr Lissman
Canteen (embryonic)	Dr Isaac
Post (insate nascendi)	H. Junge
News, Library & Pornography	H. Haber
Interior decorative demolition squad	Prof. Hollfreter
H.M. Opposition	E. Nenstein
Hygiene & Physical Fitness	W. Moss Knight of the Garter
Order & Discipline	Dr Rothberger
Antiques & Decontamination squad	Messes Selmer & Frenkle
Envoy to England	Dr Glacksmann
Regional Defence	Dr Manishaima

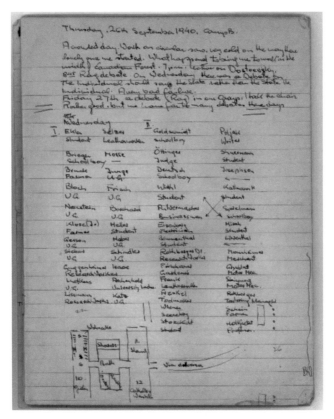

Page from Peter's journal showing space allocation and floorplan
of barracks. Canada, twenty-sixth September 1940.

He described how activities were organised:

Not surprisingly, amongst some six hundred men, we also had
other, more valuable intangible luggage. Naturally enough, it
fell to our group to set up classes. Dr Lissmann, a biologist
from Cambridge, took charge of it. Several in our group and a
number from other huts became the teachers. Even some of
the students held classes for School Certificate. Isolated from
the world, thrown onto our own resources without outside
stimuli, there was a great need to teach and learn, to question
and listen. Within a few weeks, we ran forty courses in the
arts, maths and science for the School Certificate,
Matriculation and Higher School Certificate.

We had journalists. A few copies of Canadian papers came in
daily. From them, they produced a camp newspaper.

Tragically, another transport destined for Canada was torpedoed off the west coast of Ireland with the significant loss of crew, along with over six-hundred internees: four hundred and eighty-six Italians and a mixture of Jewish refugees. The public outcry following the sinking of the *SS Arandora Star* contributed to the end of mass internment. Interment should only be for individuals who posed a realistic threat.

Peter commented on the tragedy:

> Then we read that another ship carrying refugees to Canada, the fifteen-thousand-ton *SS Arandora Star* had been sunk by a U-boat. Six hundred and thirteen internees and most of the ship's company drowned. We held a minute's silence and the officers and guards joined in.

> In August, we read about the battle of Britain. We all worried; many prayed. We asked the major to give us radios and he gave us several sets. Watching us listening to the bulletins finally convinced him and his men exactly where we stood. The RAF defeated the Luftwaffe and the Germans gave up daylight raids. The British had won the vital first phase. The night-raids over Britain were to come. In the camp, life went on with lighter hearts.

Peter's journal entries show that a highly effective programme of liberal arts education was rapidly established within the camp. He dutifully recorded that he was reading politics and philosophy, attending lectures on art, history and philosophy, as well as psychology from one of Freud's pupils. He held discussions with other internees.

Some of Peter's carefully typed pages included quotes, ranging from Plato to Marx questioning the role of individuals and society, show the liberal questioning of a curious young man:

> *'We call Man a gentle animal and, if nature has been kind to him and his education has been right, he is the most gentle and God-like of creatures. But if his education is inadequate or bad, he becomes the most savage of all products of the earth'.*
>
> *Plato*

'It is not easy to make the best of both worlds when one of the worlds is preaching a Class War, and the other is vigorously practicing it'.

'The force behind evolution, call it what you will, is determined to solve the problems of civilization, and if it cannot do it through us, it will produce some more capable agents. Man is not God's last word. God can still create. If you cannot do his work, he will produce somebody who can'.

'Powers of destruction that could hardly without uneasiness be entrusted to infinite wisdom are placed in the hands of romantic schoolboy patriots'.

G.B. Shaw, Back to Methuselah

'Any narrow patriotism, however necessary it may be at the moment in practice, is not a thing that you accept as an ideal. The emotion that must inspire our purposes is an emotion of pain in the suffering of others, and happiness in their happiness'.

'That is the only emotional basis that is any good'.

B. Russell, Education for Democracy

'The essence of democracy is the belief in the ultimate importance of every individual, that the State exists for man, not man for the state'.

Sir E. Simon

'We say that our morality is entirely subservient to the interests of the class struggle of the proletariat'.

Lenin

Once the Commandant obtained instruments from the Red Cross, concerts and music lessons joined the curriculum. They internees performed plays – *Faust* and ingeniously used cigarette papers to construct a lion's mane for *Androcles and the Lion*. Camp officers were invited to plays, concerts and spoke in debates organized by the Oxford students:

'Life is a big compromise' carried.

'The press is mightier than the sword', carried.

'Our time in camp will be a gain rather than a loss', the notices announcing it were torn down, and the motion was heavily defeated. "Count me in with the no's," the commandant was heard to mutter.

To our good fortune, we did have one genius: the pastry cook from a well-known Viennese coffee-house. He was an artist. We had the best patisseries in Canada, some said in North America. We had the best coffee; we had whipped cream in our coffee-house as good as in Vienna. The officers themselves, sneaked in.

A continuous thread running through Peter's journal is anxiety and the need for news of family and friends and of Britain and the war. He was relieved by the absence of dramatic news from Windermere, cheered by letters from Rita Freedman and David Summerfield and clearly pleased to have his supply of 'baccy' and soap replenished:

Parcels arrived. For me, from mother and from the Freedmans. Cigarettes, pipe tobacco, soaps. Parcels mean so much more than they contain.

Internees were paid twenty cents a day to work. Peter classified the work and provided a schedule used at the time. In August, he generally spent four half days and one full day per week working at a range of outdoor activities that included wood cutting, digging, outside engineering, surveying, painting and less frequently, unspecified indoor work.

Prisoners-of-War must not be forced to work. We weren't POWs but we rarely objected. We needed the exercise and a dollar a week went a long way at the camp's sales counter.

There was an exception. The worshippers were in deep trouble. Naturally, they could not work on Saturday and would be tortured and killed rather than carry a feather on a Sabbath. Once again, an unstoppable military machine hit a fundamentalist rock. Our wiser camp commandant would not have made much of it, but his CO heard of it. There were memos and meetings.

Eventually Lt Col H. Statham, Assist Director of Int. Ops wrote to the District Officer Commanding, Military District No 7. St John, N.B. It was an eight-hundred-word lulu of a letter:

'.. it is becoming increasingly evident that the group of Orthodox Jews do not propose to adapt themselves to the circumstances in the which they are placed.'

Perceptive fellow, the Lt Col, doesn't miss a thing.

'… internees who decline to labour on Saturdays will be compelled to do all the camp fatigues that are required on Sunday, including any fatigue work which the camp commandant may postpone till Sunday or create on Sunday … e.g. chopping wood for the following week … no pay'

' .. may result in charges being laid … judicial action'

'.. take away some of the privileges [mail, newspapers, magazines, radio, etc.] … all in camp will suffer'

The worshippers laboured on Sundays, presumably sustained by their zeal.

Peter's journal records his mixed feelings over release following rumour, counter-rumour, confusion, and conflicting information. Immediate release was promised in exchange for signing up for the Pioneer Corps! Was emigration to the US, avoiding the dangers of Europe, possible? In January, Dr Freedman and Lord Eustace Percy's entreaties requesting Peter's release so that he could continue his studies, were successful and his release papers duly arrived. However, the boats were full and his return was delayed until there was an available berth.

As he was no longer an internee, Peter was paroled to help Canadian foresters' survey remote forests, deep in snow as he described:

I set out with four Canadian lumberjacks and a pile of food and equipment in a battered old truck. Hidden under a sack, they had a crate of bourbon. The lumberjacks were six foot three tall and weighed fifteen stones each. We drove through snowy lanes to some place on the map that looked like every other place. They showed me how to use a theodolite and we measured a square kilometre, then a tenth of the kilometre this way and a tenth that way. We cut down trees in that hundredth of the square-kilometre, measured the trunks and counted the rings. They told me what sort of tree they had cut down and I entered it on a form.

They were kind and helpful. We made campfires and ate enormously. At night, we put up in a farmstead not too far away. It got colder still and the lanes froze solid. They taught me the only way to drive the truck, jamming on the brakes and sliding round corners. The truck took a bit of a beating. I found that they could read but hardly write. I wrote some of their letters to their wives. They were not in the least embarrassed, any more than I was by my lack of their far more relevant skills.

Peter recorded that he left Canada on board the SS *Warwick Castle* at three o'clock in the afternoon but not the date. The ship's captain announced that the internees were to be considered free as soon as the ship left harbour. He docked at Greenock on the first of March 1941. The following year, the *SS Warwick Castle* was torpedoed and sunk by a German submarine two hundred miles from the Portuguese coast on the fourteenth of November 1942, the captain and sixty-two others were killed.

In retrospect, Peter's views on his experience of internment were moderate and fair:

I've heard people go on about the internment, the injustice, the infringement of liberty. I don't go along with this. Sure, it was a nonsense. A mistake was made, without evil intention. But the whole country was in peril; we were only one concern amongst very many. Infringement? If Britain hadn't given us a home in the first place, most of us would have finished in gas chambers. The Canadians were decent and helpful. It was hard for them to understand what was going on in Europe and religious tolerance was in short supply. Paradoxically, a number of British children were sent to Canada for safety. The *SS Arandora Star* was a misfortune. It wasn't the British who sank her. Like many other civilian ships, she was torpedoed by a German submarine.

The internment of enemy aliens by the British Government in 1940, remains controversial. It was one of the two examples of imprisonment without trial during the twentieth century when innocent people lost their freedom for a period of time. Peter said repeatedly that the most dangerous part of his war had been the two Atlantic crossings, to Canada and back. Because the refugees were able to set-up such effective study programmes, both on the Isle of Man and in Canada, Peter gained an extensive education in the liberal arts to which he would not otherwise have been exposed. He also remembered his time as an incompetent lumberjack with great affection. Cesarani and Kushner, although critical of the process, report that the reactions of many internees were similar, including gratitude for being rescued from the horrors of the Holocaust, feeling that the time spent incarcerated was an unfortunate interlude although many emphasised the positive social, educational and cultural opportunities. Some of the children and grandchildren of internees, the 'Second Generation', are angry that their relatives were effectively imprisoned. Peter's account largely describes a benign regime, albeit one that at times spectacularly failed to understand the requirements of an unfamiliar set of religious practices. Clearly, it was difficult for the Canadians, many of whom would never have met a Jew before, to understand the dietary complexities of some Orthodox believers or that the Sabbath was observed on Saturday. Generally, issues were dealt with and compromises reached.

Newcastle

By the time Peter arrived back in Newcastle, it was too late to prepare for his first-year exams. To avoid having to repeat the year, students who had been sent abroad were allowed to enter their second year directly without having to sit them. He returned to Roseworth Tower and was issued with a duplicate Registration Book by the local police on the twenty-eighth of March 1941 and instructed, kindly, to report to the police station once a week.

As he recalled:

> There were lectures and labs, the news broadcasts had to be followed. The college had a rota of firewatchers. I was welcome to volunteer provided, as an enemy alien, I had a permit. So, I had to get permission from my police sergeant to spend my nights on a roof and look out for German bombs.
>
> The town was lost in blackout; you sensed its expanse rather than saw it. We couldn't black out the Tyne. When the moon was out, the river became a silver signpost for the Luftwaffe. We had our barrage balloons holding up metal wires that could down a plane, our pencil searchlights bounced off the clouds, the boom of our AA guns cut into the German's steady roar.
>
> It was freezing cold; it felt colder than it had done in Canada at minus twenty centigrade. When a bomb landed nearby, we rang the control post. When an incendiary dropped on one of our roofs, we covered it with sand from a bucket. When you heard the whistle of a high-explosive bomb, you ducked and hoped. Fortunately, we never had one landing on the college.

Peter lived with the Freedmans for the remainder of his course with brief visits to his mother in Windermere. His fellow students worked in factories during their vacations but aliens were prohibited from visiting factories as they were a possible security threat.

Fortunately, the college was kind and arranged for him to spend the summer helping an academic in the engineering department as a summer project, as he recollected:

> The finals came. I drank a lot of strong tea and worried. My maths wasn't good enough, I wasn't one of the clever students who somehow took it in their stride. Every single paper was a menace, so much was riding on it.
>
> There were anxious, slow weeks waiting for the result and a very apprehensive walk along the Town Moor to college on the day the results were put up in the entrance. I'd passed.

I hired a gown and a square cap and my mother came to Newcastle to watch the procession from King's College down to the cathedral.

Peter's duplicate registration book issued
on his return from Canada.

Paula always complained that being so short, she had not been able to see Peter as the graduates processed into the cathedral. In reality, to avoid going to the cathedral, he had not joined the procession, so she was surprised and cross to find him standing behind her also watching the procession.

Chapter 11

Holland: The Royal Navy

A willing new combatant

Once Peter graduated, he wanted to sign up and fight for the country that had given him a home when he needed one. His classmates rapidly joined the services as electrical officers and engineers but enemy aliens were barred from the navy. Refugees generally joined the Pioneer Corps, a motley group of individuals who, for some reason or another were considered unsuitable to join regular troops. Too short-sighted for the RAF, Peter visited the Admiralty in London to see if he could persuade the navy to consider him.

His strategy paid off:

I didn't appreciate the beauty of St James's Park as I walked towards the tall buildings in Queen Anne's Gate. Step by step, the chutzpah of the enterprise became more pertinent.

My long-dead grandfather on my father's side came to my rescue. "If you stir in the mud," he used to say, "there will be bubbles." So, stir, stir, I told myself.

A uniformed guard asked if he could help me.

"I would like to become an electrical officer." He wrote a room number on a chit and gave it to me, directing me to the third floor.

A civilian woman ushered me in to an officer with three gold rings, a commander. I told him I had done electrical engineering and wanted to join the Navy.

"So, what's the problem, why come here?"

"I'm Austrian."

"Ah." He shook his head.

I told him about Eric having been here since ever and serving in the army.

He kept on shaking his head. "Can't be done, I'm afraid. Not the Navy. Not this Navy."

I must have looked as depressed as I was.

"You might just try Other Nationals. They're keen on electricals just now." He rang a colleague.

"I've got an alien here. Have a word?"

He gave me a chit with another commander's name and room number.

That one was a Scot.

"It's not on, laddy," he said, or whatever is 'No' in Scottish.

"Tried the Poles? French? Czechs?"

"They won't have me, and besides I wouldn't speak the language."

He was sorry for me.

"A long shot. There's a lieutenant somewhere here who gets them in by the backdoor." I got another chit.

"I've had some strange ones," the lieutenant told me. "Never yet an enemy alien. Beats everything."

He didn't give me another chit. I was back in the passage in thirty seconds flat.

It was the end of the line. I stood in the corridor, contemplating my return to Newcastle with under two pounds left and Crushing, Screening & Engineering looming large.

A wren walked briskly towards me along the long corridor. A wonderful wren. A wise and patriotic wren, and I never even knew her full name.

"Can I help you," she asked me, "you look lost."

I told her about my troubles.

"Have you been to room ..." she gave the number of my first room, on the third floor.

I nodded.

"Commander ..." the second one.

I nodded. "And the lieutenant along here."

"Lieutenant Commander Watson?" I think she asked. Or Wilson. I hadn't been to him.

"Follow me."

We walked up a flight of stairs and past a few doors. At one of them, she stopped, knocked, and opened it.

Lieutenant Commander Watson, or Wilson, or similar, looked up.

"Hello, Mary," he said. "What have you got there?"

"A hopeless case, sir."

He looked at me.

The time for niceties was over.

"I want a commission but I'm a bloody enemy alien, sir," I said.

"Have a seat," he pointed to a chair and waved to the Wren. She said good luck to me and left.

"Tell." He instructed me.

I told him.

"Why the Navy? Have you tried the RAF or REME?"

"I tried the RAF, but I can't see enough for aircrew and I don't want to be a penguin, the bird that doesn't fly. The army is hopeless. I was told the Navy is more flexible."

It hit a button.

He smiled. "For this absence of bullshit, my Lords of the Admiralty thank you. Here." He gave me a form. "Fill it in. Put in Electrical Division."

It was an application for selection as commissioned officer.

"You'll be called for interview, just like everybody else. If you pass, you start as midshipman for three months. You should hear inside four weeks. Good luck."

Somehow, his gambit had paid off as Peter was invited to an interview with the Royal Navy:

"If you were accepted," the chairman put the last question, "and if you were given a choice between Fleet Air Arm and minesweeping, what would be your preference?"

"Minesweeping," I said without thinking.

"Why?"

"It is dangerous but you don't kill anybody, sweeping," I said, far too quickly, and wished at once I hadn't.

They were far too experienced to show what they thought. "Thank you, we'll let you know."

Peter returned to Newcastle and waited. The answer came in a thick OHMS envelope with the appointment as Midshipman (L) RNVR, directions to report in Portsmouth in two weeks' time, a list of uniform items and a draft to pay for them, a travel voucher. Doctor opened a bottle of champagne. My mother was anxious and angry and pleased.

Peter spent three weeks in barracks at Portsmouth. In that time, by some clever alchemy, the Royal Navy turned college students into young officers.

Peter, looking very young in his smart, naval uniform.

He was sent to Roedean, the girls' boarding school in the Sussex downs, which had been requisitioned by the Royal Navy and was used as a training college.

> I want to confirm an old story. Yes, there were notices in the dormitories saying, 'If a Mistress is required during the night, ring the bell.' We were all twenty-one and deprived. Yes, the bell had given out long ago.

Following intense technical training, Peter was posted to the minesweeping base at Queenborough on the Isle of Sheppey under the command of Lieutenant Commander Hugh Boyce:

> And I was lucky to have Lt Cmdr. Boyce as my commanding officer. Forgive me if hero-worship is showing. In any textbook on management, Hugh Boyce would have been the role model of the rising executive. Born in Devon, he still had a soft west-country accent. He had trained in electrical engineering and gone to South Africa where he worked for an electrical power company. There, he joined his South African bride in wedlock, and the Royal Navy at the outbreak of war.

> He had blue eyes as befits a sailor and a good-looking, clean-cut face. Whenever duty allowed, he was chasing after a ball with a hockey stick or a tennis racket. In time, I was to watch him play tennis for the Navy at Wimbledon. He didn't carry a spare ounce of weight, which made him look taller than he was. A man of few words, yet friendly, a teetotaller who stood his round of drinks in the bar, a religious believer who didn't preach, a strict boss who let us get on with our jobs.

Ships were essential, not just for defence against attack from German ships, but for transporting food and fuel around the country. Lives were lost when British ships struck mines. The technical and research departments: *HMS Vernon*, the underwater weapons experimental station at Portsmouth, and *HMS Lochinvar*, the mining laboratory in Edinburgh, worked continuously to identify new types of mines as they were developed and to find ways of neutralizing the threats they posed. Keeping the estuaries and English Channel free of mines was an essential contribution to the war effort. As Peter said at his interview for the Royal Navy, minesweeping was dangerous, if the small wooden boat you were in was too close when a mine exploded, survival was unlikely. Most refugees serving overseas were made to anglicise their names in case they were captured by the Germans. Peter's stepbrother, Erich Stössler, became Eric Stanley when he moved from the Pioneer Corps to a service corps and was posted overseas. Unusually, Peter was able to keep his name as minesweeping crew were unlikely to be taken prisoner.

Peter in uniform before joining hostilities.

D-Day

By Christmas, Peter had passed his training and was made a sub-lieutenant on active service. He was twenty-three years old. It was only six years since he had left Vienna. He remained at Queenborough but swapped his berth in the *HMS St Tudno* for a shared room on shore. The *HMS St Tudno* was one of the minesweepers that Peter manned during sweeping. On Christmas Day, he wore his Canadian prisoner of war shirt to lunch and provoked a response, laughter! They continued to sweep the Thames estuary and the Channel until May 1944.

The D-Day landings were an important allied invasion of Northern France that led to the end of the war. The German occupation extended across Holland, Belgium and Northern France. A meticulously planned co-ordinated invasion was carried out by British, American and Canadian troops who crossed the Channel and landed on five beaches along a fifty-mile stretch of the heavily fortified Normandy coast. The invasion was the largest amphibious military assault in history and is recognised as a key event in the Allied victory as they led to the liberation of northern France three months later. By spring 1945, the Germans had been defeated. D-Day has been called the beginning of the end of war in Europe.

Peter described the build-up:

On a misty morning, over half of our sweepers slipped out of Queenborough in twos and fours. We were heading for the Isle of Wight. On the chart, it looked conveniently placed for France. We sailed out of the estuary, turned right at North Foreland and made our way along the South Coast, past Dover, Folkestone, Eastbourne, Brighton, and Worthing. It took us twenty-four hours to get there.

The sea was crowded with our ships, the further we went the more of them we saw. Ships in their grey war paint at anchor, ships steaming in line astern, ships tied up in bunches along piers. We passed Selsey Bill into the Solent. None of us, so long as we live, will forget the sight of that armada. Row on row of our ships. Motor launches, minesweepers, motor torpedo boats, motor gun boats, corvettes, cruisers, battleships and aircraft carriers with their retinues of escorts, tugs and tankers. Shoals of landing craft led to moorings by ubiquitous destroyers. Our white ensign everywhere. Signals flying and Aldis lamps flashing in the radio silence.

Three of our flotillas anchored off a deserted strip of coast near Brightstone Bay on the south of the island. Others were further along the coast. It was Tuesday, the twenty-third of May. The day, though of course none of us knew it until later, when General Eisenhower informed his C-in-Cs that D-Day would be the fifth of June.

The ships remained hidden by the Isle of Wight in glorious weather for a week of anxious waiting, checking and rechecking equipment. Meanwhile, minesweepers cleared the lanes to be used by our ships crossing the Channel, after they had been cleared the RAF kept German aircraft away:

Sailors washed the decks, again. Officers studied charts, again. We electricals were lucky. We rowed from ship to ship. I spat at some diaphragms and checked the specific gravity in batteries that were in perfect condition.

Tuesday. Wednesday. Admiral Ramsey, the admiral in charge of 'Neptune' which was the naval part of the invasion, issued his Order of the Day. The CO's read it out to their ships' companies. "It is to be our privilege to take part in the greatest amphibious operation in history ... which in conjunction with the great Russian advance, will crush the fighting power of Germany ... the hopes and prayers of the free world and of the enslaved peoples of Europe will be with us ... let no one underestimate the magnitude of the task. The Germans are desperate and will resist fiercely until we out-manoeuvre and out-fight them. I count on every man ..."

"Blimey," said one of the wiremen, "Nelson."

We were grateful to him for so English a response to any unbecoming sign of emotion.

For the rest of the day: nothing. Sailors polished the metalwork.

The week crept on slowly. Thursday, the beginning of June, another perfect day. A few of us went for a dip over the side.

Friday, at last, lines of white bow-waves here and there, stern-waves catching the sunlight. The giant was stirring.

Saturday, and wherever we looked, the sea was alive with our ships moving east, towards France, the water pricked by masts and flags. Overhead, white lines drawn in the blue sky by RAF fighters who were keeping off Luftwaffe sightseers. It was a great day to start an invasion.

Ominous clouds gathered during the day. The barometer fell. A storm hit us during the afternoon and worsened by the minute. At midnight, we had gale-force. It was damnable. After weeks of the finest weather, this had to come now, with our fleet on the move. At five fifteen on Sunday morning, our flotilla officers told us, General Eisenhower had postponed the invasion. It must have been one of the most difficult decisions ever made in warfare.

After the initial beach landings, two hundred and seventy-seven minesweepers were involved in the Normandy landings. The assault on the beaches by British, Canadian and American troops took several days. German soldiers were firing down on the troops as they moved up the beaches booby-trapped with mines and other obstacles.

Small wooden minesweepers berthed ready for action.

Peter and his minesweepers remained, frustrated, moored by the Isle of Wight:

And what about us, stuck at the Isle of Wight? We were wet, morose and raring to go. A week into the invasion we heard of the German's new mine. None of our sweeps worked and it was taking its toll of men and ships. It only added to our frustration.

At long last, on D plus sixteen, the twenty-second of June, we were told to pull up our hooks and cross to France. The Channel was astounding. Streams of craft were coming and going on lanes marked by buoys, the hum of the RAF overhead was unbroken.

There were happy faces in the ships. We were heading south to where the action was. We blew up, in fact, far fewer mines than on normal patrols at home. The invasion channels were well swept already, new German minelaying was earnestly discouraged by our ships and fighters. The numbers didn't matter to us. Illogically, what we were doing now seemed to us far more important than safeguarding our home waters.

Sweeping had to be co-ordinated day-to-day with the battles on land. Our force split up; different flotillas doing different approach channels and harbours as they were taken. St Malo fell and I was with the flotilla that swept the harbour. We were not allowed ashore. The town was virtually destroyed, short of food; there was fear of epidemics. The army did not want anybody about in the streets who was not essential.

On a pleasant evening when we were at anchor, I rowed ashore by myself to stretch my legs and climbed up the cliff. There, I met a Breton farmer walking home on the cliff path. I also met Calvados; the Frenchman fetched a bottle. It was white, home brewed on the farm and had been hidden under straw from the Germans. It was as deceptively smooth as it was lethal. The Breton had no English, and I had next to no French but the entente was cordiale. For the good name of the Royal Navy let it be said that I returned to the farmer a few days later with cigarettes and a bottle of whisky from the ship's store.

By October, Peter was in Holland. The allies had taken Antwerp so quickly that the retreating forces did not have time to blow up the harbour, leaving the estuary heavily mined. Access to the port would save a two-hundred-mile land journey, getting desperately needed food and supplies to the army as it advanced towards Germany. Without access to the river, most supplies had to be delivered via the Normandy beaches or the port at Cherbourg. The further the army advanced, the overland journey became longer and slower. General Montgomery identified clearing the Scheldt, a top priority but underestimated the difficulties involved. With the exception of D-Day, it was the largest single minesweeping operation carried out during the war.

The *HMS St Tudno* led 'Minesweeping Force A' in 'Operation Calendar' commanded by Captain H.G. Hopper:

> Captain Hopper RN, BIG, square jawed, with a broken nose and you should have seen the other fellow. He went rowing a dinghy every morning at six and God help the skipper if a rope was seen trailing from his sweeper. The base looked kindly on this excessive energy of his. Remote as he was, as a captain in the Royal Navy is intended to be, he was greatly respected by us all. He did a first-rate job, and we knew it. Plus, he looked very jaunty in his uniform with his cap always a little tilted.

Between the third and twenty-fifth of November, two hundred and sixty-seven mines were swept from the River Scheldt in challenging conditions caused by the fast-moving river, currents, silt and hidden sandbanks. A local Dutch pilot who understood the river helped to navigate the small flotilla upstream.

> The plume of the first mine went up a few minutes after we started to pulse, the next one not much later. And the next. Then two together, one at the front of our convoy, the other near the back. One was so close to my sweeper that the crockery shook and the water splashed over our deck, but nobody was hurt. Two hours into the sweep, machine-gun fire started up against us from Walcheren Island on the left bank. Our gunners fired our machine guns. It was good for morale but, as we couldn't see the enemy behind the trees that

bordered the river, it was unlikely that we would hit an enemy gun. One of the flotilla leaders, was having an ill-timed pee. Bullets went through the thin wooden walls and missed him by inches.

"Must be something I drank," he said when he got back on deck.

The captain radioed the RAF. In minutes, two Typhoons came in low from upriver. They fired a rocket each, turned and came back to fire again. The explosions were less than a mile from us. They were tremendous.

Trees crashed; earth sprayed up. In seconds, a strip of landscape had been erased. The planes circled, waiting. There was no more gunfire from the island. We waved our thanks and the planes returned to their runway. We sailed on, and nearly lost count of the mines we exploded. As the light was failing, we anchored.

Each sweeper made its usual report to the flotilla leader: number of casualties - dead, injured and missing; damage; participation in mines swept. The flotilla leaders made their reports to the captain. A minimum of fifty mines swept in the day was confirmed - it may have been more. It was the largest total from any single inland sweep ever. Miraculously, all reported Casualties: Nil, Damage: Nil."

Electrical teams rowed to the ships for checking. Engineering officers did the rounds. We didn't have a celebration; we realised only then how tired we were.

We moved at snails' pace. Our backs hurt from the explosions; our legs shook with fatigue. We flopped down on the deck. The CO of my sweeper, bless him for it, passed a bottle of whisky and a bottle of gin around the company, breaking nobody knew how many naval orders and Admiralty instructions. The cook dished up corned beef hash. We hadn't known how hungry we were.

Night fell. The river lapped against our grateful ships. Our entire fleet was unharmed.

It was officially confirmed that we had swept a total of two hundred and sixty-seven mines, two hundred and twenty-nine of them magnetic, thirty-eight moored. Twelve days after we started, three coasters went safely up the river to Antwerp. Two days later, two deep-laden cargo ships sailed upstream. We watched them. So did a crowd of Germans, their heads bowed.

As the merchantmen passed the white ensign outside our makeshift workshop, they blew their sirens for us and waved. Success is sweet.

The river was declared open. Soon, eighteen thousand tons of urgent supplies went up every week.

Sweeping continued, the Germans were laying new mines with tiny submarines, radio-controlled motorboats and volunteers prepared for suicide missions. Newly taken Dutch ports needed clearing and access to the large ports of Amsterdam and Rotterdam was essential to support the army as it moved across Europe towards Germany.

In places upstream, the rivers and basins were narrow with awkward bends that made sweeping difficult. There was not space for the standard method of two boats moving side-by-side up the river to lay cables. Alternative methods carried much higher risks. If one of the boats was to accidentally hit and explode a mine, it would be wrecked risking the lives of those on-board and blocking the shipping lanes. Clearly, sweeping would be safer and easier if they knew where the mines were. Peter had the idea of asking the Germans for their plans that showed where the mines had been laid, how they had been laid and the type of mine used. His commander, Hugh Boyce, gave leave for him to work onshore.

Along with a sailor with a rifle, Peter went in search of those plans:

We trudged through acres of warehouses, huts, and open stores. Most of them were deserted. Here and there, small groups of German soldiers weren't doing much. There was not much for them to do. In effect, they were prisoners, waiting for somebody to capture them and take them somewhere else. Some Dutch stevedores were half-heartedly tidying up racks. They would have liked to help us but couldn't. I found the German civilian who acted as harbour master.

"Mines?" he asked, hurt. "What mines? Where mines? Here mines? Never. Here no mines!"

Without exception, we had found mines in every harbour vacated by the Germans. Strings of mines.

"Just in case," I put forward a bizarre hypothesis, "if anybody had laid a mine, who would have put it down?"

The army, he thought; it had taken over from the navy.

It was surprising, but anything was possible in the upheaval.

"Where was their office?"

It had been moved just before we arrived, he did not know where to. We trudged on. In time, we found a German sergeant who told us mining was a Major Poltz or Pols or Pölz and his office was in that direction, probably.

We found another group of Germans playing cards. One of them showed us the way.

The building was a one-floor concrete warehouse. Nearly all of it was taken up by wooden racks full of old friends of ours, magnetic mines. A corporal was on duty guarding them. The major was in his small office at the back of the building. I told the corporal to go away to his barracks.

"But my place is here, with the Herr Major," he objected. I liked him for it.

"I'm afraid, your place is where I say it is." He picked up some belongings, put on his shabby greatcoat, and we watched him leave the store.

I told my sentry to stay where he was outside the office and not to let anybody in or out. And on no account to load his artillery.

It was hardly an office. It was no more than a small part of the storeroom. All it had by way of furnishing was a large wooden table, a hard-backed chair and some metal filing cases on the cold concrete floor.

The major was wearing his greatcoat against the cold and working on some lists. Germans are great on lists.

He was elderly, around forty, ancient compared to the youngsters the Germans were putting into their army by then. Balding, short sight corrected by thick glasses. He had a row of medal ribbons but I did not know what they signified. First, he looked up angrily, I assumed because I had disturbed him without knocking. Then, he looked at my uniform and became apprehensive. He was a major, in the invincible German army, a man of consequence, surely, not to be interrupted. I was a rank below him and much the younger. But I was a victor and he was a prisoner. He had not become used yet to defeat. Uncertain what to do, he stood up and made a gesture which could be taken as an incipient salute.

I did not know the rules of this encounter myself: it was the first time I was alone with an enemy at close quarters.

I took off my cap and told him my rank and name. He muttered his, Major Polz, Pols, Pölz, I didn't ask. I pointed to the chairs and we sat down across the wide, rough table. I offered him a cigarette and lit his and mine.

"We are minesweepers," I explained. "We have to clear the basin."

He nodded. At least, he did not offend me by pretending there weren't any mines.

"The basin is difficult, with magnetics." He understood at once.

"Your famous floating tail," he said.

So far, so good, we were technicians talking about a technical problem.

"We need the laying configuration; it will save a lot of trouble."

Instantly, it was something else entirely.

He did not pretend that they had not kept a chart. He sat up and squared his shoulders.

"There, I am afraid, I cannot help you."

"We do need to have it. It may save life and damage."

"It is not what I can do."

"Can do, or will do?"

"It is not what I have to do."

Damn him, the orderly little man said exactly what I hope I would have said myself in his place.

I made myself keep silent.

"Besides," he added, "we moved twice in the last ten days, with all the records. Much was lost."

We had seen the confusion in the dockyard. Without his help, searching the warren of warehouses would be hopeless.

"You will have to look."

"There is no way I would find it."

I was sure he knew where their charts were kept.

From the start, at the back of my mind, I had a vague plan what I would do in such an impasse. Now I was terrified by it. In spite of the cold, my shirt was sticking to my back.

"A pity," I said and got up to go.

At the door, I said, "Auf Wiedersehen."

"How do you mean, Auf Wiedersehen?" he asked.

"You will be collected in the morning when we start sweeping and sit in the bows of the sweeper until the basin is safe. We are unlikely to find survivors so near to a mine as is likely here."

It was nasty. It broke the Geneva conventions. It was a totally empty threat: I would not have dreamt of harming the major (and quite rightly been court-marshalled if I had done).

My theory was simple. The Nazis would not hesitate to exert such pressure. A German army officer might think we would do the same. If he didn't and called my bluff, I'd send him home and it would be the end of my search.

He was quiet.

"Look," I said, from the door. "The war is nearly over now and you're lucky to have come through. All we are asking is that you help us save life and damage." I left the room and closed the door.

"Any luck, sir," the sailor asked me. I didn't know.

I asked him to stay where he was; I'd be outside the storehouse.

I hadn't finished my cigarette before the sailor came to tell me the major wanted to speak to me. I went back into the major's office.

"Perhaps," he said, "the chart might be found."

He led the way.

Hidden by the mine racks, at the back of the store, he extricated a cylindrical metal container a yard long. Not a word was spoken. He pulled out a bundle of rolled charts and gave me two of them; one was of the entrance to the harbour, the other of the basin. Mines were shown in red.

I returned with him to his room.

"Thank you," I said. "I hope you will soon be safely home with your family." I meant it, too.

Six mines were marked in the basin. Next day, the flotilla officer put one of the sweepers in a safe place and laid the cable over the jetty towards the first of the mines. It went up a treat.

Five mines were exploded before lunch. The sixth never went off and was considered a dud. The harbour was opened.

Knowing where the mines were saved a great deal of time, trouble and probably lives. Soon, the team were able to move on and sweep other areas of the Dutch coast. Peter continued to talk about the way he had frightened the major in order to get the plans and questioned for the rest of his life whether his actions had been reasonable or legal.

He continued to describe what happened:

The river was declared open. Soon, eighteen thousand tons of urgent supplies went up every week.

Admiral of the Fleet, Sir John Tovey, Commander in Chief of the South-East of England was pleased with us, "… one of the most difficult and dangerous minesweeping operations of the war … high efficiency and unremitting energy … inspired leadership of Captain H.G. Hopper … effected in twenty-two working days, six days inside the estimate."

Captain Hopper was awarded a Distinguished Service Order, Hugh Boyce, a Distinguished Service Cross and did not have to wait very long for his brass-hat as a full commander.

There was no time to sit on these laurels. There was a war on, as we kept on telling each other; there were battles still to be fought by the army, and ports to be cleared of mines.

In due course, I got promotion to lieutenant. His Majesty's Enemy Alien Lieutenant (L) RNVR.

Peter was clearly shocked and upset by the conditions he saw amongst the newly liberated Dutch:

Surrounding us was heart-breaking poverty. The Dutch were starving, freezing, threadbare. They came and offered us heirlooms, delftware, paintings, in return for food. Our sailors pilfered food for them from our galleys and the ships' officers closed their eyes to it. Our wardroom ran out of packets of cigarettes and we rolled our own. I was told women were smuggled on board of minesweepers only to be given hot meals and sent home with bags of foodstuffs.

He also saw German prisoners of war:

A lot of German prisoners were coming our way to be rounded up. A straggle of soldiers a mile long came shambling towards us.

They were dishevelled, scruffy, demoralised. Everything about them was worn out. Some of their boots were held together with string. Their uniforms were ragged and ill-fitting, off a peg, any peg, as if it had not been worthwhile to kit them out properly for the short time they would survive. Buttons were missing, shirts were open at the neck. Their ages were an eye-opener. There were boys too young for any army and middle-aged men easily old enough to be their fathers. Hardly any were of military age.

They needed a shave if they were old enough. They all needed a wash.

Wholesale destruction, piles of rubble and broken buildings
in northern Europe. Holland, 1945.

Shortly after the Hiroshima and Nagasaki bombs were dropped, the war was officially over. Peter was called to the Admiralty in London, where he was instructed to transfer to Naval Intelligence Division to become a NID 1 PW (Naval Intelligence Division Europe Prisoners of War).

He described his visit to the Admiralty:

> It was awesome walking into the Admiralty building itself. On the left was the Mall and Buckingham Palace, in the sky above was Nelson on his column, in the basement, Churchill had had his ops room. There were four different sentries to satisfy on the way and several officers with different questions.

After his initial training in a country house in Surrey known as 'the place in the country', Peter was posted to the British Naval Gunnery Mission, based in Minden, close to Bad Oeynhausen, which hosted the British Control Commission for

Germany. The Admiralty needed technical information, particularly about German gunnery. Peter's role was to find factories that had manufactured equipment of interest, identify staff who understood the process, and interrogate them. Peter travelled across Germany and Austria; he asked the office if he could be considered for any jobs involving travel to Vienna. The Admiralty, mindful of his personal situation, not knowing what had happened his family, arranged for him to visit Vienna several times.

Few buildings remained after bombing, only piles of rubble.

Again, Peter was shocked with what he discovered:

We had all seen the results of bombing at home. In our different earlier postings, we had seen them in France, Belgium, Italy, Africa, somewhere. We weren't prepared for Germany. Not for whole districts in rubble, for the thousands of messages stuck to ruined walls put there by relatives appealing for hints about their missing next of kin. Four million displaced persons were roaming around Europe; millions of others were hoping for scraps of news of them.

We weren't prepared for the drawn, impoverished Germans coming out of the holes in the ground where they lived, for the empty shops - what was left of them - for the many cripples in the streets, for the shortage of able-bodied men. There was not enough to eat for the ordinary family. Meat was scraps of fat. Coffee was made of acorns. Clothing was thin and worn and nothing could be replaced. In innumerable homes, there were no walls or windows, let alone windowpanes, against the freezing cold, no wood or coal and often no electricity.

Chapter 12

Bergen-Belsen: A Tragic Scene

A corps full of refugees

The Pioneer Corps was formed in 1939 to provide labour to support fighting units, rather than active fighters. It was the only British military service that refugees could join, many German and Austrian Jews joined what became known as the King's Most Loyal Enemy Aliens. Once members of the Pioneer Corps were allowed to join the fight in Europe, George Clare recognised that they were at particular risk if captured, as their Germanic names would identify probable refugee origins. For their own protection, refugees were made to change their names but they usually chose to keep their original initials. Erich Stössler signed up and on the thirtieth of April 1940 and became Eric Stanley; the religion on his identity tag was Buddhist. Paula, Karla and Peter were at Euston station waving bravely as his train departed.

Following his initial training, Eric took part in the Normandy Landings and helped to liberate Northern France from the Germans. In time, the value of a native German speaker, used to European customs, was recognised and Eric was transferred from the army to the newly formed No. 1 War Criminals Investigation Team (1WCIT).

As Germany collapsed, camps were emptied and the few survivors were condensed in the larger camps. Bergen-Belsen had been receiving additional prisoners since the summer of 1944. The British Army liberated the camp on the fifteenth of April 1945. The horrors they found are well documented: thirteen thousand unburied bodies, sixty thousand louse-infested inmates held without food or water and who were dying from starvation and typhus at the rate of about five hundred a day. A young Richard Dimbleby, accompanying the British troops, gave a memorable report on the horrors of what was discovered at the camp describing that day as 'the most horrible of my life'.

Despite efforts to care for the survivors by the British Army, Red Cross, medical students, Quaker and Jewish relief teams, a further nine thousand died by the end of April and four thousand the following month. Some died because their digestive systems were unable to cope with the food they were given. The army captured a few of the SS officers and other Germans who had been responsible for running the camp before it was liberated and forced them to bury the dead in the mass graves. Some of these prisoners contracted typhus from handling the bodies and died. The army set up a hospital nearby which became the largest in Europe. Once all the survivors had been moved to nearby villages, barracks and hospitals, the lice-infested site remained a health hazard. Eventually, it was burned to the ground by Royal Engineers equipped with flame throwers.

Eric with his new family name, Stanley, in his army uniform.

The 1WCIT arrived to take over a month after liberation. Leo Genn was a Jewish actor with legal training. He had signed up in 1940 and was promoted to lieutenant-colonel before volunteering to lead the investigation. His jeep led the small team into the camp.

The second vehicle, driven by Eric, followed with his aid, Major Savile Champion, a solicitor in the Royal Artillery. The team built up a camaraderie as a way to diffuse the intolerable horrors of their jobs. Perhaps the thespian activities of Eric's earlier life helped him to bond with his superiors. Handmade dinner cards for the 'Crime Club' with a skull and crossbones motif are amongst Genn's private papers. Presumably, this black humour was a minor defence mechanism.

After a few gruelling months working with the victims, translating, assisting with the collection of evidence, Eric returned to London on two weeks' leave. Feeling too dirty to be near Karla, he disappeared from the Streatham flat. Some days later, she found him crying and trembling in a small bed and breakfast hotel. He had spent several days walking the streets, with no idea where he was. He must have had some sort of nervous breakdown. Today, we would call it Post Traumatic Stress Disorder (PTSD). Eric returned to Bergen-Belsen and continued to work in Germany until he was demobilized. He never received treatment or counselling to help overcome his experiences of the camp.

Vienna – Terrible things had happened

Naval Intelligence were sympathetic to Peter's request to be posted to Vienna should the opportunity arise and sent him there on a mission in 1946. Naturally, he took the first opportunity to visit the cinema. Although the building was still intact, the Palast Kino looked drab and rundown. Peter did not recognise the manager or most of the staff but he knew Frau Strand sitting with her knitting at the sweet counter. She had survived, working at the cinema throughout the war. The counter was empty bar one small plate of dry biscuits. Frau Strand remained on duty, partly because she could not afford to heat her tiny flat if she stayed at home, nor would she have had the chance to meet and chat to others. She was shocked and scared to see a tall young man in a long, dark uniform coat but after she realized this was little Herr Peter from before the war, she began to help him to understand the terrible things that had taken place since his mother's departure eight years earlier.

Peter recalled:

I said, "Good evening, Frau Strand," and told her who I was.

"Jesus Maria," she was startled and frightened, "never young Peter!"

She hurried out of her kiosk and into the entrance hall to give me a timid hug.

To her, I must have been another kind of ghost. She had known me since I was a child. When I left Vienna, I was a schoolboy. Now I came back, an adult and one of Austria's many new occupiers.

"First, tell me about the family."

She burst out crying. I made her sit down on the bench under the mirror, designed by my Uncle Ernst, and waited until she was calmer.

Then, quietly, she told me about my Aunt Selma. Her husband, Julius Haas, had suffered from a heart condition for many years and had died in a hospice on the fifth of March 1938, shortly before the Anschluss.

"She never even tried to get out, Frau Haas, didn't," Frau Strand told me. "She had a suitcase packed and that was all."

Fritz, the cousin with epilepsy, was taken first, in broad daylight. His mother, Aunt Laura, disappeared in the night. The milkman reported the empty flat.

"I still saw Frau Haas nearly every day. She'd come in for a chat when the Nazis weren't here."

She fell silent for a little.

"Until," she went on so silently that I could hardly hear her, "one morning, she was gone. Three days later, an SA man and his woman took over her flat."

Having expected something like this did not make it easier to have it confirmed.

"What about Ernst and Muschi?" I asked after a while.

She shook her head.

"They went back to Czechoslovakia, to Brno. Frau Ticho being a Christian, they thought they would be safe there. Herr Ernst stayed 'underground' as we called it. Frau Muschi had a job. They managed."

She told me the rest; they were living with a friend of Ernst's, who told her what had happened when he visited Vienna. Frau Muschi became sick, an operation failed and she was dying. Although it was too dangerous for Uncle Ernst to visit, he stayed with her, holding her hand until she died. He was then arrested before he left the hospital and sent to one of the Eastern camps.

My uncle, Ernst Ticho, one-time dashing army captain, with a medal from the Austrian army for bravery in the First War. He had taught me rowing and swimming and making campfires.

Despite Paula's phone calls and letters urging her to travel to England, Selma stayed in Vienna and continued to manage the cinema. She must have expected to be taken, the single suitcase that was all she would be allowed to take, was packed and ready in the hall waiting for the knock on the door. She gave her friend, Denise Sellner, a neighbour who lived in another of the Josefstädter Straße flats, documents proving the Ticho-Hass-Sieber family owned the Palast Kino. Presumably, Selma hoped the papers would be helpful once the horrors were over and it was possible to try to claim restitution for the cinema.

I must acknowledge the generosity and help I've had from several people in Vienna who have sent information about my family and the Palast Kino. The Austrians were meticulous record keepers and recorded every transaction as they appropriated Jewish property. These records are now available from the Archive of the Austrian Republic. Dr Steiner, the archivist responsible for financial papers of the first and second republics, kindly sent me a large parcel of photocopies from the archive. Faced with a huge pile of letters and forms, I was shocked to see the Nazi insignia at the tops of pages, and the signature, 'Hiel Hitler!' at the bottom. In documents, the Nazis called Jewish women 'Sarah' and added 'Israel' to male names. So, Paula became Paula Sarah Sieber, whilst Peter became Peter Israel Sieber.

There are several on-line databases with digitized papers containing information collected from concentration camps, so if you know a person's date of birth, it is possible to find their death certificate. Other Shoah databases list deaths by family name, giving the place and date of death. Of course, I was shocked when I found Selma's documents. Perhaps even more shocking whenever I searched, I was faced with such long lists of the slaughtered, I could not unambiguously identify the individual I was looking for amongst the many others of similar ages and initials. This brought home the scale of the genocide.

Selma

The database of Jewish residents of Josefstadt (1938 to 1945) and papers from the Austrian State Archive has entries showing that Selma Hass (née Ticho) was collected by the State Police from 52 Josefstädter Straße on the twenty-third of October 1941 and taken, initially, to the central location for the collection of Jews in Vienna.

A notice from the State Archive states that:

Selma Sara Hass born 1.6.1880
Everything she owns was confiscated. If you have anything belonging to this person, please hand it over to Landbank to this account number A2 VII/872

Selma Hass, Paula's sister. Vienna, 1936.

Selma was then moved to Litzmannstadt umgesiedelt, the Łódź ghetto (Litzmannstadt and Łódź were the same place but with different names in German and Polish), and along with thousands of other Jews, herded onto closed cattle trucks for the unimaginable journey across Austria to Poland, no longer treated as a human being. The space in the trucks was so limited that individuals of all ages had to stand, wedged against one another without food, water or toilet. When someone died, they simply slipped down onto the rough wooden slats that formed the base of the truck. Those standing close by recited the Kaddish, the prayer for the dead, silently. At first, stronger members of the group moved these bodies to the side of the truck, but after many debilitating hours standing, these stronger individuals became too weak to continue moving bodies, so the dead were left where they fell. Selma, wedged between other terrified people, in soiled urine-soaked underwear must have smelt and shared the collective fear. The journey was slow. Cattle trucks had to give way to trains carrying troops or essential supplies. The train stopped and started, was moved into sidings and bumped across branch lines. Fear increased each time the train stopped at a station. Had they arrived at their final destination? There were no windows in the cattle trucks; they had small slats to allow ventilation. Those pressed against the sides of the vehicle might have been able to see passing autumn countryside and small deserted stations, whilst those crushed in the centre had to rely on rumours whispered across the truck. After several days, those that had survived were roughly pulled from the train by police and Nazi guards. They had arrived at the Łódź ghetto, conveniently close to the Theresienstadt concentration camp.

After Warsaw, Litzmannstadt was the second largest ghetto in German occupied Europe. Jews were deported there from across Europe. It was a major industrial centre, manufacturing textiles, mostly uniforms for the German army. Internees were crammed into the ghetto with limited food, no electricity or running water and they were made to work long hours in factories. Malnutrition and disease spread rapidly through the population. Even when not selected for deportation to an extermination site, life expectancy was only a few months. Any genetic protection from tuberculosis that may have come from the Tay Sachs mutation that is carried in the Ashkenazi Jewish population, was irrelevant in the horrendous conditions of the ghetto. Prisoners were moved to the gas chambers at Auschwitz for minor transgressions or once they were no longer fit to work in the factories.

I searched the Czech Holocaust Portal and found a copy of Selma Haas's death certificate. She died on the eighteenth of September 1942 from, so stated on the certificate, a cerebral embolism. The last ten months of her life must have been of unimaginable horror as she lived in the overcrowded, disease-ridden ghetto, worked as a slave in a factory making uniforms for German soldiers, before being shipped to Theresienstadt to die once she was too weak to work.

Selma Hass death certificate. Eighteenth of September 1942.
Ghetto Theresienstadt. (Czech Holocaust Portal)

Alfred's family
Paula's brother Alfred had died in September 1936 leaving his widow, Laura, and two sons Fritz and Franz.

Laura automatically inherited Alfred's twenty per cent share of the Palast Kino and her name appeared in some of the papers from 1938 onwards.

Poor cousin Fritz

Fritz was congenitally weak, epileptic and needed constant care. Peter referred to him as 'poor cousin Fritz'. The Gestapo collected Fritz from an apartment at 43 Josefstädter Straße on the twentieth of October 1939 and took him to the Nisco transport centre.

The Holocaust Survivors and Victims Database shows that he was then taken to the Terezin ghetto but his final destination is unknown as it could have been Auschwitz (Poland), Baranovici (Belarus), Bergen-Belsen (Germany), or Treblinka (Poland). Because of his medical condition, he probably died en route or was sent straight to a killing centre.

Franz escapes

Franz managed to escape from Vienna to Palestine on the third of July 1939. Keen to reduce the number of Jews in Austria, the Nazis appear to have condoned or even collaborated with those who helped emigrants escape. Franz's name appears on the list of six hundred and ninety-three Austrian, Czech and stateless individuals listed on the ship's manifest of the SS *Agnoyis Nicolaya*, which was included in a collection of papers classified as 'Illegal immigration to Palestine'. He must have paid to make the dangerous and difficult journey across German occupied countries to the Black Sea. Other passengers on the list included men who may have been distant relatives: fifty-nine-year-old Max Ticho and twenty-year-old Ignatz Bock. Whilst both Franz and Ignatz were young and single, Max was older and was recorded as being married. As these names appear close together on an otherwise unordered list, perhaps they had arrived at the boat together and their names were written down as they boarded?

Franz probably began his journey by river boat from Vienna to Bratislava, embarking at the Danube Canal on the outskirts of the city. He would then have continued downstream from Bratislava to one of the small ports at the mouth of the Danube where he most likely joined other refugees waiting for a ship to Palestine. The ship he finally managed to board, the SS *Agnoyis Nicolaya* may have sailed via Athens and Cyprus. Just as today, the journey across the Mediterranean is dangerous for refugees travelling in the opposite direction, towards Europe, it was dangerous then with overcrowded ships and limited supplies of food and water. In December 1939, the *SS Astria*, empty apart from the nine crew who all lost their lives, sank in a heavy storm. Safety was not assured even when the SS *Agnoyis Nicolaya* had managed to make the treacherous sea crossing to the Palestine coast safely as Britain, then in control of Palestine, made Jewish immigration illegal. To escape detection, refugees had to transfer to small boats and land secretly along the coast. The British authorities captured refugees from three ships in 1940 who they then deported to Mauritius for the remainder of the war. Franz appears to have completed his journey to Israel safely.

Laura (Luisa)

Alfred's widow, Laura was deported from Cerningasse 12, Vienna on the twentieth of May 1942. She was killed only six days later in a new killing centre: Maly Trostinec. The Germans initially built the camp there on an existing collective farm outside Minsk (which was then in Russia but is currently in Belarus). Their intention was to create a holding centre for prisoners captured during Operation Barbarossa, the German advance into the Soviet Union, the battle for the Eastern Front. With the arrival of the first transports of Jews from Western Europe, Maly Trostinec became an extermination camp on the tenth of May 1942.

A written report for the Reichskommissariet by Minsk Security Police described the activities of the police and SS in the camp in 1942:

> *Jewish transports arrived regularly and we serviced them.*
> *On May 5th, we prepared new pits, and on May 11th, 1,000 Jews from Vienna were brought to the pits.*
> *On May 13th, men were detailed to prepare new pits for the Jewish transports.*
> *On May 26th, 1,000 Jews are brought to the pits.*
> *On June 1st the Jewish transport is brought to the pits.*
> *On June 15th, 1,000 Vienna Jews are brought to the pits.*
> *On June 28th, the Jewish transport arrives … The following days are filled with weapons' cleaning [and] digging of pits ...*
> *July 17th, the Jewish transport is brought to the pits ...*
> *July 24th, another transport with 1,000 Jews.*

Laura must have been on the transport that arrived from Vienna on the twenty-sixth of May. Again, there was an agonizing train journey for the thousands of individuals who were crammed into a cattle truck, standing in the dark without food or water, as the trains travelled from Vienna across Czechoslovakia and Poland to Minsk in Russia. Old and young were crammed together, unable to move. Some families managed to stay together, consoling each another quietly. Most were alone, silent and terrified for themselves and the ones they loved but were unlikely to ever see again. A few prayed.

When Laura arrived, the killings had only recently started at Maly Trostinec. As the camp had originally been designed to hold prisoners of war rather than as an extermination camp, it was not equipped with even mobile gas chambers. Prisoners were marched into the woods surrounding the camp where huge pits had been dug. Guarded by local police and SS officers, they were instructed to undress and place their shoes, clothing and underwear on separate piles. Then they waited, comforting one another silently, until groups of twenty were called to walk forward to the edge of the pit. The horror of looking onto a heap of dead and dying compatriots, knowing that you are about to join them would have been beyond understanding. Eyewitness reports of similar slaughter at a range of extermination camps describe in harrowing detail how Jews were herded into death pits across German occupied Eastern Europe. They noted that victims behaved with quiet dignity: there was no shouting or requests for mercy, families comforted children and quietly said goodbye to one another. In most cases, a combination of local police (Poles, Lithuanians, Ukrainians, or Russians) and SS officers managed the killings, even though in the majority of reports, shooting was restricted to the SS.

Ernst loses his wife and his protection

Paula's brother, Ernst adored his Catholic wife Maria, (known as Muschi). As a Christian, Muschi could work and support Ernst while they lived in hiding in Brno. Ernst was protected from persecution until Muschi became sick.

Following a failed operation, she died in hospital in Brno with Ernst by her side in 1942. No longer protected by his wife's Aryan status, Ernst was arrested before he could leave the hospital and forcibly moved to Prague. His name appears amongst the list of Auschwitz victims.

Ernst Ticho, Peter's uncle. Vienna, 1936.

Fritzi's suffering

Fritzi Grossova, Paula's niece, married Walter Deutsch in the 1930s and they lived in Brno. At some point, they were both arrested and taken to separate camps. Unusually, they both survived incarceration and eventually returned to Brno. Walter worked as a civil servant and, with gradual promotions, he gained a senior position. He died during the 1970s. The starvation and beatings that Fritzi had been subjected to whilst she was in the camp were the probable cause of her infertility.

The survivor databases are smaller and easier to search than the databases of those who were killed. I searched the Holocaust Survivors and Victims Database and found Fritzi on a list of the four hundred and eighty-nine survivors in Terezin on the fifth of February 1945.

Uncle Manu

Peter's Uncle Manu was barely a year older than his father, Hermann. After Hermann's early death, Manu had been a father-figure to Peter and they had always been close. Emanuel was taken from an apartment at 32 Novargasse and died in Auschwitz on the twenty-fourth of October 1942.

Robert Coen

Karla's parents did not survive. Her father Robert was killed on the first of June 1942 in Maly Trostinec, Minsk, Belarus. The fate of her mother, Paula, is currently unknown.

Incinerator in an unidentified camp. Germany 1946

Chapter 13

Windermere: The Hostel Empties

The horrors of the Holocaust

The Nazis opened Dachau, their first concentration camp, in 1933. Initially camps were built to house anyone they wanted to remove: Communists, homosexuals, the unfit, Roma, Jews, resistance fighters and prisoners of war. By 1945, there was a complex network of many hundreds of camps. These included extermination (death) camps (Maly Trostinec where Laura was murdered); slave camps - built close to factories where individuals were forced to work (like Łódź where Selma was forced to work before she was killed in nearby Theresienstadt); holding camps for people the Nazis thought they might be able to barter; and transit camps which held individuals until they were transported east to a killing centre. The Final Solution emerged at the Wannsee conference in Berlin on the twentieth of January 1942. Jews capable of working would be transported to the labour camps in the East, those unfit for work would be eliminated in the death camps, most on arrival. News of Nazi plans, the appalling treatment of Jews, and others, filtered back to the Allies throughout the war via escaped prisoners, intelligence agents and even local inhabitants. There are many examples where detailed information became available; in autumn 1941, someone from the Chilean embassy in Prague sent information about the Reich citizenship law, the establishment of Theresienstadt, and even predicted the Final Solution. Although the Allies knew something of the abuse perpetrated by the Nazis, little about this appeared in the British press presumably to maintain morale and protect the public.

In January 1943, Germany was losing against Russia on the Eastern Front. Operation Barbarossa had failed for multiple reasons: the distance was too great to maintain a supply chain and feed the army, their strategy was wrong and much of the equipment, particularly the tanks, was obsolete. Hitler had underestimated the Russian strength once they were fighting to defend their motherland. As the German armies retreated westward, the Nazis abandoned the death camps they had created. The few prisoners that survived these camps were then forced to march across Poland to concentration camps in Germany. Already starving, sick and with little clothing to protect against the weather, few survived these death marches.

In July 1944, Soviet forces captured the concentration camp at Majdanek, then they found the abandoned killing centres at Belzec, Sobibor, and Treblinka before they liberated Auschwitz in January 1945. In April 1945, the Americans found twenty thousand emaciated prisoners in Buchenwald. Shortly after, they liberated Dora-Mittelbau, Flossenbürg, Dachau, and Mauthausen. As camps were liberated, the extent of the genocide and the true horror of the conditions of survivors were recognized by the Allies, possibly for the first time.

As descriptions and pictures of concentration camps began to appear in British newspapers, in BBC news broadcasts and in Pathé newsreels shown at the cinema, Paula and Alice realized the probable fates of the children's families and of their own relatives. Although the matrons attempted to shield the girls from these atrocities, it was inevitable they would discover news of the barbarity. The matrons prohibited the normal weekly visits to the local cinema to prevent the children from seeing pictures of camps in the newsreels that prefaced the main film. But the girls, many of which were now teenagers, learnt the news anyway from the radio, from newspapers, and from their school friends. One child, desperate for news of her parents, sneaked into the cinema anyway. Shocked by what she saw and realizing that her parents might be amongst the piles of dead bodies, or one of the walking skeletons she had seen in the newsreel, the poor girl fainted. The young cashier phoned South Wood to alert the matrons. When Paula arrived to collect the poor child, she was being given sweet tea and comforted by the cinema staff. As Windermere's only taxi was not available, the cinema had arranged alternative transport, a police car was waiting to take them back to the hostel. Yet another small example of the kindness of this community to the hostel.

Peter described the poverty and destruction he had seen in Holland, Germany and Austria during his time in intelligence. Europe was in chaos. Cities bombed to extinction were without essential services: water, electricity, gas and transport systems. Many lived in poverty, with multiple families in one building, sharing a single bathroom. Without electricity and fuel, it was very cold. Windows broken by bomb blasts were hastily covered with cardboard that gave no protection from the wind. Food was scarce; few had any possessions left to sell to buy food from the black market. Some had to walk miles from their homes in towns and cities to the countryside to search for food and firewood. The population had been drinking acorn coffee for several years, so people were used to adapting to what little they could find. Displaced persons began searching for their families. Soldiers slowly returned, often on foot, from the Eastern Front.

The Red Cross began to try to care for and identify camp survivors. There are many photographs of buildings, monuments and even lampposts plastered with handwritten notices, pleas for information about lost family members. It is difficult to underestimate the time needed to begin to piece together information following the wholesale destruction caused by the war and to unravel lost familial connections. It took some years before people were discovered, returned to their homes and reunited with their families.

Wall with notices seeking information about missing persons.

As information filtered down to the hostel, a few girls heard from, often distant, family members scattered across the globe. Others slowly began to realize that they would never hear from or see their parents again. Some were luckier.

Lisl's father was still serving in the British army when a telegram from the Red Cross arrived for her at the hostel. Her mother had survived and had been taken to Sweden to recuperate. Once her father had been demobbed in 1945, Lisl joined him in Glasgow. It then took nine months before her mother had recovered sufficiently to be fit enough to travel from Sweden to Glasgow. Modern techniques, clinically induced comas and parenteral nutrition were not then available. The family were reunited in January 1946 and moved to Israel to join her sister in 1949.

Lisl described the moment when she received the telegram:

On the fifth of May 1945, I go to work and I am passed by the telegram boy. And then Ruth comes to my workplace and says the telegram was for you. And I say, has something happened to my father? And she says no, you have to come home now. I come back and all the girls are standing there saying: You have a telegram!

The ladies waited for me with a cup of coffee and a tranquilizer. The telegram was from the Red Cross telling me my mother was alive. I was the only one with a dad and now I have a mum! Nineteen girls are standing behind the closed doors, the ladies are sitting with me and the telegram and I hear, "why does she not come out and tell us who the telegram is from?" I say to them, how can I tell them my mother is alive. I am the only one with a dad and a sister in Palestine, they have no one. I go out and tell them. And they say how nice. Perhaps we will hear something as well. But they never do.

It was addressed to my father who was a British soldier. I was his private address in case he was arrested by the Germans. It says: Stockholm. Fourth of May '45 S... Your wife saved. Arrived here Red Cross transport from Germany.

She was in Sweden because my father had a friend in Sweden, and my mother remembered him. And that is how I got the telegram. My father tried to get her to England but she was not in a good condition to travel. I left the hostel in fall 1945 and we rented a room. I was shivering with excitement. My mother saw me but kept saying, "where is Lisl? She expected a little girl and I was sixteen.

There was no money in the bank so after three days, my father had to go back to work. I kept holding her hands and we were mother and daughter again. She told me what had happened to her."

Some of girls had already moved on from the hostel. Ilse was fortunate as her mother had escaped to Britain in 1938 and had a job that allowed her to live near to the hostel. Mother and daughter moved to London in 1943. Ilse briefly worked in Boots library in Golders Green before joining the WAAFF (Women's Auxiliary Air Force) in April 1944. She served in the WAAF for eighteen months before marrying in September 1945. She had two children before moving to the US in 1959. Ilse trained and worked as a dental assistant for many years before retiring to do voluntary work.

Back row: Sophie, Elfie, Ruth ?, Lisl, Middle row: ?, Ruth A., Margot, Lore, Hilde, Front row: Inge, ?, Lea, Frieda.

By 1945, the frightened children that had arrived in the hostel at Windermere in 1938, had grown into young women.

Ruth intensely disliked everything about the hostel, the matrons, the discipline. She continued to be very unhappy about her time there. Unlike the other girls who had to get a job or training as there were no funds available for them to continue their studies, Ruth was able to continue with her education whilst living in the hostel. She bicycled the ten kilometres or so to and from school each day and was expected to contribute to the general chores that kept the hostel operating while she lived there. Eventually, she moved from the hostel to the grammar school and gained a scholarship to read French at Bedford College, London.

Others had to leave the hostel to continue their training as the distance was far to make commuting possible. Sophie moved to Barrow-in-Furness to train as a nurse whilst Eva moved to the cottage hospital in Bowness before moving to London in 1949. Eva married and had two children and, later, two grandchildren.

In one case, siblings were reunited. Annie joined her brother and cousins in Cardiff. At first, her brother paid the rent on a small room for her but as she had been working as a seamstress in Windermere, she quickly got a job as a dressmaker that enabled her to pay her own rent. She met her Viennese husband, Rudolph, in 1944. Rudi was an American GI stationed in Cardiff with the US army prior to the invasion. Annie's family invited two of the GIs to join them for the Seder meal that marks the beginning of Passover, the festival where Jews celebrate their escape from slavery in ancient Egypt. Annie and Rudi dated a few times, corresponded regularly whilst he served in France, and married just before the end of the war in Europe. After her marriage, she worked at the Sully Tuberculosis hospital in the Vale of Glamorgan for a year before moving to the US as a war bride.

Dasha moved from the Windermere hostel to a Czech school in Wales in 1944 in an attempt to help her retain her mother tongue (Czech). By the time that the school in Wales closed at the end of the war, the Windermere hostel had been disbanded and so she faced yet another dislocation as she was sent to a hostel in London.

She was only thirteen years old:

It seemed a very long time that a decision was to be made about my future. By this time, all the girls in the hostel in Windermere had found relatives who would care for them somewhere in the world. The hopes of finding my parents were still my great hope. Once again, I was sent to another hostel in London. New faces, new schools awaited me. I was given an allowance which I had to clothe, feed and save for myself.

At this time, I was thirteen years old. Names of survivors were circulated. I went frequently to Bloomsbury House in the hope of seeing the names of my mother and father. As the lists grow shorter and shorter, I realized that my hopes were shattered. I was on my own and had to think of my future. At this stage, I had contact with my brother who was by then studying at Oxford. I visited him fairly frequently. He became my mentor. I looked to him for guidance and considered his opinions very seriously. He was the only person, at this stage of my life, who actually cared for me. We became very close after the separation caused by the war years. I had an aunt and uncle in London who I went to visit a few times. We corresponded and they sent me parcels of clothes for which I was grateful.

In 1945-46, the hostel in London was closed. I seem to have been a problem for the Czech Trust Fund which had now become my guardian. A new home had to be found for me. This time, I went to stay with a Christian family with two small children. I went to school, did some household chores and looked after the children. This was my home until I managed to get a bursary to become a junior schoolteacher.

As the girls, now young women, moved on, gradually the hostel emptied. It closed finally in 1946. I spoke to Lisl by phone recently. She is a strong, independent, eighty-eight-year-old, living in London. She said that as the youngest, she and her sister were the last to leave the hostel as they were too young to live independently. They were sent to another hostel in Manchester.

Paula the landlady
By saving most of her three shillings a week that the hostel committee had paid her, plus the profits from the sale of her

night-time cottage industry, Paula had accumulated enough to place a deposit on a small, terraced house in Gosforth. In September 1947, she took a short-lease on a two-up, two-down house in Windsor Terrace and became a landlady. Her letters to Peter show that she was worrying about finding four suitable tenants who would be able to pay her six guineas a week in rent. The furniture was supplied by George Wilkes of Harmony Hall, Shields Road, Newcastle and the High Street, Gateshead. Later in the year, her letters show that she had found four gentlemen and was providing them with a cooked breakfast every morning.

Paula's health continued to trouble her, as it would for the remainder of her life. Over the years, she spent time in nursing homes in Sunderland and Vienna. The fate of the cinema troubled her greatly. Paula needed the proceeds of selling the Palast Kino to support herself.

South Wood shortly before it closed. Windermere, 1946.

Alice, once more a teacher

Both of Alice's sons had managed to escape from Austria to the US, Karl by the skin of his teeth via Dachau. Otto was still serving in the US army based in Europe, with the Counterintelligence Corps in Stuttgart, hunting SS men and then, from 1948, in Vienna. Karl had moved from Oregon to the Northwestern

University when he began the research which led to a PhD in Chemistry. Alice longed to see them; to see for herself the fine young men they had grown into during eight years they had been separated. She travelled to the US as soon as her responsibilities at the hostel were ended. Alice continued to visit Europe regularly, staying in London with Paula. Most years, the two friends took a holiday together on the Austrian lakes where this story first began. The ladies spent a great deal of time together and corresponded regularly when they were apart.

Eventually, Alice followed Karl to California but instead of settling down to a quiet retirement, she resumed her teaching career. She approached a local college which gratefully accepted her offer and she began teaching again. As before, her reputation spread rapidly. She began to appear on local television demonstrating how the Viennese cook. Also, she gave interviews to the press. She continued teaching into her late eighties.

Amongst others, Elfie and her late husband visited in San Francisco when they were travelling in the US in the 1970s:

I mean, Alice was incredible! For her age, she didn't stop talking and was teaching in a cookery school. They must have thought her credible as she was on television and in the local press.

When we talked about her teaching, she said, "All I did was just talk. I didn't actually do any work. I told them what to do and I told them about stories from Vienna."

She was a natural teacher. I think with hindsight but I think at the time also, we must have heard an awful lot about Vienna and the people who went to her cookery school in Vienna from her. She always told us that if she met anybody who had been a pupil at the school in Vienna, she didn't remember their name and so always said, "Oh hello. How is the old complaint?" She said there was always something to say about the old complaint!

Chapter 14

Vienna: The Fate of the Palast Kino

A crippling pain

By the time I was old enough to begin to understand my grandmother's life story, I knew she was very unhappy. I had always known that terrible things had happened to her family and that few had survived but I could not understand her crippling pain. She felt guilty at escaping to safety when they had perished and she was angry that she had failed to convince them to leave. Individual ties prevented each one from abandoning their familiar lives for an unknown life in a foreign country. Recently bereaved, Selma was grieving for her husband Julius. Laura's disabled son Fritz was too weak to travel. Ernst had already moved to safety in Brno and assumed he would be protected as his wife, Muschi, who was a Christian. Paula seldom spoke of her siblings as individuals and never talked about Hermann's family. Occasionally, she had terrible conversations with Peter about brutalities that had taken place inside concentration camps. In contrast to the trauma and pain of losing her family along with a visceral mixture of fear and hate of Nazis and Germans in general, Paula's complaints about the cinema were different. She had been badly treated and had not been given her fair share of the business she had created. She was afraid of authority, obsessive about obeying regulations and keen to avoid attracting attention. Fear of being noticed must have set-up an innate struggle for this tiny and once extrovert woman. Her immediate friends and neighbours were also Jewish refugees who shared and fuelled her unhappiness in a polyglot of languages and broken, accented English.

Shortly before his death in 2000, Peter cleared his loft of many of the items that I remembered from my childhood. Paula's collection of rather ugly, large jugs and other ornaments, my childhood stamp albums, and his suitcases of wartime photographs were gone. He left some cardboard boxes that contained assorted photographs and papers. These were sorted into large manila envelopes, their contents clearly written in his characteristic writing, 'Mother – Paula', 'Hermann's family –

Peter's father'. There was also a battered attaché case, covered in hotel stickers, some too torn and faded to read. Others were from the Hotel Austria, Badgastein, HotelRostt, Bad Aussee, Salzkammergut, Hotel d'Italie, Bauer Griniwald from Paula and Alice's visits to the Austrian lakes, the Giorione, Venice, with a picture of a gondola; the Continental Hotel, Nice and the Hotel Astoria, Menton from her holidays in the French Riveria.

Paula's battered old attaché case with stickers from the many hotels she stayed in.

Inside the case was a random collection of letters, papers and official documents, along with a couple of packets of photographs. Mostly written in Paula's strong, black, sloping handwriting, on flimsy blue airmail paper, they are incomplete, difficult to read and not all are dated. I was surprised by how quickly Paula started writing in English and how well she wrote in a language she had known nothing about only six months previously.

My exploration of the old attaché case containing random bundles of letters, postcards and photographs gained momentum as I became increasingly absorbed by the family story. We visited snowy Vienna in February 2019, gorging on food remembered from my childhood. Viennese cooking captures the finest examples from across her earlier empire, with strudels, goulash, crescent-shaped almond biscuits, vanillekipferl (their shape based on the Byzantine crescent), red cabbage and sauerkraut, (sweet by comparison with German kraut), and schlagobers, whipped cream, similar to the French Chantilly cream, immortalised by Strauss in a ballet. Although Paula had not been interested in cooking herself, her best friend Alice had written the city's definitive recipe book.

Bundles of assorted letters inside Paula's old attaché case.

On a clear cold day, under a penetratingly blue sky, we took the tram to my grandfather's grave in the Jewish cemetery, the *Zentralfriedhof* in Simmering. Hermann shared his grave with his brothers Josef and Emanuel which was next to his father's, Chaim Schieber. Rosa Hirsch had been added to Chaim's plot in 1956. The large granite headstones were well maintained, the Hebrew lettering on Chaim's was weathered but legible whilst the lettering on Hermann's stone remained crisp and well formed. All the graves in this new part of the cemetery are beautifully maintained by the Jewish community.

Gravestones in the central cemetery.
Chaim Schieber's and his daughter Rosa's grave on the left; his
sons Hermann, Josef, and Emanuel Sieber on the right.

Cheekily, I had written to all the inhabitants of the Schreyvogelgasse apartments explaining about my grandmother and asking if a visit might be possible. I was lucky enough to receive one reply, an invitation for coffee and homemade strudel. This kind couple invited us into their home. Our host had already asked several questions about Paula and Hermann by email in advance of our arrival. He had worked out that they were now living in the apartment that had once been Paula and Peter's home. Although there was a photocopy of the list of the occupants dating back to the nineteenth century, there was no entry for Sieber. Over the years, the page had obviously been folded many times, some of the folds had torn apart and the paper had been stuck back together with Sellotape. The entries covering 1920 to 1938, were black, as Sellotape is opaque to some old photocopiers. Once we had recovered from this extraordinary co-incidence, our hosts conducted us round their palatial apartment, explaining how over many years they had restored and altered it. After the war, the property had become run down. It was used for cheap lodging rooms and student accommodation. Restoration only began in the 1960s. Fortunately, many of the original features remained.

I recognized the huge hall, ideal for playing skittles with Dachshunds, and could almost see the small dogs sliding along the ornate parquet floor on their stomachs. Seffi's room tucked behind the kitchen was close to Peter's which was recognisable from photographs.

Our host, intrigued by my imposition had, in anticipation of our meeting, visited the Austrian State Archive, the Österreichischen Staatsarchiv, and uncovered parts of the story. He already knew about the cinema and assumed much of the rest. The couple then kindly advised us how to visit the archives and who to contact when we got there. From this, my mild curiosity grew into a quest. We spent the remainder of our time in Vienna running around the metro visiting archives. Intriguingly, the City of Vienna archive is housed on the eleventh floor of a converted gasometer. Alighting at Gasometer Station, we found an eclectic mix of shops, cafes, sound centres and an elevator to the library. At both the Wiener Stadt-und Landesarchiv and the Staatsarchiv, the staff were unfailingly courteous and eager to help, despite our arriving without an appointment and unable to speak German. They searched the catalogues for us and called colleagues asking for papers to be retrieved from the stack immediately so we could have copies to take with us. We were shown how to find out where people had lived using the details from their 'Meldezettel', the registration cards that were collated annually and then helped to find the address of the flat Paula had lived in before she met Hermann in Gonzagagasse.

Dr Hubert Steiner is a head of division at the Austrian State Archive and has spent his career creating a database of Jewish property appropriated by the National Socialists, the 'Vermögensverkehrsstelle'. He has been instrumental in the restitution of stolen property. Dr Steiner kindly posted me large bundles of copies of papers about Paula, Peter and the Palast Kino from the State Archive. With great generosity, further bundles arrived from the archives in response to my questions. I have only been able to reconstruct the probable sequence of events affecting the Palast Kino from correspondence retrieved from the City Archives of Vienna and the Austrian State Archives.

Palast Kino 1938

Working slowly through the papers from both the archives, perhaps most striking feature was the extent and detail of the information that was still available. Official correspondence about the cinema from early 1938 shows that the process of Aryanising Jewish businesses began before the formal annexation of Austria by Germany, the Anschluss. Nazi influence had seeped across the border for some time before they arrived in person. From the early 1930s, Germany had refused to show films made by Austrian studios that employed Jews. This placed the industry under a great economic strain. The correspondence about the Palast Kino was precise and detailed and began twelve days before the Anschluss on the twelfth of March 1938.

The first letter from the Central Film Bureau regarding the value of the Palast Kino was dated the first of March 1938. It gave a detailed description of the cinema including the landlords, Sommerlatte and Marschall (the original architects), a list of the business owners and the proportions shared amongst the family:

Selma HAAS	Wien VIII	3/8
Paula SIEBER	Wien 1	3/8
Laura TICHO	Wien VIII	1/6
Fritzi GROSS	Brünn (Brno)	1/24
Walter DEUTSCH	Prag (Prague)	1/24

Five staff were listed (all described as Aryan): Florian Fischer the projectionist; two ushers, Robert and Johann Krall, both single, presumably brothers; Paula Dafert, a cashier and Marie Zawodsky, the cleaning woman. There were also several pages of a detailed inventory which appear to have omitted nothing: detailed technical descriptions of the projector, film licenses given, along with the quantity of coal stored and the number of toilet rolls. The account stated the cinema had made an operating profit of 1,5512 Schillings (about 7,750 RM) and showed that outgoings included assorted taxes, including an entertainment tax of 25,000 Schillings and interest on a loan. On the fourteenth of March, only thirteen days after the initial inventory, a second set of papers showed about one third of the items on the original valuation had been crossed out in pencil. It also stated that the business had an outstanding loan of 12,413 Schillings (6,000 RM) with the Central Savings Bank.

It is difficult to convert these figures into something we can usefully compare with current values. Historical currency converters only provide a rough guide as they rely on conversions between multiple currencies or the value of gold. The value of the Austrian Schilling was manipulated by Germany. Inflation was rampant and, as goods disappeared from the shops, barter and the black market prospered. The Schilling was forced to devalue by a quarter but was then subsumed into the German Reichsmark and it then ceased to be legal tender when Hitler liquidated the Austrian National Bank on the seventeenth of March.

On the twenty first of March, the Palast Kino was Aryanised. The Reichsfilmkammer (Office of the Reich Cinema), appointed Carl Fischer as the acting director of the cinema on the grounds that the jobs of party members were at risk should the current owners of the business want to sell the lease back to their landlord. There was no previous mention of a lease or that the family were trying to sell it, so this was probably spurious. Correspondence between the cinema owners and the authorities continued between March and May. Each official letter produced a further reduction in the valuation of the cinema or demanded more evidence to support the valuations the family put forward. Paula's brother, Ernst Ticho wrote a long letter in immaculate cursive script detailing the interior renovations and technical innovations that the family had made during their tenure. Monthly accounts were presented each month from March to June on Palast Kino letter-headed paper. The cinema's accounts showed a surplus of RM279.82 for the spring quarter from the thirtieth of March to the eighth of June. A letter from 'Sasko' dated the fourteenth of June, reminding the Palast Kino that they had still to pay S10.45 outstanding for their advertising in the former 'Neues Leben', despite several reminders and a promise to transfer the funds, is further evidence that the business was struggling.

Carl Fischer, the acting director of the Palast Kino, wrote a long letter on behalf of the Reichsfilmkammer supporting Ernst

Ticho. Written on Palast Kino letterheading Fischer pointed out that Ernst had been sent on leave on the thirty-first of March and had received neither salary, compensation nor severance pay for the period. His only source of funds was a meagre income from subletting his flat. He also mentioned that Ing Ticho was a Czech citizen who had been wounded at the front during the last war. Fischer recognised that the cinema's finances were weak but suggested that payments might be made in instalments as funds became available. This letter, clearly written to support the family was one of Fischer's final actions as acting director. It paints a bleak picture of the Ticho family circumstances. Having lost almost all their income from the cinema, they were subsisting on their savings, anything they could scrape together by letting rooms in their flats and, presumably, selling whatever they could.

A rather surreal parallel set of correspondence took place alongside the valuations of the cinema as a range of individuals proposed themselves as suitable prospective owners of the Palast Kino. Essential requirements for the role were being able to prove honourable service for Germany in the SS coupled with an excellent veteran's record during the previous war; internment in Wöllersdorf detention camp an optional extra. Wöllersdorf was a former ordinance factory that was used as detention centre for political criminals and following the Anschluss became an early concentration camp.

By the end of May, a formal offer to buy the cinema appeared from SS Hauptscharführer Otto Model and SS Hauptscharführer Ferdinand Spizka. These two good Nazis had achieved the highest rank for enlisted officers in the SS. They both wrote letters describing the excellent service they had already performed for the Führer. Model's claim was that he had joined the National Socialist Workers Party (NSDAP) – Nazi party, aged seventeen. He was discharged from the army for dishonourable conduct, presumably for NSDAP-related activities. His active involvement in the occupation of the German Chancellery resulted in arrest and he had spent time imprisoned in Wöllersdorf.

Over the summer, there were a number of other letters to the Chamber of the Commissioners of the Reichsfilm similar to those from Messer's Model and Spizka. Essentially, each of these letters gave evidence which supported the applicant's claim to be a good Nazi and therefore, worthy of being given the Palast Kino. Like Otto Model, some boasted of spending time in jail as a result of the terrorist activities that they carried out in support of the party. It is possible that this was just a front to divert funds from the cinema to the NSDAP.

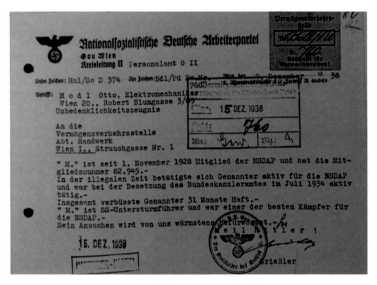

Otto Model's application for the Palast Kino.
Vienna, December 1938.

On the tenth of June 1938, Franz Hahnemann, then a second lieutenant in the SS, put forward his claim on the grounds that he had been born in Vienna in 1905. After working for his father, he had then worked for a lawyer before moving to work at 'Adolf Hitler House'. Hansmann currently worked in security at Junker's Aeroplane and motor works. His political activities and therefore, Nazi credentials, were that he had joined NSDAP in 1927 and he had gained several promotions until he reached his current level in the SS. He was interned in the Wöllersdorf prison for sixteen and a half months for high treason following his involvement in a tear gas attack on a department store. There followed a long and detailed account of the many placements with the SS that he had held in Germany. He had returned to Vienna once it was safe for him to do so, in 1938, and currently worked for the SS.

Another, similar, letter was sent by the leader of the NS administration for the Reichsstatthalter, who were essentially the representatives of the German Reich overseas, dated the sixth of October 1938, recommending Otto Spangaro for the job.

Spangaro had been a member of the party since 1929 and had been awarded the Gold Cross. His actions during the 'uprising' which had led to him spending ten months in Wöllersdorf proved that he was a worthy candidate. It concluded, 'To show our gratitude to Spangaro for all his services, acquiring the Palast Kino will give him a secure livelihood'.

On the twenty-first of July, Dr Richard Padlesak's father made a case for him to be given the Palast Kino on the grounds that he had graduated with honours from the higher engineering school before attending business school. He had been a loyal party member since 1932 and had to flee Vienna after illegal employment led to detention in Wöllersdorf. After a period of unemployment, Dr Padlesak was currently employed by the Reichsbahn in Berlin but would like to return to his mother country. He continued to make the case saying, 'I can provide RM 200,000 towards establishing the estate'.

This clear offer of funds to support Dr Padlesak's case suggests blatant bribery, supporting the suggestion that funds from Jewish businesses were being diverted to the NSDAP. Over that summer, there were several similar letters that eloquently put forward impeccable Nazi credentials for assorted individuals. On the thirty-first of August 1938, Otto Model and Ferdinand Spitzka were formally made the owners of the Palast Kino. Paula and Selma continued to run the cinema but were hardly paid for their efforts as the profits went to the new owners, Model and Spitzka.

Paula completed a form listing her assets for the 'Directory of the Fortune of Jews twenty-seventh of April 1938'. On the fourteenth of July 1938, she stated that the value of the Palast Kino, minus any operating debt, was 7,382 RM and that her share of the business was just over a third of the total.

The relentless reduction in the value of the cinema each time it was valued left Paula without the funds necessary to pay the ever-increasing escape tax, let alone leave anything for Selma. Before she could leave with her single suitcase, Paula had to appeal to her former lover Ing. Sambul to send funds. Selma must have continued to run the cinema on a shoestring until she was arrested at her Josefstädter Straße flat in September 1941 and taken to Theresienstadt.

Section 3

1946-2000:
Lives Built and Rebuilt

Chapter 15

Vienna: Paula Fights for Her Cinema

One simple question

In the summer of 2019, I asked Professor Heinz Rupertsberger, who is the conservator of the Jewish database for the Josefstadt area, what I thought was a relatively simple question, "How can I find out what happened to the cinema after the war?" I was hoping for information about an archive or database. Surprisingly, he visited the archives on my behalf and a few weeks later, he kindly sent a summary of events whilst his wife had generously photographed one hundred and seventy pages of documents which she then shared with me via Dropbox. Together, they had created a timeline of the events surrounding the Palast Kino which formed the backbone of this reconstruction. Since then, Helen and Heinz have been extremely helpful providing me with additional information and continuously patient with my uniformed questions.

The Palast Kino remained open throughout the war. The two Nazi managers, Modl and Spitzka, who had taken over in 1938, were both killed in different battles on the Eastern Front in 1942. Spitzka's widow, Grete, then assumed ownership of the cinema and installed a man called Arkadij Osadtschyl as the manager. At some point during this period, the name of the cinema was changed from Palast Kino to Palast Lichtspiele. Presumably, the name change was another effort to eradicate any trace of Jewishness from the business.

The Soviet army was easily able to enter Vienna on the second of April 1945, as there was only a single German Panzer corps left to defend the city while the remainder of the German army retreated. Stalin rapidly restored sovereignty to Austria. American troops entered Austria a few weeks later on the twenty-sixth of April, closely followed a few days later, by French and British troops. Vienna had been ravaged by allied bombing. The majority of the once glorious buildings were damaged, and some destroyed entirely. The population was starving with basic services disrupted. There was no transport, water, electricity or gas. If there was anything left to sell, people tried to use it to barter for what little food was available on the black market. Without transport, some walked miles into the countryside in search of potatoes or other root crops. The police force had been decimated. Many were Nazis and had either been killed, fled or were in hiding. Without the police to keep order, assault and looting were common. Russian soldiers rapidly gained a notorious reputation for raping civilians, looting and drunken brawling and were greatly feared by the general population. In July 1945, just as in Berlin, Vienna was partitioned by the allies, Britain, France, US and Russia. The city was effectively divided into four regions, each of the allies became responsible for the one sector assigned to them.

The Palast Kino was initially taken over by Russian administrators who reopened the cinema for public performances on the twenty-eighth of April 1945. Three weeks later, on the eighteenth of May, Selma's friend from the Josefstädter Straße flats, Denise Sellner, wrote to the chairman of the Federation of Austrian Cinemas asking to speak on behalf of the family. She presented evidence that in 1938, prior to Aryanization, the Palast Kino was owned by Selma Hass, Paula Sieber, Laura Ticho, Ernst Ticho, Walter and Fritzi Deutsch. Presumably, these were the papers Selma had given Denise for safekeeping before she was arrested in 1941. Denise asked that the cinema should be returned to the family, adding that Paula had emigrated to England with her sons in 1938 and that whilst Walter and Fritzi had been living in Brno in 1938, she did not know their fate. She also asked that further business arrangements concerning the Palast Kino should be made through her. Denise may have worked in the cinema. She was clearly a close and trusted friend. Paula used her familiar nickname, Didi.

After liberation, the police removed Grete Spitzka from the cinema and forced her to leave her flat in the Josefstädter Straße complex. It is not entirely clear what happened to the widow Spitzka. However, correspondence from November 1945 shows that the director of the Business Department of the Public Administration of the Vienna Theatre, had granted a monthly maintenance payment of 100 RM to a Margaretha Spitzka, a minor. It is possible that Grete had died leaving her young daughter, Margaretha without any means of supporting herself.

Denise Sellner (Didi) Selma's close friend from the Josefstädter Straße flats who during the war took care of the paperwork proving ownership of the cinema. Vienna, c1950.

When Vienna was partitioned between the allies in July, the whole Josefstadt area, including Josefstädter Straße and the Palast Kino, fell within the American controlled sector. However, because its owner, Paula, was in England, responsibility for the cinema was then transferred to the British Property Control Office. In July 1945, Vienna City Council appointed Mrs Ethel Marachalek as the public administrator of the cinema and she was given the task of unravelling what had happened during the Nazi occupation. Strangely, there were no files available for Mrs Marachalek regarding the period 1938 to1945. Fortunately, the accountant who had worked for the cinema before the war, still lived locally and was able to give her an outline of the situation. Some records remained, including cash books and receipts. Claims for expenses had all been maintained properly, presumably because they continued to follow the processes that Selma and Paula put in place when they first started the cinema.

On the first of November 1945, the American authorities requisitioned the cinema for the entertainment of US troops. The only income the cinema then received was from the single performance per day that was available to the paying public. Clearly, this did not cover the running costs: staff, heating, lighting and hiring the films that were being shown. In January 1946, the British Property Control Office noted the cinema was operating at a loss which they attributed to the free showings for American troops. They referred the matter to the Americans on the grounds that the cinema was only making a loss as they were not paying to use it. Correspondence passed between the English and the Americans while the cinema continued to make a loss. Eventually, it became clear to the protagonists that because there was no paperwork associated with the American requisition anyway, the matter could not be resolved amicably and the whole chaotic business was dumped back into Mrs Marachalek's lap for her to sort out.

As Paula was still working at the hostel in Windermere, she asked the authorities to let Peter represent her in negotiations with the authorities regarding the restoration of the cinema to her and any surviving members of her family. Papers from the Vienna State magistrate show that Paula applied for ownership of the cinema in October 1946 which was granted in November 1947. In January 1948, the cinema was officially restored to its owners but public administration continued until the end of the year. Although the building was still intact, the premises were very shabby as there had been no redecoration and only minimal maintenance during the ten years since Paula had last managed the business. Constraints such as the free performances for US military, meant it had been forced to operate at a loss for some time.

Also inside the attaché case were air-mail letters in Paula's strong looped writing from this period. Fortunately, Peter's replies were generally typed. One batch was from the period when Paula was trying to assert her claim to the Palast Kino when either Peter was posted to Vienna in 1945 to 1946 or later, when Peter was working in London but Paula was in Vienna pursuing her claim between 1950 and 1952. Her writing was always difficult to read. In later letters, she reverted to German when she was upset or discussing financial matters. Few can still read gothic German script, particularly when written in slanting handwriting.

I trained as a biologist specialising in ecological genetics, and faced with this odd collection, I wondered how I would examine a field populated with strange plants. I decided that taking samples at random until some sort of pattern emerged might be the best initial approach. This strategy worked surprisingly well despite the limitations of incomplete, illegible, undated pages. Nonetheless, they help to unravel a story that must remain made up partly of conjecture.

It is impossible to overestimate how long the chaos prevailed across Eastern Europe and how long it took for some families to be reunited. At some stage, possibly in 1946, Paula discovered that her niece Fritzi, had survived and had returned to Brno. Unusually, Fritzi's husband had also survived in a different concentration camp and eventually, he too had returned to Brno and they were able to live together again. The Red Cross and other charities did an excellent job tracing lost relatives and putting them in touch with one another. Letters were incredibly important.

As she was an enemy alien, Paula had to remain in Britain until 1948 when she was naturalized and became a British citizen. She required permission from both the British, to be sure of re-entry, and Austrian authorities, for entry, before she could travel to Austria. Paula's frustration with the system showed in her letters to the Austrian legation requesting permission to enter the country. In 1947, she was living at 35 Windsor Terrace, Tynemouth but was in poor health, suffering from high blood pressure and heart problems. She spent some time in a nursing home in Sunderland in April but she was ill again in 1949. This time, Alice Urbach cared for her.

In June 1949, Paula's notebook recorded:

I have been ill and two months to bed with high blood pressure and heart enlarged. Alice nursed me wonderfully. I am much better now.

Paula spent several years arranging the management of the cinema and fighting for her share of the equity, initially from England then, once she was naturalized and could travel freely, she had several protracted visits to Vienna. She needed funds to support her throughout her later life and the cinema was her prime asset which she needed to sell as a thriving business.

In 1946, Paula was stuck in England, an enemy alien unable to travel to Vienna. Her sister Selma, who had also managed the cinema, was probably dead, along with her niece Laura and at the time, there was no information about her niece Fritzi's whereabouts. (Fritzi must have resumed corresponding with Paula at some point late in 1946 or 1947).

Peter recalled the approach that many adopted:

Gradually, as people realized that many of their closest relatives were dead, they sought more distant ones. If your brothers and sisters had perished, it must have been good to find even a distant cousin.

With Paula still in England, clearly the cinema needed a manager. It is likely that in those difficult times any relation, however distant, was better than a complete stranger. Helene Bock appears to have been a distant relative of Paula's, possibly via her cousin Louisa (Laura) Ticho who had married a Jan Hans Bock. Ignatz Bock had travelled to Palestine along with Franz Ticho on the *SS Agnoyis Nicolaya* in 1939. It is likely Denise Sellner worked in the cinema in some capacity throughout the war and continued with the few original staff like Frau Strand from the sweet counter after the end of hostilities. Peter may have made contact with Helene Bock while he was stationed in Vienna in 1946.

He described her as:

A distant cousin of my mother's. Helene was hardly Jewish. Before the war, she had run a rough wine bar in a poor, outer district of Vienna. Her story of the war years was gruesome, a man had taken over her wine bar and she had cleaned, scrubbed, scrounged to survive. On the day the Russians arrived, she had thrown the man who had taken over her wine bar into the street.

Helene was all wrong for the cinema: too loud, too crude, from the wrong district, she had never employed any staff, hadn't a clue about films or the cinema trade. But she was there, and I thought she would leave a little of the takings over for my mother.

Again, documents from the archives help to illuminate what happened to the cinema in the years after the war. In order to operate, all cinemas needed an official licensee, a named person, the concessionaire. Each licence lasted only two years so they were renewed regularly. These documents identify the concessionaire at a particular time, helping to trace the management of the cinema during this period.

There was a regular correspondence between Paula and Helene. Helene addressed Paula as 'Tante' (aunt), appeared affectionate, and expressed her concerns about Paula's wellbeing, along with detailed operational questions about running the business. Paula's replies show that she was directing the cinema from a distance. She also regularly asked for cocoa, chocolate and saccharin to be sent to Gosforth as it was difficult for her to sustain her sweet tooth locally as sugar rationing continued in Britain until 1954, nine years after the war ended. Their correspondence suggests that Paula was giving Helene detailed advice on how to run the business from a distance as Helene asks for permission to pay larger invoices. At one point, she even asks if she might use funds from the cinema to pay the Central Cemetery for the upkeep of Hermann's grave. Initially, the two women appeared to get along and when she wrote, Helene was always carefully respectful and considerate of health matters. As time passed, Paula began to discuss the possibility of Helene becoming the concessionaire and managing the cinema.

Following a meeting with Major Micklethwaite of the Property Control Office on the twenty-sixth of November, Peter wrote to him a few days later sanctioning Helene Bock as the person who could act on his behalf with all matters relating to the cinema. Also, that she should run the cinema until such time that the establishment could be returned to his mother and the heirs of its former owners.

In January 1947, Paula also wrote from England, whilst Fritzi wrote from Brno, requesting that Helene Bock should be made the concessionaire. Unfortunately, tensions developed between the two women and Helene rejected Paula's initial financial proposals.

Paula and Didi (Denise Sellner) corresponded regularly. The parcels of chocolate and other Viennese delicacies Didi sent her friend were clearly received with much appreciation. Didi must have kept Paula abreast of news from the cinema. Several of Paula's letters to Peter mention Didi's unsuccessful attempts to mediate with Helene. Paula's letters to Peter continuously mentioned problems with the cinema, problems with Helene and her concern about her own poor health. Helene and Paula continually failed to reach an agreement. Otto Urbach, Alice Urbach's eldest son, who was then stationed in Vienna by the US military counterintelligence corps, must have talked with Helene on Paula's behalf as there is a long letter from him to Peter making helpful suggestions of a way forward. Negotiations appear to have continued throughout 1947. In August 1948, a retrospective agreement was reached between Paula and Helene. Helene was appointed as the business leader with a monthly salary plus a one per cent share of the profits. She was authorised to make cash withdrawals from the business which were a necessary part of running the cinema. There were detailed letters from Helene to Paula accounting for routine expenditure and requesting access to more funds or money for special items. Helene continued to address Paula as 'Beloved Aunty' and sent profuse good wishes for her health and wellbeing. In March 1949, Helene noted that although she had repeatedly written to Franz Ticho (Paula's nephew who had escaped to Palestine), she had not received a reply.

When Paula was finally able to travel to Vienna in June 1950, she was again ill and spent a month in a sanatorium in Vienna. She was very upset to find the new sign Lichtspiele had replaced the familiar Palast Kino in large letters across the sign above the entrance and that the business was in such a poor condition. The building was dilapidated and as the décor her brother had so proudly designed had received no attention, it was faded and shabby. When the concession came up for renewal in 1950, Paula nominated a new manager, Alfred Breither. Perhaps Paula and Helene had fallen out? Though in letters to Peter, she remarked that she remained on good terms with

Helene. Paula remained in Vienna trying to work out what had happened to the business during her absence. After she had extended her stay a couple of times, she moved from her modest hotel and took cheaper lodgings in an apartment in the Opernring, 8th District, not far from Josefstädter Straße. Her stay became further protracted and she remained in Vienna for over a year, finally returning to London in 1952 for Peter's delayed wedding.

The new name and fascia of the Palast Lichtspiele, 1949.

Aside from Fritzi in Brno, Paula's only close family that had survived the genocide was her nephew, Franz Ticho. Although he was only twenty-five in 1938, he ran a boutique dress shop along Josefstädter Straße near the Palast Kino. Clearly, following in the Ticho footsteps, Franz had established himself in textiles, just like his grandparents in Brno and his uncle Ernst, who ran a successful shop in the Bauernmarkt, the Farmer's Market. The Bauernmarkt is a smallish street at the centre of the smart cosmopolitan area leading up to the pedestrianised shopping area and the pretty, baroque Catholic St Peter's Church in an old part of the city. St Peter's may be the site of the oldest church in Vienna. In 1921, Ernst's shop at 19 Bauernmarkt stocked a glorious array of goods, ranging from textiles, wools and throws, cooking utensils, ironmongery, building materials to oils. The street with its tall, rather austere secessionist buildings, clearly catered to an affluent clientele with the Pollitzer Brothers ornate fashion store along the road at numbers 6–8. With his entrepreneurial fingers in many pies, Ernst had another business with a partner, Vega Taussig, which traded in textiles and manufactured lampshades, ornaments and teepuppen - doll-shaped tea cosies. The business was also located on Josefstädter Straße. Franz clearly followed the family example. Indeed, he boasted of his dressmaking heritage in an advert in the Official Journal of the City of Vienna, the *Amtsblatt der Stadt Wien*, on the twentieth of January 1938, claiming that he was, 'building on his dressmaking heritage', to create ladies garments at 8 Josefstädter Straße 43 – 45.

Franz had escaped to Palestine alone leaving his mother and infirm brother in the Josefstädter Straße flats back in 1938. He travelled on the *SS Agnoyis Nicolaya* and probably spent the war years in Palestine. By 1950, Franz had married and he was running a ladies fashion business in Tel Aviv. As neither his mother nor brother had survived, Franz should have inherited Laura's sixth share of the cinema. Paula could only communicate with Franz via his lawyer in Vienna, Dr Hans Bablik, which caused additional delays each time the lawyer needed to consult his client. Franz may have moved back to Vienna in 1951 as some of Paula's letters to Peter at that time mention seeing Franz, sometimes using the more affectionate diminutive, Franzi, used for a younger relative.

Paula's letters to Peter continuously identified new problems. One described how Bernard Zeisel, a former manager, who had not been seen for six months, had helped himself during his tenure. In a letter to Peter written in 1951, Paula talks of Didi Sellner arranging a secret meeting with a specialist accountant at her Josefstädter Straße flat to examine the cinema's books. It is possible that mismanagement had descended into fraud and theft. One intriguing letter written on notepaper from the Hotel Albert, Ier Place Rogier, Brussels was from a private detective called Lumuruni that Paula had engaged.

On the second of June 1951, Lumuruni described part of his investigation:

> On my way to Germany, I broke my trip at Brussels and spent a day making investigations about Mme Magdalen Pilaar. After

prolonged inquiries, I have found her and lodged an official complaint with the Belgian police authorities at Uccle. She is known to the police, has previously been charged with dishonesty and is 'walking the boulevard'. I will have to sign a 'prosecution' at the Belgian Consulate and submit further evidence, but at least we know now, this woman's recent address. The police have been most helpful and we have started the 'process judiciare' which will make her pay up, if anything does ...

Although the detective had formally lodged a claim with the Brussels Police, he reported that as Miss Pilaar was a known prostitute, there was no prospect of recovering anything from her. There were letters from a London lawyer to a lawyer in Hamburg about a claim against the same Magdalen Pilaar and another letter about missing jewellery.

It is clear from her letters to Peter that Paula was very upset about the way Helene had managed the cinema. She said that 'Helene has done badly for the business' and wrote of her determination to sell the cinema and return to England. Around this time, Paula appeared to ask Helene Bock to swap a reduction of duties for a very slight reduction in remuneration. Helene's reaction to this idea was not recorded. On a postcard written in July 1951, Paula mentioned finding 35,000 Schillings (a substantial sum which would be worth approximately 13,000 euros today) 'hidden in the account books'. Paula's letters to Peter in London also document her deteriorating relationship with Franz Ticho. After a visit from Franz in August 1951, she complained that 'he started terrible and was very impudent', later adding, 'I flatter myself to hold the strings and to drive according to plan'.

Although friends and acquaintances in Vienna suggested that Paula should remain there and run the cinema for at least a few years, in her letters to Peter, she is clear that she wanted to sell the business and return to London. Other, comments from the odd pages of letters that remain indicated that Franz also wanted to sell his share of the cinema but that he expected twenty-nine per cent and wanted the business sold for a high price whilst Paula wanted fifty per cent plus the concession. Their relationship continued to deteriorate.

Helene Bock (left), Paula Sieber (centre) and Denise (Didi) Sellner (right) pose in the foyer of the Palast Lichtspiele, Vienna c1950.

She wrote to Peter around this time:

Franz Ticho arrived and he has permitted himself to behave extremely badly to me. He is more overdressed with a lot of diamonds on his fingers. ... Franz dared to say that I have never done anything for him, yet I have bought beautiful flowers last year when he was operated on! And I should have sold my ring for him. When I must say to him whether he has forgotten that I and my dear sister have voluntary resigned on the inheritance of my late mother in favour of his father (my brother). He most impertinently said I don't want to talk to that topic and I have the circumstances. Fortunately, I did not get agitated. Nothing from the corrupt boy can get to my heart and I am finished with him.

I hope the Lord will give me further health and strength to finish my difficult task under these disgusting circumstances. I am glad about Eric being "British".

Helene Bock (left), Paula Sieber (right), and Denise (Didi) Sellner (rear) posed outside Palast Lichtspiele, c1950.

Paula's letters frequently digress to describe the problems her friends were having selling their businesses, often having to involve expensive lawyers to help with their claims. Clearly, she was not the only woman in Vienna who was struggling to recover what had been taken.

Normally, the concession was valid for two years but when Paula applied for a routine renewal on the twenty-ninth of December 1951, she was only given a one-month extension as a competing claim had been submitted from her nephew, Franz Ticho. Franz and Helene Bock appear to have combined forces to create their own claim for the cinema and may have claimed Fritzi's portion of the business along with the one per cent of profits that Paula had agreed to give her in 1948.

Unable to reconcile their differences, the matter of ownership of the cinema was referred to the courts. In a long letter to the Vienna magistrates, Paula made her case to be granted the licence for the cinema. In it, she explained that the Palast Kino had been purchased by her parents in 1915 to be shared amongst their children. Paula acknowledged Franz's claim that his grandmother, her mother, Bertha, had changed her will shortly before her death, removing both Selma and her from the inheritance. Paula and Selma had continued to manage the cinema after her death in 1924. She explained that there was no dispute that the cinema had been confiscated by the Nazis in 1938 or that Selma had died in a concentration camp. Paula argued that Selma's third share had reverted to her and that Franz should have only inherited 17.5% of the company. Combining Franz's share with Helene's would then still leave them with less than fifty per cent of the business. She urged the court to consider which of the two competing claimants could better manage the cinema by pointing out that she and Selma had run the cinema from 1915 and consequently, understood how it operated. Furthermore, as she was currently living in Vienna, she would be available to manage it properly whilst Franz currently lived with his wife in Tel Aviv and was working in the fashion industry. Paula also submitted the historical documents that had described the fractions of the business that were allocated amongst the family. Paula was the only survivor of her generation, two of her siblings Olga and Laura had surviving children, Fritzi Gross in Brno and Franz in Tel Aviv. Earlier dispositions had given Paula and Selma 3/8th of the shares each, Laura Ticho, Franz's mother, 1/6th whilst Fritzi Gross and her late brother Walter Deutsch 1/24th each. Paula also argued that on the second of December 1949, the Cinema Union had allowed Helene Bock to apply for the concession in Paula's name and refuted the claim that when Bock had applied two years earlier in 1947, her application had been refused on the grounds that Selma might have survived and be living in the US.

The court ruled that it was unable to decide on the claim and that the case should be referred to a higher court. It is not clear from the papers that are currently available what happened or how the commercial court ruled and the outcome is currently unknown.

Arguments about ownership of the cinema continued. In June 1952, Paula returned to London in time for Peter's wedding, which had already been deferred twice, so that she could attend the modest celebration. Paula moved back to her flat in 81 Hatherley Court, Bayswater, where she had taken over Eric and Karla's flat when they had moved to a smarter apartment block in the next road. Paula sublet 91 Hatherley Court whilst she was in Vienna. Several of her letters to Peter ask that he checks when her tenants are due to depart and could he please arrange to have the flat prepared for her arrival, or if it had not been vacated in time, to find her alternative accommodation locally until the flat might be ready for her. Huntley, the younger son of Dr and Mrs Freedman, who had offered Peter a home in Newcastle, had lived there briefly. Paula's fight to retain her share of the business continued from a distance. She instructed Viennese lawyers to act on her behalf and Didi Sellner continued to help with the matter locally.

Paula must eventually have come to some form of agreement and sold her share of the Palast Kino. She was unhappy that she had never received a fair share of the business that she and her sister had created. Indeed, for the rest of her life, she maintained that she had been cheated out of what was rightfully hers. Peter said that she and Franz had a huge argument which resulted in them never speaking to one another again.

A company was formed in 1954, the OHG Palast Kino (the Offene Handelsgesellschaft) by Ing. Franz and Elisabeth List-Listopad, Eschler and Ticho. Since Paula was not part of this company, it is likely that a separate agreement had been reached over payment for her share of the business in advance of the company being formed. Franz List became the manager of the cinema. A further agreement was then reached between Helene Bock, the former manager of the cinema and its owner, Franz List, the following year. Presumably, Helene sold her interest in the cinema. On the eighteenth of September 1957, the Vienna State magistrate issued an order that gave the concession for the Palast Kino to Ing. Frans and Elisabeth List-Listopad, Eschler and Ticho, that would be valid for six years until the thirty-first of October 1963.

Franz and his wife, Pauli Ticho, eventually established themselves in a very smart location on one of the main shopping streets, Wollzeile 12, around the corner from St Stephen's

Cathedral, and sold designer furs from their shop, the Boutique Caprice.

The Palast Kino ceased operating as a cinema in 1977 and the site was sold. It became a supermarket and currently operates as a SPAR. Although the fascia of the cinema has been replaced, it is still possible to see the outline of the former circle seats embossed on the shop ceiling.

Whilst I was trying to unravel this part of the history and wanting to know more about Helene Bock, I googled her and found that from 1958 to 1998, Helene Bock and Margarete Ebner had been the managers of the Admiral Kino in Vienna. Consulting a map, I became aware just how close the Admiral Kino was to the Palast Kino. I contacted the current owner of the Admiral Kino and, overnight, received a courteous and helpful reply from Michaela Englert. She said that although she did not know about Helene Bock, she had put me in touch with the son of the other owner, Margarete Ebner. Henry lived in London.

A few days later, Henry Ebner called and in perfect, unaccented English, as he had been educated at an English boarding school, brought Viennese charm alive again during our conversation. He remembered meeting Helene Bock when he had returned to Vienna after the war as a teenager with his mother to sell the Admiral Kino. (Like Paula she needed to release the capital from her cinema to support herself and her child). Reminding me that he had only been a child when he met Helene, he described her as 'a stocky, spinster in her forties who was kind to him and had taken him to the cinema'. He also said that Helene had been desperate to buy the cinema. Although he knew nothing of the Palast Kino, we both thought it was likely his mother must have known Paula as the distance between the two cinemas is only a ten-minute walk and not many Jewesses ran cinemas in the 1930s. We wondered if the funds that allowed Helene to buy the Admiral Kino had come from the sale of her interest in the Palast Kino?

Sadly, Henry Ebner died in October 2020. When we spoke, he said he was being treated with chemotherapy. I am so pleased to have had the opportunity to meet him, however briefly.

Chapter 16

London: From Redcoat to ATV

Getting on with life

Eric never fully recovered from his experiences of Bergen-Belsen. Nor did he think of asking for counselling or support to help recover from the trauma as there was little recognition of PTSD in those days. He returned to Karla who had lived in the Streatham flat throughout the war. Her occupation was listed as 'housewife', so she probably did not have formal employment. She may well have done odd jobs on the side to make extra money as funds were always short.

Eric was thirty-six years old with no professional training to fall back on when he returned to London, following the many men who had already been demobbed from the forces. Eric had inherited his mother's flamboyance and had always enjoyed acting and entertainment. Photographs recording the thespian activities enjoyed by the family in Vienna in the 1920s, show them in elaborate costumes striking poses in theatrical tableaux. A youthful Paula even appeared alongside Eric and Karla in a couple of photographs. Eric maintained his interest in acting during his time in the army as he enjoyed his performances for ENSA (the entertainment company of the armed forces) and even organised local productions for his comrades.

One of Eric's friends was the young pianist, Walter Landauer who met the Polish pianist, Maryan Rawicz, accidentally whilst they were both holidaying at an Austrian resort. They bonded instantly and began to perform together as Rawicz and Landauer. Landauer's four-handed arrangements of popular classics became successful in Vienna. They left Austria together with their wives in 1935 as antisemitism became more prevalent.

Peter described how Eric tried to help his friend:

In more affluent days, he had brought a pair of young pianists called Rawicz and Landauer to England. Walter Landauer was an old friend of his. They wanted to make their name in England. Eric took after our mother; he loved the entertainment business. He bought them dinner-jackets, gave them an advance and tried to get bookings.

Eric and Karla, Walter Landauer and others by the pool at 'The High' with Eric and Walter joshing one another.

Rawicz and Landauer became very successful. They performed regularly on the BBC, made over a hundred recordings and were a particular favourite of the Prince of Wales. In 1957, they were interviewed together by Roy Plomley on the radio programme *Desert Island Discs* and in 1961, they appeared on the long-running television programme, *This is Your Life*, compèred by Eamonn Andrews.

Eric eventually found a niche that combined his need to earn a living with something that allowed him to use his theatrical talents. He became a Redcoat at one of the Butlins holiday camps. Billy Butlin opened his first holiday camp in Skegness in 1936. Butlin's vision was to replace dreary guesthouses with economical self-catering accommodation with inclusive activities and entertainment. He was initially disappointed to find that rather than joining in the entertainment offered, his visitors were shy and remained isolated in family groups. He employed Redcoats in eye-catching red jackets to break the ice, encouraging visitors to interact by creating a buzzing atmosphere. The role suited Eric's flamboyant character as he increasingly appeared on stage as the compère orchestrating proceedings. He must have been good at his job and respected by Billy Butlin as he was sent to the ill-fated venture in Barbados as part of the cabaret in a double act with Peter Kent in 1949.

In January 1955, he contributed to Butlins Pageant of Butlin History, a glittering annual event at the Albert Hall that celebrated ten years of post-war history and hosting over five million holiday makers. Interspersed between dancing to the music of Eric Winstone and his orchestra, a display of formation dancing and the final of the Miss Vanity Fair competition were held. The competitors were the finalists from shows held in the assorted holiday camps over the summer. Eric was the compère and the judges included Thora Hird, Jean Jupp and Kenneth Horne. There is even a Pathé Film of the next part of the proceedings, the presentations of sports trophies by Chris Chataway (TV Sports Personality of the Year 1954). I tried to convince myself that the largish man in a dinner jacket with extremely wide lapels might have been my Uncle Eric. This was followed by more dancing and the Pageant of Butlins History. Billy Butlin then presented further trophies for another ten minutes before the finale, *Penny on the Drum* and the Butlins half-hour with Eric Winstone that featured *Goodnight, Campers*, followed by *God Save the Queen*. These events were an opportunity for Eric to meet many people from the entertainment industry along with some of the stars.

Independent television franchises were first formed in late 1954. Associated Rediffusion began broadcasting programmes with commercial advertising in the London area the following year. Eric, excited by the opportunities offered by commercial TV, joined the second commercial broadcaster, ATV, which broadcast at weekends in London. His role was to find and persuade potential advertisers to invest in the new medium by demonstrating the potential sales opportunities that it offered. A sequence of advertisements had always been included at the start of the programme in cinemas since the beginning of cinema history. Independent television brought advertisers into people's homes. Eric's experience at Butlins and his contacts in the entertainment industry gave him a strong background to help television advertising develop from its infancy. After all, he had been brought up in a cinema and must have learnt the importance of pleasing his audience from his childhood experience of the Palast Kino.

Eric prospered in his new role, rapidly forging a niche that allowed him to use his talents. Lew Grade's family, the Winogradskys, had escaped violent antisemitism in Ukraine in 1912. They moved to England and settled in Shoreditch, then a poor area of London with a large Jewish community. Lew and his brothers, Leslie and Bernard, were all highly successful in the entertainment industry. Leslie was an agent, a dancer, and one of the founders of ATV. Bernard was an impresario. Both Lew and Bernard were made life peers. By then, the latter had changed his family name to become Bernard Delfont. At times, Eric worked directly with Lew Grade, a man he revered. Eric's career took off. His days of scratching around to make a living were gone. He was forty-six years old and not only enjoying his work but also making good money.

Eric and Karla did not have children, possibly a result of the termination she had as a very young woman in Vienna when she first became involved with Erich. Soon after Eric returned from Bergen-Belsen, the couple moved north across the river from 'The High' in Streatham to Bayswater. Bayswater was not smart but it was cosmopolitan with growing numbers of European refugees who had chosen to live there because it was close to the West End with its shops, theatres and restaurants and cheap rents. Soon, shops that catered for European tastes began to open: a Polish baker, Pâtisserie Françoise, and a couple of delicatessens. In many ways, Hatherley Court was similar to the Streatham flat they had just left. Built in the 1930s with four identical blocks, each with curved steps leading from the pavement up to the front door. The basement and ground floor were covered in cream stucco whilst the upper four floors exposed the tired, red bricks from which the building was built. Again, there were draughty metal Crittal windows. A second block, built behind Hatherley Grove, faced Westbourne Grove Terrace. The rear courtyard between both buildings was filled with a maze of shared metal stairs, walkways and rectangular metal shoots with small flaps opposite the rear door of each flat that allowed rubbish to fall straight into the communal bins below. In 1950, as Eric became more financially secure, they moved to a smarter apartment in Ralph Court, literally around the corner at the top of Queensway. Paula took over the lease of their flat at 91 Hatherley Court.

One set of papers the Österreichisches Staatsarchiv kindly sent, covered the claim for the Lustspieltheater on the Prater rather than the renamed Palast Kino, the Palast Lichtspiele on Josefstädter Straße . Although these papers were not entirely relevant, there were remarkable similarities between the two cinemas. The Lustspieltheater was built as a music hall in 1850 and only became a cinema in 1929. By 1950, the claimants who had managed to escape from Vienna before the Nazis arrived were to be found spread across the US and in London. As in Paula's papers about Palast Kino, the proportions of the business owned by each individual were detailed, along with balance sheets and valuations, strangely though the accounts themselves for 1938 to 1945 had been lost. Another co-incidence was that one of the claimants, Alice Weinstein née Weil, lived at 29 Ralph Court and lived in the same block as Eric and Karla. They must have known one another and shared stories in that tightly knit community of continental refugees.

Eric was established and doing well at ATV. For the first time in their married life, they were financially stable. They had some spare money and did not have to live hand-to-mouth. Eric and Karla embarked on having their flat refurbished. Both the remodelling of apartments and interior designers were novelties in the early 1960s (it was several decades before Habitat and Ikea were born). Eric and Karla basked in praise as almost everyone in Bayswater visited and admired the results. As a child, I could not see why anyone was so excited by the recessed ceiling lights and silk wallpaper but I did appreciate multiple helpings of Karla's hedgehog cake with whipped cream. Sadly, just as life was going well for him Eric lost his bounce. He was always tired, developed a persistent cough, began needing to sleep during the day and lost weight. In 1961, he was diagnosed with lymphatic cancer that had spread throughout his body. Eric was only fifty-three when he died after a long and painful illness. Although lymphoma, particularly if it is diagnosed early, is now considered relatively treatable, in the 1960s, treatment options were limited.

Karla was left with a recently designed flat, a small widow's pension and seven thousand pounds. She had no training, nor had she been employed during their marriage. To make matters worse, she made a disastrous investment with Bobby Pollack, a man who promised huge returns but absconded with half her inheritance. Peter then had the ingenious idea of combining her passion for bridge with the stylish apartment and helped her to create a bridge club. Ladies would spend afternoons at the flat, playing bridge and gossiping whilst Karla provided tuition, coffee and cake. The club was a success, it worked well and supported her both emotionally and financially until she died from breast cancer in 1976.

Chapter 17

London: The Sound of Music

Bayswater Paula

Paula took over Eric's lease on 91 Hatherley Court in 1950 when she moved from Tynemouth to Bayswater and he had moved to the more prestigious apartment in Ralph Court. A year later, she moved to number 81 in the third block. Paula's flat was on the first floor, with a front door leading from the lift and stairwell and a back door leading onto the metal walkways running behind the flats. The hall was short, with a pair of sliding doors concealing cupboards along the left-hand side. Carefully constructed, the panels and doors were solid wood, each with four matching horizontal panels. The doors had inset curving brass handles and the whole wardrobe was painted a cream colour that had darkened to a dull beige. Behind the doors, the shelves were stacked with vases, huge, continental eiderdowns with their paisley covers, towels, curious suitcases and boxes stuffed with mysterious memorabilia. One of the glorious, Persian carpets that Paula had saved from her flat in Vienna ran along the corridor, its rich colours gleaming through the border made up of diamonds, lozenges and intricate lines.

The main room, first right off the hall, was always overheated and crammed with heavy Germanic furniture, navy velvet armchairs, whilst a strange and very uncomfortable sofa bench arrangement occupied one corner of the room behind a round table. The table was covered with a green, chenille cloth with tassels overlain with assorted, embroidered tablecloths including one with an almost transparent design, white with flowers, embroidered in pastel colours, circling the centre, picked out in shadow stich sent by Didi. Terrible portraits of chickens, in gold frames, hung above the seating area, undemanding landscapes, with or without peasants, adorned other walls. One entire wall was filled with the compactum, a collection of Bauhaus-like oak shelving units with a wardrobe and a bureau with a pull-down writing table that had initially been made for Peter's teenage room in Vienna. Any remaining space was taken up by another velvet armchair, writing table, a couple of standard lamps and the vitrine, a glass cabinet displaying Paula's treasures. Her Persian carpets were spread round the room, vibrant reds and purples emerged from the deep, blue background of the largest which dominated the room. There were several smaller, more intricate rugs under the writing table and in front of the compactum. A couple of convector heaters, complete with trip-hazard trailing electric cables, augmented the electric fire built into the wall to ensure the room was constantly stuffy.

Lisl, Elfie with Paula at the Hatherley Court flat, July 1971.

Paula's bedroom was next along the corridor, a symphony of pink, across the corridor from the bathroom whilst the corridor ended at the kitchen. An external door from the kitchen opened onto the metal walkways and service hatches behind the flat.

When I was researching the story, an identical flat was on the market. Although the kitchen and bathroom had been refurbished and laminate floors installed, the skeleton remained unchanged. The reception room, described as expansive, was sparsely furnished with a grey corner seating unit, a tiny table with three plastic chairs stand by the window. In place of the compactum, a flat screen television took up much of the wall. In the centre of the room, there was a low table covered by a red cloth sitting on a shaggy pile red mat. The colour theme was emphasised by red cushions on the sofa. Gone are the rich colours of the carpets and velvet furniture. The overfilled Victorian apartment has been replaced by sparse furnishings from IKEA. The floorplan showed how essentially unchanged the flat was. Although the agents described Hatherley Court as 'an impressive period mansion block', the street was still scruffy. Bayswater, still a little run down, remains cosmopolitan; the European refugee population largely replaced by a more diverse range of ethnicities.

Shortly after his marriage, Peter moved into a flat in Block Two Hatherley Court, one block along from his mother. It was my first home and we remained there until shortly after my sister was born, two years later. We had moved north to a house with a large garden in East Finchley by the time I was three. Geographical separation from her mother-in-law was a wise move on the part of my mother.

Pembridge Gardens

Although Paula was bitterly disappointed with the small amount of money she had received for the cinema, it is likely that she used this, along with whatever she made from the sale of the Tynemouth house, to buy a short lease on a large house in Notting Hill. The rent from multiple separate bedsits within the house provided Paula with the income she needed to support herself. In the early 1950s, Notting Hill had neither been discovered nor gentrified. A right turn at Notting Hill Gate underground station from the Bayswater Road leads to Pembridge Gardens. The fronts of these big, Victorian houses were grey and shabby, with cracked plasterwork, broken stucco, whilst doors and windows had faded and much of their paint had peeled. There was neither coloured paintwork nor fancy planters with matching bay trees on either side of a front door, nor discreetly designed front gardens. Galvanised dustbins disgorged rubbish across front areas, their lids at rakish angles. Cracks ran across the steps leading up to the front door, almost to a point of danger. Multiple bells with or without faded names, indicated that rooms in this, like most of the other houses in the street, were let. Paula installed a housekeeper, Mrs O'Leary who lived in the ground floor rooms so that, like the concierge in the

Josefstädter Straße flats, she was able to keep an eye on the comings and goings of the tenants and discourage any visitors.

Equally shabby inside, each room was a bedsit with a hand basin. There was no separate kitchen. In one corner of the room, there was a Baby Belling, a tiny, enamelled oven with hotplate on top, a wall cupboard and basin. The cupboard was cream whilst the wooden sliding doors had been at some distant time in the past, painted the dull green normally favoured by public buildings. Stuck to the centre of each door was a cut out wood lozenge embellishment that ensured that the doors stuck monotonously. There were no en-suite bathrooms, the shared toilets and bathrooms were distributed along draughty stairs and landings. Showers still had to be invented. The tenants were generally polite when they passed each other on the stairs; less so if they thought it was their turn to use the toilet or bathroom.

During the day, the street was busy with mothers and children and passing tradesmen. Women pushing huge prams, with their shopping in the tray below, took babies and children to nearby Kensington Gardens for fresh air. Friendships were made as prams were pushed around the Round Pond. Older children were encouraged to go and play whilst their mothers sat, smoked and gossiped. When the weather was warm, they might make a day of it, bringing sandwiches and squash for the kids.

Few landlords allowed families to store their prams and pushchairs in the hall. The poor women would have to make multiple trips upstairs transporting baby, pram, and shopping up to their room. The bin-men came once a week, tipping a mass of unsorted waste into the refuse lorry's noisy crushers. Beer and lemonade bottles could be returned to shops and pubs for pennies. The milkman would collect empties when delivering orders. Food was bought fresh, cooked quickly and eaten as the rooms were not equipped with fridges. In cold weather, milk was kept on windowsills. In very cold weather ice formed on the glass inside the windows and the milk froze inside the bottle, whilst in warm weather it went off.

The housekeeper was responsible for maintaining order, cleaning, weekly rent collection and selecting replacement tenants when people left, which did not happen very often. Along with detailed descriptions of Paula's physical health, the treatment of European Jews, or how badly she had been treated over the cinema, Mrs O'Leary became an integral part of Paula's conversation. Complaints about Mrs O'Leary or fears that Mrs O'Leary might be unhappy and leave were constant themes. It would be a disaster! How would we manage without her? She isn't washing the hall or cleaning the stairs often enough but how could we say anything? When not talking about Mrs O'Leary, grandmother would worry about the rent tribunal.

Paula lived in Hatherley Court for twenty-five years. She held regular afternoon tea parties for other elderly ladies, all continental refugees like herself, who generally lived in flats in the other blocks of Hatherley Court. They were all short with large chests and thick legs. They wore dark-coloured, shapeless dresses, cried a lot, and spoke in a polyglot of broken English, German, Polish, Hungarian and a little Yiddish, accompanied by considerable arm waving for emphasis. To native English speakers, their European accents ranged from strong to unintelligible, but they appeared to be entirely comprehensible to one another. Paula had always had a quick ear for languages so her English bore more evidence of her time in the North East of England than of Vienna. She had an uncanny ability to match the accent of whoever she was talking to in either German or English. As each new visitor arrived, there would be a ritual chorus of the question, "What language should we speak?" followed by a brief negotiation and they would resume their conversation in simultaneous German-broken English.

During the 1950s and 1960s, individual concentration camps began to create their 'Book of the Dead' by collating death certificates and other information of those who had been murdered in each of the camps. When these books began to reach the old ladies in Bayswater, they would sit, as a book was passed reverentially from one member to another, in order to check for names that they recognised. Each cried quietly as they remembered family and friends lost or relived personal suffering. The crying intensified when someone came across the name of business associates, acquaintances, friends or family. Memories were shared, the horror of these experiences reiterated and relived repeatedly.

Paula settled into the normal life of an aging, continental refugee. Her two sons, their wives and, when they came along, children were expected to attend every Sunday afternoon for *Jause*.

Peter explained:

> A Jause is tea (without milk) and a trolley groaning with Aufschnitt - large platters of assorted continental sausages - patisseries, wafers, cakes and whipped cream.

Literally, an aufschnitt is a selection of cold cuts. Sunday afternoons with Paula, involved platters of assorted sliced cooked meats, sausages and salami along with thin slices of Gouda or Austrian smoked cheese served with baskets of buttered dark and light rye breads. Next, came sweet bread, butter and jam served in the Meissen Zweiblemuster comfiture bowls with the little roses for knobs that Paula had managed to rescue from the Schreyvogelgasse flat before her escape from Vienna. The finale was a platter of cakes from Pâtisserie Françoise or the Polish baker. Great balls of choux pastry filled with whipped cream and covered in glossy chocolate or coffee icing, millefeuilles, individual tarts covered in a cornucopia of seasonal fruit and slices of torte held rigid by their cellophane enclosures. This was accompanied by tea, cigarettes and conversation. However hard Paula tried to be English, her failure showed each time she poured tea and forgot to add milk to the cup first. Although her sons teased her relentlessly over this omission, she seldom remembered to put milk in an empty cup.

Shrinking as she aged, Paula was barely one and half metres high, her voluptuous charm had turned into fat, so she became a formless cylinder on stout legs, although her hands and feet remained small and neat. Despite this, she remained completely feminine and continued to wear the same perfume she had worn for Hermann, Narcisse Noir, a mixture of sweet orange blossom and aromatic sandalwood immortalised by Gloria Swanson in the film *Sunset Boulevard*. Her assiduously applied lipstick was the Parisian Rouge Baiser that Peter was tasked with buying each time he visited France. Her manicured nails were always coated in shell pink varnish. When Eric died in 1962 she went into mourning; from then on she only wore black for many years. Eventually, she was persuaded to diversify and she began to include burgundy or grey in her wardrobe. Like her,

her clothes were generally shapeless and bulky. When she reached seventy, she was finally persuaded, after many years of dying her hair black in the continental fashion, to revert to her natural waved white.

Picasso retrospective Tate Summer 1960

Peter escorted his mother around the Picasso retrospective exhibition held at the Tate Gallery, Millbank in summer 1960. Dressed in her customary shapeless long, dark coat, a beige velvet hat with a square brim and small net veil, neat dark shoes and a large black bag, Paula clicked her disapproval as they moved through each room. Like a Geiger counter approaching a radiation source, the clicking intensified as they proceeded through the packed exhibition. When they finally reached the end of the exhibition, Paula drew up all of her four foot eleven inches, turned to the throng and announced, 'Me, I like Rubens!' and swept out.

Sound of Music 1965

I was eleven when *The Sound of Music* was first screened; Julie Andrews and Christopher Plummer, many noisy children and plenty of snow-covered mountains. My mother delivered me and my younger sister to grandmother at the Dominion Theatre at the top of Tottenham Court Road in time for the matinee. Tickets were bought but no sweets as they were seen as a waste of money. Granny had her usual grey hat with the small veil, her usual shapeless, dark coat, neat shoes and a large bag. The cinema wasn't very full. Strangely, the audience was entirely made up of small, continental ladies in their usual hat and coat, each with one or more grandchildren.

The sniffing began with the titles; it rapidly turned into crying and worse. At one point, granny clutched my hand wailing, "That is where your father broke his collar-bone." It had never been entirely clear whether Peter had broken his collarbone falling down some basement steps or out of a window. What was clear was this selfish teenage action had not improved their vacation.

Ours was not the only crying granny, as the swastikas appeared, the grannies howled in unison. Other children looked as embarrassed as we felt. *The Sound of Music* played at the

Dominion for three and a half years, the longest run of any production in the world.

Paula on an outing in her shapeless dark coat with hat and bag.

Like many refugees, Paula horded food and overvalued her possessions compensating for all that she had lost. Amongst the cluttered living room was a trolley with two clear plastic containers with ill-fitting lids that contained permanently stale Jaffa Cakes. On the rare occasion my sister and I were allowed one, they were so hard that we were able to extract the jelly layer intact. The glass cabinet became a repository for childish drawings and gifts we made for her along with treasures rescued from Vienna. The contents of the mysterious silver-topped glass jars at the back of the cabinet eventually turned out to be a gallstone preserved in formalin.

Prague Spring 1968

Following the partition of Europe after the war, Czechoslovakia became a communist country, ruled from Moscow. A wave of Stalinist-like terror was unleashed with the accompanying show trials and forced labour camps, built along the same lines as Nazi concentration camps with a central square for roll call and Spartan wooden barracks where inmates were housed. Although there was a slight increase in freedom following Stalin's death in 1953 and the de-Stalinization programme that followed, change was limited. Soviet control remained as Antonín Novotný, a hard-line communist who had been imprisoned by the Nazis in Mauthausen, became the Communist Party Secretary in 1953. Over time, there were slight reductions in press and artistic censorship but the economy remained weak and personal freedoms were limited. Many Czechs were angry that their economy was being destroyed by Soviet doctrine whilst the fruits of their labour were enjoyed at a distance and not by the workers.

The Soviets resisted change, even though the methods of collective farming and centralization of production they had introduced after the war had reduced output. Discontent continued to ferment until Alexander Dubček was elected First Secretary of the Communist Party of Czechoslovakia in January 1968, replacing the hardliner Novotný. There were peaceful mass protests against the communist regime and Soviet repression. Dubček attempted to reform the government from within, whilst trying to placate Moscow. These changes were branded, 'Socialism with a human face', as he worked to increase personal freedoms and to release the country from the failing Soviet planned economy. The Prague Spring was brief as on the twenty-first of August 1968, after only six months of relative freedom, two thousand tanks from the Soviet Union, Bulgaria, Poland and Hungary invaded Prague to crush the uprising. Seventy-five people were killed and hundreds more injured during the invasion. Dubček put up no resistance and was taken to Moscow. The protests and civil unrest that followed were largely peaceful led by students and young people. To some extent, these protests followed a wave of student protest that crossed Europe and the US. Students rioted in Paris, whilst in London, there were regular demonstrations against the Vietnam War outside the American embassy in Grosvenor Square.

Although Fritzi was her only remaining contact in Czechoslovakia, Paula was upset by the news from her motherland. On the eighth of August 1968, there was a large demonstration as over a thousand protestors chanted outside the Russian embassy before marching to Earls Court to protest outside a Russian exhibition that was being staged there. A few days later, there was a smaller protest held by young Czechs in their colourful, national costumes. The women wore their wide skirts, embroidered aprons, white blouses under embroidered waistcoats in reds and blacks whilst the men wore black trousers and equally intricately embroidered waistcoats. Peter drove slowly behind the sea of red and black as it paraded around Marble Arch and down Park Lane. Paula sobbed loudly from the front seat; upset both by the Soviet invasion and the sight of so many costumes so familiar from her childhood after such a long time. Following this excursion, Paula began to draw figures in Czech costumes and other motifs from her childhood in bold colours and strong strokes. She generally used felt-tip pens and drew on the shiny card Peter provided. She continued to sketch until, in her late eighties, her health deteriorated.

Six months later, in January 1969, in protest against the renewed suppression of free speech, Jan Palach set fire to himself in Wenceslas Square.

Papers from the Austrian State Archive show that throughout the 1960s, Paula continued her compensation claim from the Relief Fund. There are copies of the many forms she completed that were then notarised by commissioners for oaths. One of these was around the corner on Westbourne Grove whilst she must have taken the bus to have her signature witnessed on the Finchley Road. Identical information is repeated on many forms: place of birth, address in Vienna, date of departure and occupation. In some years, she received small payments - they varied, in 1963 she received 9,000 Austrian Schillings (about £125), there is no record for 1965 or 1966 but 4,000 Schillings were paid in 1967 (£55) but only 1,500 Schillings (£25) were paid the following year. In 1965 a pound was worth 73 Austrian Schillings. However, devaluation of the Austrian schilling in 1978 reduced the amount Paula received once it was converted into Sterling as there were only 28 Austrian Schillings to a pound. The inflation tool calculates that £100 in 1963 would be worth

£1,783.59 in 2021 assuming five per cent annual inflation over the years.

Later, as she aged, Paula applied to the Hardship Fund. Towards the end of 1977, she was frail, and her health had deteriorated. Once she became unable to stay safely in Hatherley Court, she moved into a nursing home in Golders Green. Correspondence with the fund showed that there were only limited savings left to cover the cost of the nursing home and that they would not last much longer. By then, Peter was paying half her costs. The fund made a single payment of 14,000 Schillings, which today is worth about £3,000 (3,350 euros) towards these costs. After a comfortable eighteen months in the nursing home with regular visits from family and friends, Paula refused to get out of bed or sit in a chair and after a couple of weeks, she died quietly during the night.

Chapter 18

London: His Own Business

Demobilisation

Although one third of the nation's armed forces were demobilized before Christmas 1945 and the remainder were home before the following Easter, Peter was asked to remain in Naval Intelligence. Germany had been decisively defeated by the Allies but throughout the war, their forces had been supported by a number of technical innovations which the Admiralty needed to understand. Peter's role was to find the scientists and engineers responsible for these developments and understand why and how they had made them. Peter was given some training before he was sent across northern Europe to universities and factories.

He reported to the guards at the Admiralty, Whitehall:

Eventually I was given a slip of paper with my appointment: it was to NID 1 PW.

NID was Naval Intelligence Division, 1 stood for Europe. PW meant Prisoners of War. I was delighted. I must have been the only ex-PW in PW.

"It's Commander McFadyeon you want. He's at 64 Victoria Street, Bennett Constructions."

It was a far cry from the Admiralty. Bennett Constructions had a small office on the first floor in one of the terrace houses in Victoria Street. In a large, untidy outer room were a couple of women and three youngish men. The commander was in a small, inner room. He was grey-haired, relaxed, invariably entertained by what was going on around him.

I gave him my slip, feeling silly in my best uniform. Everybody wore civilian clothes, the commander had on a dark business suit.

He made introductions. The women were Wren officers. Two of the men were lieutenants, the third was a petty officer in ciphers.

"It isn't posh," the commander told me, "but there isn't room for us all in the division. And it's a lot easier working here."

He issued information at a trot. We could come and go as we pleased, no papers, no sentries. If I wanted to talk to anyone in the office, I should just ring in, "Watch what you say, we're good at catching on. Writing in," he said, "was a lot quicker by ordinary forces mail than coded."

"'We don't use our own names," he told me. "Pick one, doesn't matter what, change it when you want to use a new one."

First, I was to go to the place in the country for a couple of weeks. Some of it might be useful, perhaps.

I reported at the office the following morning, in flannels and a jacket, with my hold-all. A car took me to a country house in Surrey. It was referred to only as the place in the country.

I never knew how many instructors there were there or how many learners. Come to that, with some of them I didn't even know whether they were the one or the other. They were sailors, soldiers, airmen, civilians, British, Polish, Czechs, French, Dutch, Americans, and Australians. They all seemed to have two degrees, spoke at least two languages, slept with at least two lovers, male, female or assorted. Food was imaginative, drink was plentiful and, I was told, vintage.

We had lectures, seminars, discussions. Some of the lectures on interrogating were memorable. The message was very loud and very clear.

You don't use violence;

Because it is immoral and evil.

Because it is not allowed.

Because it is self-defeating. Use enough force, you'll be told anything you want to hear but not necessarily the truth.

Because of the greatest danger of all: The prisoner who is innocent, who does not know anything. Torture him to death, he won't know any more.

Gleefully we were told, and were not the first so to be told, of the interrogator who gave his German suspect a cold shower every four hours, day and night. Five days on, the German was fit and frisky, new hair sprouting on his chest. The interrogator was on a couch talking to the army's shrink.

"How, then?" we asked.

"How with a suspected traitor or infiltrator do you protect your own?"

You're cleverer.

You're persistent. You're patient.

"If you have no time?"

You draw your line, as near as you can to be effective but humane (that was the word that was used over and over again). You bluff, you twist and turn, and you catch out. You make a chink. Then you work on it.

I was glad; it seemed to give me a pass mark over my German major with the mines in Holland.

For the remainder of his life, Peter continued to question whether the way he had threatened the major into revealing the whereabouts of the plans showing where mines had been laid in the River Scheldt was legitimate.

We were told to have a long nose (a superfluous instruction with my own particular profile) for liars, taught to do elementary ciphers, a sergeant showed me how to pretend I could handle a service revolver and advised me to carry a small pistol in a shoulder holster as well, in case I wanted to take the big one off.

Our NID passes, it was explained, gave a lot of rights to order people about, requisition things, commandeer transport. They also had an unwritten rider: abuse it, boy, and you'll answer for it.

Back in London, I was given my posting, to the British Naval Gunnery Mission, based in Minden. Naturally, the Admiralty and the experts in Bath - naval constructors, gunners, engineers, and electrical engineers - wanted to find out everything to be learned from the German guns and gunnery predictors. It was no secret that we had a lot to learn, especially over predictors. I drew a revolver and an Imperial portable typewriter from stores and made my way to strengthen the British Naval Gunnery Mission.

Monty, or General Sir Bernard Montgomery as we who knew him so well preferred to call him, had his headquarters as Commander-in-Chief of British forces at Bad Oeynhausen, between Bielefeld and Hanover in the north of Germany.

Admiral Sir Harold Borrough, our naval C-in-C and Monty's deputy, had his conveniently, only twenty miles away at Minden, There, the navy had taken over a large industrial building and the suburb that had housed its staff, put a wire fence around it and hoisted our white ensign.

I was given a room in the office block and a furnished flat of my own. Commensurate with my rank and very late arrival, it was a modest flat on the second floor. But it had two rooms, bathroom, kitchen, it was more than enough and it came with a steward. I also got a square four-wheel-drive Humber staff car. For much of my time, I was to be more in the car than in the flat.

....

Captain Ellison, head of the Gunnery Mission, dropped in on me in the office on my first day. Didn't send for me, dropped in. A quiet, private man with a self-effacing smile and a deep interest in, of all things, early Chinese ceramics.

I met Tim Brown, an engineer out of Oxford with a love for engineering. He was the right man for the Gunnery Mission. Captain Ellison told us what we had to do. There were long lists from Admiralty in London and from the specialists in Bath of German equipment, armour-plating, guns, predictors, stabilisers that they wanted to know about. We might find them in service in ships, in stores, factories, on drawing boards, in sketchy outlines. We might find them anywhere in Germany, Austria or in any occupied country, so long as the Russians let us in if it was in their zone, Germany was divided into four zones and administered by four armies, British, French, American, Russian.

More than anything, we needed the men (hardly any women were involved) who had thought of them, developed them, made and tested them, used them, or still only dreamed of them.

We needed them willing to co-operate with us. I remembered the place in the country. You don't get useful technical information from stone-walls.

Very quickly, over a drink, Tim and I understood each other. He really wanted to know how all those clever gadgets worked and where they were pointing to for the future. He didn't want to know what any Germans had or had not done in the war except for their engineering, and whether they loved their mothers. For myself, I could live without the intricacy of servomechanisms; but the Germans were fascinating. It divided itself up between us quite naturally: I find them, I talk to them, then Tim makes sense of what they tell us.

Our compound in Minden worked efficiently, it was Royal Navy territory. Orderly, well-dressed, well-fed, healthy personnel went about their purposes, from quarters to office, from one office to another, to dining rooms and messes, to the NAAFI stores, to ENSA entertainments in the assembly hall. We were an enclave of sanity surrounded by chaos.

We weren't prepared for the drawn, impoverished Germans coming out of the holes in the ground where they lived, for the empty shops - what was left of them - for the many cripples in the streets, for the shortage of able-bodied men. Here, in Germany, we found another world. I carried on looking for German engineering wizards.

As a member of the Corps of the Royal Electrical and Mechanical Engineers, Peter was sent to find individuals responsible for German technical innovations. The Admiralty wanted to learn from these engineers and scientists. Sometimes, parts were found accidentally and needed to be identified:

An army engineering officer called on our captain carrying a heavy, sealed package. It was an engineering component found in a German railway truck that had been immobilised in a siding by our bombs. REME couldn't make head or tail of it, the RAF could not place it. Our mission was no wiser and sent the piece to the Admiralty.

Two months later, we were told in confidence there was a rumour from London that the unit was intended for the German atom bomb. How many other units and parts and components and essential supplies had been held up somewhere in loading bays and trains and trucks, never to reach their destination?

During his travels, Peter managed to spend a day observing the trial of Nazi leaders by the allies at Nuremburg, one of the many experiences that remained with him for the whole of his life. He was lucky enough to observe the great British barrister, Hartley Shawcross in action:

I took off a day to see the tribunal at Nürnberg for myself. With my NID pass, I was allowed briefly into the courtroom. It was incredible that such ordinary, grey men could have brought about so much suffering. I expected devils and found only clerks and psychopaths.

Eventually, Peter was sent to Vienna:

I was ordered to report to London and went to near-by Bückeburg where the RAF had a landing strip. They took me to London in one of their flying machines, a Dakota with rows of metal bucket seats along its length and many cracks in the bodywork. It was very cold.

Commander McFadyeon had been given a job in Vienna and put it aside for me. It was the kind Royal Navy all over.

I was to find Herr Professor Yohute Tobluchin, professor of physics at Vienna University who knew something that was worth having. I was given a briefing paper and was none the wiser for it. As a secondary objective, could I locate Herr Ingenieur Ender who had perfected triangular transmission shafts and pulleys. Don't laugh, they could be a great advance on the circular shafts and keys we were using. And there was also some new lens made by an optical firm. I was expected to be back in Minden within a few days.

I went back to the RAF to get to Vienna. Another Dakota with rows of metal seats along its length was to take us.

Vienna was bedraggled; the nearer we drove to the centre, the worse it became. Some of the houses had been destroyed, many more were damaged, here due to shelling as much as to bombing. Some were smouldering. "Displaced Persons (DPs) use the furniture for firewood," the ATS explained to us. "Floorboards and rafters, too. It gets out of hand."

Every now and then we could hear what sounded like small-arms fire. Dishevelled people in rags were walking along the streets and huddled in doorways. Otherwise, the streets were strangely deserted.

"People stay at home as much as possible," the ATS continued her commentary, "there's a lot of looting and stealing."

"And worse," the driver added, saving her from spelling it out. "Robbery, murder, rape. There are all sorts here. Russian soldiers, they are the worst with women. Deserters, refugees, homeless people looking for food."

On many of the walls along the way were the familiar hoardings with scraps of paper advertising for lost relatives.

I had my own family to search for and no great hope of success.

....

In the morning, the sub-lieutenant and I went to the university, opposite our old flat. It was disorganised and deserted. Although I had seen it every day all those years ago, I never realised how huge it was. It took a long time in echoing corridors and many offices to find the right lab.

Herr Professor Yohute Tobluchin had died, from natural causes, in 1943. None of his papers were found after his death. It was fairly certain that his assistant, Dr Jägers, had taken them with him. Dr Jägers was last heard of a year ago in Innsbruck. The university had written several times but received no reply.

Ingenieur Ender's small engineering firm was easily found and also in the British sector. It was very interesting. They made machine components. "Of course," he said, "in recent years most went to German arms manufacturers." He shrugged his shoulders and raised his arms in a Viennese gesture I knew very well: This is how it is, it signified, we must sail with the wind under any opportune flag of connivance. Survival is the only principle.

He had developed a new triangular shaft and pulleys that required no keys. He showed us drawings, calculations, prototypes, test results. I couldn't judge it properly but it seemed to be genuinely promising.

Would he be prepared to come with me to Paris where we had a technical evaluation centre? Not surprisingly, he would be only too pleased. Trade with the German army was bound to be slow just then. I told him we'd leave in a few days' time.

One mission led Peter to spend time with a technical counterpart from the German mine laying department. Although he clearly disliked the German Admiral in charge of the unit, he enjoyed his encounter with a lieutenant commander who had been involved in laying the mines the Royal Navy had swept so effectively. They were two techies companionably sharing their experiences who respected one another without rancour:

The mission had a request for information about German midget submarines and special weapons. It wasn't our field, but we were there. Again, because of the language, I was sent to the German admiralty in Kiel. An important naval base with huge U-boat pens, Kiel had been a prime target. The damage was amongst the worst I had seen. I drove right through the town centre before realising I had reached Kiel. Most of the admiralty staff were in underground offices and in makeshift huts.

I met the German admiral who had been in charge of special naval weapons. He was gross, fat, manicured, in a well-tailored uniform and he smelt of 4711, the traditional German Eau de cologne.

He was quite happy to tell me about the mini submarines the Germans had developed, the 'Marder' the 'Molch', the 'Biber', the 'Hecht', the 'Seehund' and the 'Linse', like a collector showing off his prize items. He kept on ringing officers on his staff and barking rudely to bring in drawings and photos and operating charts for my growing pile of documents. Casualties and losses were painstakingly recorded in black ink (lost) and in red ink (killed) and in blue ink (missing, believed killed).

"I think I know the 'Marder'," I mentioned, and told him about our crossing in the *St Tudno*.

He looked up a chart.

"Ah," he was pleased with his records, "two killed, three returned. One of them, I believe, is still here. You shall meet him later."

"They caused us no damage."

"Not many did," he said dismissively.

"It is said you had heavy losses?"

"I should say so. As bad as any in the fleet."

"Why did you continue?"

"They were something different. They showed we were adventurous, imaginative."

"Were they worth the losses?"

"What's worth what, in a war? Besides, the Führer loved them. He didn't really like the navy, never did. But he always enjoyed hearing about our special weapons."

"You didn't mind sending out your sailors?" I asked and should have known better.

"Mind," he was close to shouting. "What's to mind! The Führer says send them; I send them. I didn't have to sit on a bloody 'Marder' myself."

We went for lunch. Considering the ruins and the need around us, they did themselves pretty well with white linen and stewards, plenty to eat and a choice of wines. They were prisoners, of course, but the unit was kept together while it still had many mines and torpedoes, and perhaps some information.

A lieutenant came in. The admiral beamed. "Ah, here you are. Let me introduce you."

The young officer was a survivor from the attack on the *St Tudno*.

We shook hands.

"You missed us," I said.

"I'm glad now that we did. You missed me as well."

"I'm glad, also."

There were many such meetings between previous foes. There was no hostility, only relief that it was over and done with, and, yes, something shared.

"What's that ship, the *St Tudno*?" the admiral asked me.

I told him I had been in magnetic minesweeping.

"Some of our minelayers are here still. You might like to meet them." I told him I'd value it.

The admiral gave me details about the rest of his operations. I had a stack of papers by the time we finished.

"Now, the minelayers are expecting you."

We made our farewells.

A young officer took me past wrecks and partly standing buildings to the mines department. The building was in fair state, for Kiel. The boss, a silver-striped lieutenant commander met me in his lab.

"We are very pleased to meet you," he was welcoming. A junior officer and a couple of petty officers were still working, surrounded by the familiar wires, meters and cathode-ray tubes. It could have been HMS Vernon in Portsmouth or Lochinvar in Edinburgh.

It did no good to the British Naval Gunnery Mission, but I had a great time in the German Mine Department.

We sat at the lieutenant commander's desk, smoked English cigarettes and drank German imitation coffee.

"We thought we had you licked with our magnetics in November '39," he said.

"So did we, damn you," I admitted, "and you nearly had."

"I was only a sub-lieutenant then," he told me. "My commander had a lot to do with the magnetic mine. He is a very clever man. He's retired now, as a full captain."

"He nearly closed our Thames, blast him."

"We were rubbing our hands, expecting to be weighed down with Iron Crosses. And then, suddenly, it goes phut."

"We started removing the magnetic charge. That's what saved us."

"We were furious. Furious and disappointed. We thought it would take you much longer."

"We, on the other hand, were pretty pleased. Until early in the New Year. Then suddenly it all went wrong again. We lost more ships than ever."

"That," he said, modestly, "that was me, I think."

"You? Personally?"

"I think so, yes. I was going home at night on the bus, fed up. The reports we had from the Luftwaffe and from the E-boats were very depressing. I was racking my brain, how did you English cope with our mines so soon. You couldn't sweep them, we were sure. From our flyers we had enlarged photos showing new cables around the decks of your ships. So, you were sending a current around the loops to neutralise the ship's magnetism."

I nodded.

"Then, I had this brainwave. You couldn't know how much magnetism there was in a ship. To make sure, you had to over-compensate. I jumped off the tram and ran to the commander's house. He was having his dinner with his family and none too pleased to see me. "Excuse me, sir', I burst out, 'they must be sending so much current around their cables, they have reversed the polarity of their ships'. He stared at me for a moment. Then he said: 'Good thinking', took the serviette off from around his neck and got up, saying: 'Let's go'."

We went into the mine store; he had a key, of course. Then and there we got hold of screwdrivers and spanners, took the first six mines to be loaded in the morning and dismantled the arming circuits. Then we just reversed the black and red leads to the magnetic needle. We finished around one in the morning, the mines were loaded into E-boats at six."

"By lunchtime," I took up our side of the story, "our ships were going down."

"I got my second ring for that."

"I should think so," I conceded.

It was a tiny fragment of naval history I was unearthing. Within a few days of the new sinkings, HMS Lochinvar in Edinburgh realised our degaussing had to be far more exact and wipe out all the magnetism. But nobody on our side could ever have known exactly how the Germans had reversed the polarity literally overnight.

"You improved your degaussing," he admitted.

"And once we got hold of one of your mines intact and had a look inside, we tried to sweep them."

"The big magnetic coils that kept on blowing up," we both smiled.

"We had to learn. Until we got the tails."

"Those damned tails. And you got them so quickly. That was clever."

"Saved our bacon, I can tell you. There were far fewer sinkings."

"We didn't know how you got them to float. Until an E-boat found a piece and picked it up for us. Tennis balls. Who but the English would have thought of tennis balls!"

"They worked."

"Too well, they did."

"Then you put in series impulses."

"And you changed your sequence."

"Until you foxed us again when you let the first few ships pass. Those caused losses."

We went through the whole tit-for-tat of laying and sweeping.

Their acoustics, our submersible Kango hammers.

"Your pressure mines."

"And your hand grenades going pop, pop."

It was dark and late evening when I drove him to his home a few miles out of Kiel and we shook hands.

An opponent one could respect and like.

Eventually, in 1946, Peter was recalled to London and faced the prospect of leaving the Royal Navy. He was offered a senior post, for his age, in the Civil Service; but he rejected it in favour of following a commercial career.

Of the three services, the Navy, Army and Air Force, the Royal Navy is considered the senior service partly on grounds of longevity. When Peter applied for naturalization, he was then the senior officer in the senior service so he was the first to be interviewed and proudly became a British Citizen on the twenty-second of July 1946, Certificate AZ18775. He sent Paula a telegram, 'I am now of British nationality.' He had served in intelligence for two years:

> I was only too pleased to have a few months in England still in the navy (and on navy pay). Civvy Street, civilian life was looming. We'd been looking forward to it for years, made jokes about it, designed castles in Spain for it. It was the Promised Land.
>
> Now that we were approaching it, we found it a very strange territory. I had been very lucky with an interesting war and a little room for initiative. It was not exceptional. In all ranks, war service brought new experiences, new responsibilities and challenges. For many, it brought great and frequent danger (though for most of us, in total, it was probably no greater than living through the London Blitz). What we had overlooked was that whatever any physical danger, HM Forces were an all-embracing, benevolent cocoon.

Pay-cheques came, accommodation was found, uniforms were provided, food may not always have been Ritz standard, but we didn't starve. There were medics, welfare people, and padres. There were whole networks of support.

Now, we found ourselves at the end of our last free travel voucher having to fend for ourselves. 'Baby it's cold outside' might have been written for us, the ex-servicemen.

Early computers

Elliott Brothers was founded in 1804. The company made precision mechanical equipment, adding telegraph and electrical equipment to their offerings during the 1870s. Throughout the war, they manufactured fire control equipment for the Royal Navy from their factory in Lewisham, South London. When the war ended, although Elliott's were still skilled in precision manufacturing they, like many British engineering organisations, had failed to adopt newer technologies, notably electronics, and were operating at a loss. The Admiralty then persuaded Elliott's to establish an R & D team to develop advanced digital systems, Elliott Automation, and leased the company premises, a factory at Borehamwood, Hertfordshire. Led by Professor Coales, a former naval commander, the group was setup to work on a range of classified projects. Staff were specially recruited, frequently they were young scientists and engineers from the Navy. They arrived to find an empty shell and pitched in to build their laboratories within the vast buildings. In 1947, Elliot Brothers were the only organisation outside academia to develop the world's first real-time computers with memories. The company began to contribute to the economy when they moved into civil data processing through their collaboration with National Cash Registers (NCR). Once he left the Navy, Peter's first job was with Elliot Automation and he moved to Borehamwood to be near the factory:

The new Research and Development laboratory in Borehamwood was a huge step for the company. In Commander Professor Coales OBE RN, they had an excellent head for it; an able engineer and a good administrator.

The lab was housed in a new, modern factory building with plenty of room for expansion, four floors, all empty and the paint hardly dried.

We were all new. None of the others had been there more than a few weeks. There were twelve small teams under two section leaders, for military and for civilian projects. I was assigned to work in the civilian section to develop a remote water-level meter so that the levels in reservoirs and lakes could be measured and controlled from far away.

Peter was assigned to a project to find a way of measuring the depth of a reservoir remotely. He worked hard and took five months to demonstrate that it was possible to make a machine that could measure the depth of water in a tank under controlled conditions. Elliott's automatically patented the idea. Peter thought little of his development: it would not be practical to keep visiting distant reservoirs to tend to these machines. Peter's writings show that he felt he lacked the single-minded interest to pursue a career in R & D. He compared himself unfavourably with those who apparently thought about their projects continuously, almost to the exclusion of everything else and even while they were sleeping. Peter was a polymath, interested in everything who could not confine his huge energy to a single question. Modestly, he deprecated his machine denouncing it as impractical, though systems like this are now routinely used, made possible by wireless technology and the internet, as he chose to move away from the world of pure R & D.

Peter was better suited and happier in his next job as a subeditor on the journals produced by the Institution of Electrical Engineers (IEE). Savoy Place is probably most famous for being the first home of the BBC. Built on the North Embankment, next to Waterloo Bridge, the rectangular, red and white Victorian building faces the Thames. Suitably, for an institution dedicated to electrical engineering a statue of Michael Faraday proudly stands in front of it. Like many non-native English speakers, Peter had a deep love and respect for the language. His speech was unaccented unless he was speaking with someone from the North East when he unconsciously developed a Tyneside twang, remembered from his first encounters with spoken English in

1938. His writing was succinct. Unlike most native speakers, he understood grammar and applied it correctly. Working as a sub-editor for the IEE journals developed his language further and taught him the importance of attention to detail. Peter next worked in a couple of advertising agencies as a sales executive and copywriter.

After three years as an employee, he was eager to start his own business:

> My maternal grandfather started with a barrow and finished with three drapery shops in Brno, Czechoslovakia. My paternal grandfather was a timber merchant in Rumania and then in Vienna, my father put up his shingle as a lawyer, my mother was the leading spirit in the cinema. Working for yourself runs in the family.

> Since the navy, I had been employed for three years; quite long enough, I thought. I was getting gestatory urges - I wanted a business of my own.

Graphis

Peter did not have the capital to set-up an advertising agency alone. Instead, he used his savings and a took one-thousand-pound bank loan, guaranteed by Dr Freedman, to buy a fifty percent share of Graphis Press, a tiny print works in Hackney. Like Peter, John Tomkins was a refugee. Born as Julius Teicher in Leipzig, he followed his printer father into an apprenticeship before taking evening classes at what is now the Hochschule für Grafik und Buchkunst, the Leipzig Academy of Fine Arts, and qualified as a master printer.

Once work was forbidden to Jews in Germany, as he had a Polish passport Julius had been able to travel to Copenhagen for a job interview. He had then travelled to England from Copenhagen arriving in 1938 in his only pair of trousers, with a rucksack, a single spare shirt, and ten shillings. Although Julius did manage to bring two of his sisters and their families to London, the remainder of his family were murdered in Auschwitz. He worked at low-level printing jobs, including a couple of years spent with the Blackheath Press before his military service. As the Poles were not considered to be enemy aliens, Julius served in the Sixth Airborne Division and fought in theatres of war from France to the Baltic. Like Eric, the military advised him to anglicize his name to hide his identity in case of capture by the Germans and so he became John Tomkins and his ID card stated that his religion was Buddhist, rather than Jewish.

Peter was introduced to John by a mutual friend, Ernst Hoch. They met in a pub in Fleet Street so that John could explain to him the dangers and pitfalls of setting up in business:

> After the war, he had hired a few square feet marked by chalk lines on the stone floor in the basement of a small print shop in Dalston and bought a very small machine. When he got an order, he had to ask the customer to pay enough in advance to buy the paper. But he brought the proof on the same day and the finished printing next morning.

> By the time we met, he had moved into an old factory building behind the Kingsland Road.

> He showed me samples of his designs and they were first-rate. I showed him some of my stuff. I felt sure he was an honest person and I wasn't wrong.

> I had met him only to get advice. But he seemed to be an ideal ally on the road to an agency of our own in tandem with the printing firm. John in turn was attracted to the idea of a having me as a salesman for the press, starting an advertising agency, and having me around so that he could at long last go on holiday with his family.

> Very quickly and smoothly, we had it all agreed (subject to everything). I'd buy fifty per-cent of the shares; we'd increase the printing side and start an agency as soon as possible.

> I looked over his print shop. It was a ramshackle little place as John had said it was. But it would be half mine. It would be a start and the rent was low. It was called Graphis Press Ltd. We promised ourselves that our agency would be Graphis Publicity Ltd.

> To save costs, at first, John and I shared one car, the driver meeting the other one at the nearest tube station. We had it alternative weekends for our own use.

> We had a big ace up our sleeve, as we both had known from the beginning.

> Most printing houses were poor at design. Big jobs came ready designed from publishers and from companies who had in-house designers or hired outside studios, and from ad agencies. When a printer had to do the design, it was usually very ordinary.
>
> We could turn out good design, get the artwork done, and print. For some jobs, my own visualising and copywriting came in handy. We could take on the world.

Because John had only been able to afford to buy a couple of small obsolete printing presses, Graphis Press could only print small runs on a limited range of sizes. Their output was fine rather than large and success relied on the quality of their design, printing, and the personal service they were able to offer. Soon, they were printing catalogues for several of the Mayfair galleries that exhibited modern art. Peter tramped around Cork Street and Bruton Street selling Graphis to gallery owners and taking their orders. The art scene in London in the early 1950s was challenging and exciting. Peter Cochrane at Arthur Tooth & Son brought American and European art to London. In the 1960s, Peter Cochrane promoted modern British art, exhibiting emerging young men before they were famous, David Hockney, Allen Jones, Peter Kinley and Howard Hodgkin. Round the corner in Cork Street the Waddington galleries proliferated. Victor Waddington had opened his first gallery in 1927 and was joined by his son, Leslie in 1959. Leslie exhibited the St Ives artists, Patrick Heron, Roger Hilton, Terry Frost along with Elisabeth Frink and Ivon Hitchens. Peter visited the galleries every week to discuss their forthcoming exhibitions and take their print orders. Occasionally, he met the artists. Sometimes, he went to the pub with them. One notable time, he spent an afternoon with Francis Bacon, returning home both star-struck and inebriated:

> We were right for this work. The runs were short so that our machinery could cope, and the galleries needed more attention than many larger firms could devote to them. At one time, we probably printed for more avant-garde galleries in London than any other firm. True, a single catalogue for an

exhibition at the Tate amounted to more than our entire turnover for a year.

As the company prospered, they were finally able to buy their first new printing press, a Heidelberg cylinder, and expanded into printing LP covers. As they grew, the company needed more space and they moved the heavy machines to the ground floor of a former fire station on Highbury Station Road, conveniently round the corner from the tube station. The sturdy, three floor building constructed out of yellow, London stock bricks, was embellished with odd rows of pale bricks.

I remember being taken to the factory as a child. The curious smell of cut paper and ink and the crash of the great 'slump bomps' as paper poured through the presses. Sometimes, kindly compositors would let me play with the metal sorts used to construct the type they were creating. Rather than use individual letter text, the linotype machine created text from slugs of metal created with a keyboard. Pictures were etched onto smooth metal inserted into the text. Every year, John designed a unique Christmas card for the company. Once, he made an ingenious stand out of turquoise card with a slot that held a slug bearing the message of seasonal goodwill. It was, of course, very heavy.

As I grew older, I was allowed to sit behind, and no doubt annoy, the long-suffering receptionist in her tiny cubby hole by the front door watching, fascinated, as she rapidly slotted plugs into the appropriate holes in her switchboard as calls came through. Pulling them out to let them retract automatically when the call ended.

An inexhaustible supply of off-cuts of paper and card was a luxury we took for granted as children.

Before long, they were able to start the long-planned advertising agency, Graphis Publicity, in ramshackle offices on the first floor above the print works. Huntley Freedman, Alec and Rita's youngest son, joined the partnership.

A few years later, Peter and Huntley started Export Advertising, specialising in technical marketing, particularly in Europe. As both the print works and advertising agencies prospered, the businesses became increasingly autonomous and financially self-sufficient. As they expanded, space became a problem again as they had outgrown their premises. Peter and Huntley moved from Islington to what was then a much smarter location, Tottenham Court Road, close to Warren Street tube station. Very amicably, Peter and John decided to go their separate ways but remained friends for the rest of their lives.

Shortly after he joined John Tomkins at Graphis, Peter met the woman who would become his wife, my mother. Politely, they waited until Paula returned from Vienna following the sale of the cinema before marrying in a simple civil ceremony at Caxton Hall, London.

Chapter 19

Brno: A Brave Woman

Surviving the camps

From autumn 1944, the SS began to retrench, emptying camps in the east and forcing those sick and emaciated prisoners who were fit enough to march towards the west. Many died on these death marches. Between the twentieth of April and the second of May 1945, around fifteen thousand prisoners from Buchenwald, Gross-Rosen and many sub-camps were moved into Theresienstadt, effectively doubling the number of prisoners held there. Conditions became even more inhumane as the newcomers increased the pressure on the already limited food and hygiene. Many brought typhoid into the camp which spread rapidly through the weak inmates causing an epidemic. The SS guards, some disguised as ordinary German soldiers, fled leaving their prisoners without food or water as Soviet forces advanced on Theresienstadt. The Red Cross arrived on the second of May and provided urgent medical care, especially treating those suffering with typhus to control the epidemic. Russian soldiers liberated the camp on the evening of the eighth of May. It took a month to bring the typhus epidemic under control, nine hundred and twenty prisoners along with about a dozen of the medical staff who cared for them died.

It took a further three months before the eighteen thousand survivors were released on the twenty-first of August. Fritzi was one of only seven thousand five-hundred and three survivors from Bohemia and Moravia and was eventually repatriated to Brno. Nothing was left of her former home or possessions, most of her relatives were dead and their property also gone. It is not clear when Fritzi was able to return to Brno or communicate as Paula's correspondence suggests that there was no contact between them until 1946. At some stage, she was reunited with her husband who had been held in a different camp, presumably also in the East. With nothing but memories of the horrors they had experienced, Fritzi and her husband had to rebuild their lives from scratch.

The whole question of compensating for the Holocaust is in many ways is impossible. How can killing, torture and forced exile on a mass scale ever be made good? Normally, the losing aggressor of any war is expected to pay for at least some of the damage they caused. Whilst discussions between Germany and the allies began in 1945, to some extent, they still continue nearly eighty years later. The issues remain complex with multiple nations involved; aggressor, victim, victor, vanquished and neutral. Philippe Sands describes how the terms genocide and crimes against humanity, along with the concept of global responsibility for these crimes, originated during the Nuremburg trials from the work of Rafael Lemkin and Hersch Lauterpacht. Indeed, the International Court at the Hague, which is now responsible for the trials of those charged with genocide, war crimes, crimes against humanity and aggression evolved from the Nuremburg courtroom.

Many thousands of individuals were displaced, and defeated soldiers were spread across Eastern Europe with no infrastructure for them to return to their homes in broken towns and cities. The Nazis had systematically expropriated assets and looted treasures from governments, museums and individuals in countries as they defeated them in their sweep across Europe. Hitler took great art for the Führermuseum he was building in Linz, his hometown, whilst Göring had curated his own private collection. Other treasures were carefully hidden in salt mines whilst individuals simply took things. Paula's cinema and the furnishings of the Scheyvongasse flat and Fritzi's belongings are perhaps trivial examples given the scale of events but to the individuals involved, their loss was significant. The immediate responses to the unprecedented ravages of the Holocaust were humanitarian as the allies were more concerned with dealing with concentration camp survivors and displaced persons than resolving the ownership of stolen property. Difficult though it was, these actions resulted in direct payments to Nazi victims to compensate for their personal loss and suffering were perhaps the most straightforward form of Holocaust compensation as assistance was provided in terms of need rather than losses. The 1945 Paris Reparations Agreement between eighteen countries provided twenty-five million dollars indemnification 'to those who suffered heavily at the hands of the Nazis and now stand in dire need to promote their rehabilitation but will be unable to claim assistance from Germany'. Whilst the majority of the victims of the Holocaust were Jews, there was then no central body to represent them as the State of Israel did not come into existence until May 1948. It is likely both Fritzi and her husband received something from this fund that enabled them to survive in Brno.

Along with indemnification, in her review of fifty years of Holocaust compensation, Marilyn Henry identified two further categories:

- Reparations - payments from one government to another covering war-related debts of a defeated aggressor.
- Restitution - return of assets to their original owners; these may be businesses, buildings or art collections and other treasures appropriated by the Nazis. The Nazis had also taken the gold and other reserves from the countries they had occupied.

Disentangling the history of things stolen by the Nazis, identifying their original ownership and agreeing reparations is complex and remains contentious. In part, this is caused by the number of different organizations involved, ranging from multiple governments, operating under different legal systems, civil courts, lawyers, historians, local institutions to local museums and record offices. Aside from the main protagonists, the victorious Allies, vanquished Germans and the countries invaded by the Nazis, some neutral countries might have assisted in the concealment of valuables. Was Austria, annexed by Germany in the 1938 Anschluss, an innocent victim of a hostile external government or one that was culpable as many citizens had welcomed the arrival of the National Socialists? Who had benefitted from the property expropriated from Viennese Jews? Not everything was stolen. Jews were forced to sell their art collections at rock bottom prices as they needed to fund their escape or when they were no longer allowed to own property. The Rothschilds were forced to sell their great collection. Hitler, a failed artist himself, particularly disliked abstract and impressionist art which he had removed from German galleries, while he respected traditional figurative representative art. In July 1938, the Degenerate Art Exhibition featuring modern, abstract, non-representational art, including that by internationally recognized Jewish painters like Paul Klee, Oskar Kokoschka and Wassily Kandinsky, was staged across the road from the Great German Art Exhibition composed of landscapes and statuesque Teutonic figures. Dealers, like Hildebrand Gurlitt, exploited the situation and bought works cheaply from desperate artists and collections and either horded or sold them at inflated prices outside the Reich.

Over the years, there have been some spectacular finds of lost artwork, paintings discovered in Swiss bank vaults and salt mines. Prestigious international galleries found there was a lack of clarity over the provenance of some the objects they accessed in the 1930s, 1940s and even, 1950s. When Hildebrand Gurlitt's son Cornelius died in 2014, he left to the Kunstmuseum in Bern the fifteen hundred artworks known as the Munich Horde, including works by Picasso, Munch, Matisse, Kirchner, and Klee, that his father had appropriated whilst working for the Nazis. Cornelius Gurlitt stipulated that the provenance of these items should be investigated and any looted art returned to the heirs of their original owners. Thanks to persistence, Klimt's portrait of Adele Bloch-Bauer was returned to Maria Altmann in 2004. Marie O'Connor's book about this was the basis for the film *The Lady In Gold*, starring Helen Mirren. Arguments over lost items continue as more are discovered, usually when collectors or their children die and their estates become visible once more.

In *Burning the Books,* Richard Ovenden describes how Jewish libraries and books were destroyed by the Nazis. A few survived, largely thanks to the courage of a few individuals who managed to hide them. Placing them in new libraries, for example in Israel, or restoring them to the community they came from was controversial.

If the restitution of looted treasures was and remains complex, making good personal suffering and loss was far more emotive, subject to national and international politics and global movements. The whole question of culpability, guilt and compensation has reverberated through Germany, and later, Austrian politics, since 1945. Konrad Adenauer's speech, made on the eve of Rosh Hashanah in September 1951, was called 'Attitude Towards Jews' and stated that Germany was responsible for material compensation and restitution to Jewish victims. Parallel negotiations were held in Hague between the Claims Conference, a group of twenty-three voluntary Jewish organisations and Federal Republic of Democratic Germany (FDRG) and the State of Israel and West Germany which eventually resulted in the 1952 Luxemburg Agreements. This led to West Germany paying over one hundred billion Deutschmarks in compensation to individual victims of Nazi persecution and was subsequently extended to include stateless persons and refugees living in the west.

Fritzi (Bedriska) Grossova. Bruno, 1975.

Fritzi returned to Brno in late 1945 or 1946. By then, Czechoslovakia was in the communist ruled Soviet sector. Stuck behind the iron curtain, life for the population was hard. Before the war Czechoslovakia was a rich country. Agriculture was strong and the country exported a wide range of quality produce. It was the industrial powerhouse of the empire. The country had been badly damaged by the reduced labour force caused by the war and was battle scarred. The Soviet policy of collective farming, directed from Moscow, led to further disastrous reductions in yield. Similarly, centralisation of industrial processes rapidly reduced the quality and output from Czech factories. Both food and goods were in short supply.

Fritzi's access to restitution was further complicated by Russia's refusal to compensate victims of National Socialism. The communists were busy expropriating lands and goods on their own behalf anyway. For four decades, only people living in the West received anything.

Strict currency controls were imposed by a government keen to prevent the population from obtaining foreign currency. Even after the cinema was eventually sold in the 1950s, Fritzi's share of the proceeds were stuck in Vienna and could not be transferred to her. Paula gave the funds to Didi and asked her to get them to Fritzi when it became possible. Nor could Paula send money from England. The Socialist state-run Tuzex shops which were the only places individuals could use foreign currency as the government, desperate for foreign currency, controlled them. Paula, and later Peter, could buy Tuzex coupons in London which they then posted to Fritzi. Coupons were exchanged in Tuzex shops stocked with goods that were in short supply or imports that were then considered to be luxury items. Vouchers for ten or twenty pounds were sent twice a year, for Christmas and birthday. Twice a year, we would sit in the stuffy living room in Hatherley Court as Paula read out Fritzi's thank you letter which listed what she had been able to buy with her voucher. Ten pounds bought a great many utilitarian items and the list would include things like an electric heater, toaster, saucepans, and blankets. Essential items rather than luxury goods for those of us living in the West. The Czech government must have been so desperate for foreign currency that the exchange rate was extraordinary as Paula's ten pounds converted into a great many items. Adverts for electric heaters in British magazines in 1960 range from Belling heaters that were six to seven pounds, to cheaper models for only two to three pounds. Every time a letter was read, someone, usually Peter, would comment on the extraordinary value offered by the exchange rate. Although Fritzi and her husband benefitted from Soviet policies that provided full employment, cheap accommodation and free healthcare, access to foreign currency via the Tuzex shops and later from Vienna would have enhanced their lives significantly.

In 1977, agreement between Germany and Czechoslovakia was reached and Germany provided one hundred and forty million Deutschmarks for projects to support victims of National Socialism. Fritzi must have received some funds as she wrote to Peter saying that as she no longer needed financial support, he should spend the money on his own family. As the soviet stranglehold over Czechoslovakia loosened, it became possible for Didi to gradually send Fritzi her share of the money from the sale of the Palast Kino that Paula had left with her in 1953. Much later, Peter said that he thought Didi had sent ten or twenty times more money than Paula had originally given her as she continued to send money long after the original funds must have been exhausted.

Brno 1992

The Berlin Wall fell in November 1991. A year later, I finally met my second cousin Fritzi, Paula's niece, in Brno. I took an impossibly early bus from Vienna that travelled though sloping fields with tidy rows of green vines, bunches of grapes hanging down glistening in the sun, in vineyards that curved around hilly slopes. Shortly before we reached the Czech border, we stopped at a small supermarket and passengers jumped out for last minute shopping. Many of their purchases were, to westerners, ordinary: washing powder, sugar, flour and other grocery items. As we drove through Czechoslovakia, the terrain changed, it became flatter and wetter. Along the margins of mud-filled ponds, reeds with huge silver fronds waved in the breeze. Improbably, as the bus wound slowly through this soggy landscape, *Mull of Kintyre* by Paul McCartney's band, Wings, blasted out from its sound system, bringing marching bagpipers aboard the shabby bus. Gone were the orderly vineyards, the landscape was unkempt and broken Trabbies littered the road. The Trabant was manufactured between 1957 to 1990 by car manufacturer VEB Sachsenring Automobilwerke Zwickaucar, known affectionately as a Trabby. In contrast to Vienna and Austria, the landscape was flat, monochrome and grey.

As we approached Brno, I wondered how Fritzi and I were going to communicate as I speak neither German nor Czech. I need not have worried. When I got off the bus, a little old lady, so like Paula but lacking her beauty, greeted me. To my great relief, she hesitantly asked about my toddler niece and nephew:

How are the little children?

She told me how she had been teaching herself English using the subtitles from Austrian television broadcasts. Then, matter of fact, she said:

When we were very small, we spoke German. Then, when we went to school, we had to speak Czech. Then, when we were in the camp, they beat us when we spoke Czech - if we did not speak German.

Empty trestle tables with only a few customers in the bedraggled Krautmarkt, Brno 1992.

Fritzi conducted me on a walking tour of Brno, standing in the Krautmarkt, she waved in the direction of the three shops her grandfather had owned. Behind us, the building that had once housed his largest shop had been torn down and rebuilt as a brutalist concrete supermarket with remarkably little stock. Looking down the square to 18 Krautmarkt, I realized that this had been my great-grandparents home and the apartment where Paula was born all those years ago. Our tour also included the 'crocodile over the well' at the old town hall. The cobbled roads were broken, with patches of missing stones. In places, the road and pavement were so damaged, there were heaps of earth with paving stones pointing out at strange angles almost as though the earth below had shifted. Many of the buildings were falling apart. Those at the top of the Krautmarkt, under the shadow of the cathedral, were fenced off with rickety sheets of rusty corrugated metal. Tired women, in faded clothes, sat at a few, small, folding wooden tables each with only a single cabbage, a few onions or a small bunch of herbs on display. So different from today's bustling market with multi-colour parasols over stalls piled high with bright green salads and stacks of red capsicums. There was little on display in shop windows. The plate glass monstrosity that had replaced my great-grandfather's shop only had two small boxes of washing powder and a bottle of bleach. Clearly, life was very hard for the population.

Although the roads and pavements were a mess, the trams operated smoothly and the system appeared extensive as Fritzi escorted me back to her apartment on the outskirts of the city. One of many brutalist, concrete blocks the Soviets had built in the bleak suburb. Rows of identical grey rectangles loomed above the street. The tram stopped outside Fritzi's block and we climbed the stark, concrete stairs to her apartment.

Stalls loaded with vibrant fresh fruit and vegetables in the bustling Krautmarkt, Brno, August 2008.

Fritzi explained that like many apartment blocks built in the Soviet era, hers was a rectangle arranged around a central open space that the tenants had divided into allotments. As she was too old to cultivate her allocated area, it was worked by her neighbours who then gave her a share of the produce. She said how lucky she was to have been able to stay on the apartment after her husband died but this was just another example of how clever and thoughtful, he had been. Under the Soviet system, on being promoted, he had been offered a larger more prestigious flat in keeping with his status but he had declined the move. He hoped that, by staying in the more modest flat, Fritzi would be able to remain there after his death. Had they taken the larger flat, she would have then been forced to move to a much smaller place if he died. By Western standards, the flat was small but practical, the living room dominated by a couch covered in a bright shiny orange plastic fabric. The small kitchen faced the road. The grey enamel stove, smaller and older than the 1950s model that I had seen Paula use in Hatherley Court, stood on sturdy utilitarian legs opposite an old enamel sink. The bathroom was similarly utilitarian and Spartan.

The circular table, covered in a clearly new tablecloth with the blue and white Zwiebelmuster design, was laid with plastic crockery, again with the Zwiebelmuster pattern. Fritzi had prepared bread, meat and cheese and sweets. One neighbour had contributed potted meat and preserves, another pickled vegetable, whilst another had made biscuits. It was an embarrassing largesse from people who had so little, nor could they buy much as the shops were empty, yet they had produced an aufschnitt for me.

Fritzi said that as she had access to foreign currency, she was relatively well off. From time to time, her neighbours would travel across the Austrian border to shop and would kindly fetch goods for her at the same time. She was positive about everything, keen to look at photographs of the family, even our pets.

Of course, I was loaded with gifts for the family: cards, a bottle of Jelinek's Borovička, a fiery Slovakian juniper brandy, jars of preserves, sweets and little hand-carved toys for the children. As we were leaving the flat, she handed me the remaining section of what must once have been a pretty necklace wrapped in tissue and refused to let me decline her gift.

The beautiful, baroque monastery where Mendel carried out his famous experiments, crossing round and wrinkled peas, is opposite the ugly bus station. As we walked round the unkempt garden, I tried, but failed, to explain how we now know that Mendel must have fiddled the data as his results were too perfect. They lacked the natural variation statisticians expect. I did succeed in explaining that my training as a geneticist made the visit to his monastery special and how wonderful it was to finally meet Fritzi.

I watched Fritzi, a tiny old lady in her best and probably only suit, overshadowed by the drab, post-communist, brutalist, concrete bus station, cheerfully waving, but she looked tired after a long day and she still had a long tram ride to get home. I wondered how she had remained so positive and had not complained once about the injustices she had lived through.

Epilogue

Austria: Holocaust in Retrospect

Reparations

In 1945, the Allies recognised the necessity of preventing Auschwitz from ever happening again. The Potsdam conference declared that 'German education shall be so controlled as completely to eliminate Nazi and militarist doctrines, and to make possible the successful development of democratic ideas'. The Americans tried to identify and remove individual teachers who were found to be sympathetic to the Nazis. However, they found that all had been subjected to indoctrination by the National Socialists. During the regime, teachers had been forced to swear allegiance to and promote Nazi values in their teaching. Dissenters had simply been removed from their posts. By the end of the war, those individuals who were still teaching, were typically older as their younger colleagues had been called up to fight. The remaining teachers were conservative and preferred to follow rigid pedagogical lines. Whilst the Americans tried to identify and remove these tainted practitioners, teachers were in such short supply that even Nazi sympathisers were re-hired. Although new textbooks were created, little emphasis was placed on the fate of Jews. Many teachers chose not to cover the period at all; whilst others presented the German people as victims whose sufferings were a direct consequence of following Hitler. The Holocaust was largely overlooked by mainstream German education until the 1960s.

Following the liberation of Austria by the Russians, the immediate reaction was that the Anschluss had made Austria the first victim of German invasion. The population had suffered from deprivation, Allied bombing campaigns had destroyed much of Vienna, and conscripts had been injured, killed or taken prisoner whilst they were fighting for Germany. The 'victim's doctrine' conveniently overlooked extermination camps and the mistreatment of Jews and other marginal groups. Although evidence of war crimes by Austrians emerged during the Nuremburg and Dachau trials, and thirty Austrian Nazis were sentenced to execution, the myth of Austrian innocence continued until the late 1960s.

There was an intriguing pair of letters to Peter, one from Paula and a second from Alec Freedman who, by chance, were both holidaying in the same resort in the Tyrol, Bad Gastein. Paula's letter to Peter complained about the way Jews were behaving in the hotel as they were loud and showing off, whilst the Austrian behaviour towards them was openly antisemitic.

Dr Freedman's letter repeated Paula's allegation of antisemitism and asked Peter to meet them at Heathrow on their return.

Attitudes to the Holocaust in both Germany and Austria began to change in the 1960s when there was a move away from general denial of acceptance of these events and developing determination that they should never be repeated. Several factors influenced this development, amongst them, youth protest movements, social change, and mass consumerism. As changing political attitudes swept across the world, students protested noisily about the Vietnam War. In 1968, demonstrators in London marched from Trafalgar Square to the American Embassy in Grosvenor Square where Vanessa Redgrave handed in a letter protesting about the war. It was a pretty orderly affair. The following day, there was a sensation at my school; one of the sixth form had been arrested at the demonstration and had spent a night in police custody. In contrast, students in Paris occupied the Sorbonne and rioting broke out across the city as they protested against capitalism, consumerism, and American imperialism but also for sexual liberation. Activists moved across Europe and stoked discontent in Czechoslovakia promoting the Prague Spring.

In the west, the 1960s were a time of great social change as the anti-establishment counterculture movement that promoted individualism, women's rights, minority groups, and nascent environmentalism, became established. It was partially driven by the post-war boom in the global economy and increased consumerism as goods became widely available once mass manufacturing was established after years of wartime deprivation. In turn, this led to increased access to information as domestic televisions became common. The contraceptive pill, that made birth control available, underpinned the sexual revolution.

The sixties were a time for the young post-war baby boomers and change was exhilarating. The Prime Minister, Harold MacMillan, even announced his view that the people "had never had it so good."

In 1979, both Germany and Austria aired *Holocaust*, a fictional American mini-series on domestic TV. Starring Meryl Streep, the series contrasted the lives of a Jewish family from a successful doctor to their deaths in the gas chambers with that of struggling lawyer who joins the SS to become actively engaged with Nazi killings. The series attracted huge viewing figures and sparked discussion of the Holocaust amongst friends and families. Although criticised for presenting an oversimplification of history, the programme was reputed to have been responsible for introducing the Holocaust to a new generation. It opened the question, 'What did you do during the war?' within families, whilst survivors of Nazi persecution were invited to talk of their experience in schools and the wider population. Holocaust education was embedded in the German system during the 1980s. In an attempt to present a balanced view that avoided the stereotypes where most were either willingly complicit or that most resisted Nazi atrocities, it was presented in the context of promoting wider discussions of current global discrimination and genocide.

In the summer of 2009, I was at a woman's networking dinner in one of the Oxford colleges. That I had received the invitation was probably more due to a badly managed email distribution list than my eligibility. Whilst I do not normally participate in anything on grounds of gender, this time, I was curious.

It was a gloriously warm summer evening, sweet, summer smells floated through huge open windows as, sitting in a semi-formal mismatched circle, we drank rather good champagne. Languid sounds rising from student cricket and tourist picnics on Christ Church Meadows completed the idyll. Alongside, was a trio of famous lady professors. There were two young German academics I knew slightly, both young mothers, one neat in tailored trousers and white shirt, buttoned to the neck, the other in an extremely fancy party dress in shimmering metallic shades of blue and grey.

Later, in the oak panelled private dining room downstairs, we sat at a mahogany table gleaming with the patina of at least a couple of hundred years of polishing by college servants. The meal started with huge swirls of excellent smoked salmon and crisp white wine, followed by lamb. After the meal, we moved back upstairs for coffee and the talk was of children and childhood. Moving from current difficulties of managing work and child-care back to their own experience, the party dress complained of how her German childhood had been spoiled by a country determined not to allow anyone to forget its past.

"In school, we were always reminded of the horrors; never allowed to forget what happened. We couldn't have normal lives." I thought about my strange childhood: crying grannies with strong accents, strange cousins suddenly appearing from around the world and Fritzi's quiet dignity while she spoke so simply about being beaten in the camp but said nothing.

In 2017, the Körber Foundation reported that forty per cent of the schoolchildren they surveyed had not heard of Auschwitz-Birkenau. Last time I flew from Stuttgart Airport, in 2019, there was explicit antisemitic graffiti on the inside of the ladies' toilet door which did not look particularly new.

In Austria, the victim-perpetrator debate changed more slowly in response to the social reforms of the 1960s than in neighbouring Germany. Collective amnesia helped to maintain the illusion of victimhood. However, in 1986, the furore surrounding Kurt Waldheim contributed to a re-evaluation of attitudes to the Nazis in Austria. He had neglected to mention the time he had spent as a Wehrmacht officer between 1940 and 1944 on his CV when he stood for either Secretary General of the United Nations or President of Austria. After the scandal became public, attitudes to the Holocaust and restitution began to change and discussions of culpability, guilt and the restitution due to victims of National Socialist persecution started. The government came under increasing political pressure from foreign governments. In both the US and Europe, momentum towards restitution resulted in pressure on Switzerland to reveal the looted treasures stored there. Although Austria had been a founding member of the Organisation for European Economic Cooperation when it was founded in 1948, the country remained neutral. The existence of the Russian sector retained vestigial attachment between Austria and the Soviet bloc. Once the stranglehold of communism weakened, interest in joining the European Union grew within Austria. In turn, existing members of the EU applied pressure on Vienna to openly address their Holocaust legacy. Along with Finland and Sweden, Austria became a full member of the EU in January 1995.

In the early 1960s, Austria began supporting individuals who had suffered as a result of National Socialism. Paula began to claim and received financial support from Austria via Hilfsfonds, the Austrian Aid Relief Group. The State Archive sent copies of the lengthy forms and correspondence both Paula and Peter submitted, beginning in 1962. Because Peter had still been at school when he was forced to leave Vienna, he was credited with a number of years of social security payments in the Austrian system and was then allowed to continue to make annual payments into the system from the UK. When he reached retirement age, he was then entitled to an Austrian pension. To prove he was still alive and, therefore, still entitled to receive the pension, Peter had to present himself at the Austrian consulate in London every year.

The reunification of Germany, and pressure from the US government, coupled with a number of high-profile lawsuits, resulted in further funds being released primarily by Germany and Austria. These were used to provide restitution to individuals, to maintain and record events of the Holocaust and to promote education on the subject. Much of the information I have obtained researching this book came from projects developed using these funds, Yad Vashem in Jerusalem and some of the Shoah victim's databases. Education projects included the development of education centres at former death camps. During the 1990s, large sums were made available to victims. In 1991, Austria provided $23.5 million for projects to aid Austrian born victims. Many say the compensation was too little, too late. Fifty years after the end of the war, many of those who would have been eligible to receive it were already dead.

Peter only visited Austria a couple of times for holidays, preferring to ski in Italy or German-speaking Switzerland. He said that every time he saw men of his own age or older, he began to think about what they had done in the war. Peter was too reasonable to think everyone was a Nazi and he respected men who had flown for the Luftwaffe even though they had bombed Britain. However, he could not forget the enthusiastic welcome average Austrians had given German troops when they entered Vienna. Although two or even three generations have passed since then, incidents keep occurring that remind us of the tentacles of National Socialism. In September 2019, the *Independent* reported that the owners of a Tyrolean hotel attempted to sue German visitors who gave them a bad review on social media as they had complained of the photographs of grandpa in uniform with an eagle and swastika badge on display in the lobby. Old uniforms lie musty and forgotten in the back of unused wardrobes. Of course, current generations cannot be responsible for things their parents did but they are responsible for their attitude to these events and to stop them happening again.

German citizens who were forced to leave Germany to avoid persecution and lost their citizenship as a result have been entitled to apply to reclaim it since 1949 when the right was enshrined in basic German law. However, there were strange exceptions to this right: children could only apply if their male parent was German but not if their mother was German and their father was not. Applications were only considered for births during dates between 1933 and 1945. In some cases, one sibling was awarded citizenship but not another, born after 1945. Only recently, have amendments correcting these anomalies been considered; they are still work in progress before they become statute.

> The Federal Minister of the Interior Horst Seehofer said: "It is extremely fortunate for our country if people wish to acquire German citizenship although we stripped their ancestors of everything they had. This is not merely a matter of restitution but of asking forgiveness with a deep feeling of shame."

> *21st March 2021*

In the early 1990s, as Austria began to debate its involvement in Nazi-era crimes, it began offering dual nationality to refugees who had been forced to renounce their Austrian citizenship when they fled and had gained citizenship in their adopted countries. Someone from the Austrian Embassy in

London contacted Peter to ask if he would like to consider regaining the Austrian citizenship that he had renounced when he became a British Citizen in 1946. Peter's negative response was abrupt and deeply anatomical. From the first of September 2020, the descendants of Austrian refugees could apply for citizenship without having to renounce their current nationality. I applied as soon as the website went live in August before the offer opened officially.

An old friend asked what I thought Peter might have said about my applying for and getting citizenship of a country that had treated him so badly. I replied rather vehemently that I hoped Peter would understand why I had applied but he would be saddened that I felt it necessary. In part, it was my reaction to the UK leaving the European Union. The European Community grew from the horrors of the war and the peace we have enjoyed since 1945 has been sustained by the EU. Whilst I hope that leaving the country will not be necessary, with insecurities learnt in childhood, I know how rapidly freedom and tolerance can evaporate. Justice, freedom of speech and fair reporting are easily eroded by lack of respect and corruption. So, I hope Peter would sympathise with my decision. Once confidence in democracy is lost, it takes a long time to rebuild a just and peaceful society.

By chance, I was standing in front of my house when the postman arrived with a bright orange official envelope, I squealed when I saw the Austrian embassy address on the top left. Much to the amusement of the postman, who agreed that it must be a very important letter, I ripped it open and found my certificate of citizenship and bounced around my drive. I spent the remainder of the day in a happy haze telling everyone about my good luck. Then I remembered the assorted 'I am now British' telegrams Peter, Paula and Eric sent in very different circumstances. I tried to imagine how they, as stateless refugees forced to build new lives in a foreign country with different customs, food and a language they had to learn, would have felt on receiving their British citizenship.

The hostel girls
The terrified children who arrived in Tynemouth and Windermere over fifty years ago and grew up in the hostel to become adults, many with their own families and careers, then

spread across the world in another diaspora. Many stayed in touch with Paula and Alice and one another, sharing the bond of childhood, happy or otherwise.

Over the years, many of the girls Paula had cared for in Windermere sent letters and photographs. One of the envelopes included photographs on which Paula had carefully recorded the lives of girls as they became mothers, parents and grandparents. Families standing rather stiffly in formal wedding clothes, a casual picture of a radiant bride, relaxed with her new husband, babies in rockers and proud grandparents dangling a new grandchild. Cute little boys, posing proudly in matching white shirts and ties in a garden contrast with the photo of two small children squatting in a sand dune. All are annotated with dates and places, some with additional notes in Paula's strong slanting writing. As the girls migrated across the globe, they sent cards from far-flung places, though one from Newby Bridge, just down the road from Windermere, shows a happy family who had just enjoyed lunch in the Swan pub. The cars parked behind them are now vintage specimens. Over the years, the fashions and interior décor changed but the contact and affection remained.

Annie always worked as a dressmaker, costumier and wedding organiser while her husband, Rudi, returned to his pre-war career in music, worked with opera companies and eventually, became the director of opera programmes at Carnegie Mellon University in Pittsburgh in 1964. They had three children; their eldest daughter works as a labour organiser; their twin son is in IT while his sister is a physician.

I met Annie briefly in London shortly after Peter died. She spent a night with us in Hackney. Small and energetic, she dressed as befitted a bespoke dressmaker. She was acute and great fun. We corresponded up to her death. She was a kind and wise advisor. The last message we shared showed how excited she and her family were that President Obama had been elected that morning.

Margot trained as a hairdresser during her time in both the Tynemouth and Windermere hostels. She moved to London in 1946 to work as a hairdresser and married in August 1947. She had a daughter and later three granddaughters. Margot also spent twenty-six years working as the cook and canteen manager for a school in North London (though she commented, "But not to Mrs Urbach's standards!").

Elfie also moved to London, first to a hostel in West London, possibly one in Willesden Lane as described by Mona Golabek in her book about the Kindertransport. She then shared a flat in Swiss Cottage with Edith, another woman from the hostel. After a job as a secretary in the city, Elfie applied for, and received, a grant from a non-Jewish charity in Hampstead that supported her through teacher training college. Once qualified, she went on to teach for many years. She met her husband, a law student at London University. They married as soon as he qualified and moved to Birmingham as he joined a law practice there. Eventually, he became president of the Birmingham Law Society, was active in local politics and chairman of the Birmingham Symphony Orchestra for many years. They travelled widely together attending the orchestra's concerts around the world. Very sadly, Elfie died on the second of March 2021, leaving a son, daughter and grandchildren.

Ruth qualified as a teacher at University College, London and for over thirty years, she taught French in several schools in Leicestershire. She married in 1958 and had two children, a boy and a girl, but she then divorced. Ruth moved to Iowa to join her second husband, an American professor for a few years before returning to Leicester. Sadly, she died of Covid-19 in June 2020, aged ninety-one years old.

Ruth described her childhood in Fränkisch-Crumbach, Germany, travelling on the Kindertransport and her time in the hostel in her book, *A Child of our Time*. She remained severely critical of her treatment by the matrons during her time at the hostel. Ruth was a regular and respected speaker on the Holocaust, particularly telling children of her personal experiences. Her many visits to Germany and the work she did keeping the memory of the Holocaust alive was recognized when she was awarded an Order of Merit by the German government.

In June 1989, eight of the ladies, then in their seventies, met in London.

June 1989 reunion. (Left to Right)
Inge, Margot, Sophy, Ilse, (visitor), Ruth A., Lisl, Eva, Elfie.

Dasha and I began corresponding when I asked for consent to include her quotes in this book. She summarised her life briefly:

I left England in to go to South Africa in 1954 and left South Africa with my family in 1984 to come to Sydney Australia. I have five grandchildren, the youngest now is eighteen years old. I managed to obtain a government grant to become a teacher in Arts and Crafts.

Psychology was part of my training and I realise how Mrs S. and Mrs U. were totally unprepared for their challenge in looking after the welfare of the girls. However, each one did what they thought was right. Your grandmother, the kind and gentle person whilst Mrs U. was the disciplinarian who delivered the punishments.

Streatham 2019
Standing outside 'The High' late one morning on a sunny bank holiday in May 2019, the building looked much smarter in reality than it appeared on the web. Much larger than I had expected, there are five blocks, each with striking entrances: in each doorway 'The High' is set out in black ceramic tesserae, contrasting with the white. In turn, a mirror image of the text is

reflected on the polished brass plates at the bottom of the double doors. The oak doors, with shiny brass handles, have panels of clear glass set into a pattern of swirling lead that echoes the semi-circular quarter lights above them. The hallways are monochrome, art deco style with black and white checkerboard floors. The architecture is simple with curved arches leading to further corridors. White domed lights are positioned at head height along the walls at regular intervals and are framed by simple grey moulding. Each hall has a beige utilitarian fireplace set into the wall with a mirror above. The stairs, with simple black handrails, curve upwards. It is a little like the cinema building in Josefstädter Straße. A modern façade runs along the top of the ground floor units, above it, five floors of flats rise built with dull yellow bricks with steel Crittall windows and topped by a simple white cornice. The road is wide because a suburban railway once ran down its middle. Now, gentrification has led to a row of small birch trees planted in place of the railway tracks. The assorted cafes and shops, if not exactly busy, were trading steadily.

The hall and stairs at 'The High' with simple black handrail and checkerboard floor, like the rear of the Josefstädter Straße cinema.

A poster on the resident noticeboard has a QR code linked to their website. Among a range of historical records, someone has scanned the tenant register from 1943. In the space for flat 122, the entry shows Stössler Karoline, crossed out with Stanley printed above it in blue ink. Alongside the note: 'Perr Name Officer AXA 1943'. Like many, Erich retained his initials, so Erich Stössler became Eric Stanley when he enrolled in the Pioneer Corps. This name-change, noted in the tenant register for 'The High', is now available for everyone to see on the web. Whilst a few of the women listed had jobs as sales ladies, dressmakers, and secretaries, the majority, including Karla, did unpaid domestic work.

A 1943 tenant list for 'The High'. The name Stössler is crossed out and replaced with Stanley, marking Erich's name change when he served overseas in the Army. (National Archives).

Windermere 2019

I was about ten when Peter proudly showed us South Wood on our way back from a family holiday in Scotland in the mid-sixties. Only the huge Cedar tree in front of the house made a lasting impression on me.

When I visited the house again with my husband, Paul, in 2019, I recognised the tree, still majestic but now old. A number of large branches surgically removed. The front of the house was familiar but more from photographs than memory. The current owners were kind enough to let us intrude on their home, generously letting us look round whilst explaining how the rooms had been altered. I was struck by how small the kitchen must have been to provide meals for twenty-five or more children, two or three times a day. How difficult it must have been to keep the house warm without central heating. The huge, single-glazed sash windows made the rooms light but must have been draughty, offering little insulation against the cold. Perhaps that explains why several of the girls commented on collecting wood and lighting fires. Although the rooms are large by domestic standards, even the larger rooms would have been crowded once there were six beds in them, leaving little private space for the girls. No wonder they kept their prized possessions, letters and pictures of their families, under their pillows.

After our visit, we drove home along the Kirkstone Pass, the route Dr Freedman had driven so many years earlier when he travelled between South Wood and Newcastle. It was a beautiful clear day with only a few clouds scattered across an impossibly blue sky. As the road wound between the lichen-covered dry-stone walls that keep sheep on the austere shale-clad slopes I thought it was a good day to be alive. Several of the girls commented on how fortunate they were that the hostel had been forced to relocate to such a beautiful area.

This book has been an unexpected adventure. Along the way, I met many kind, interesting, and a few inspirational individuals and discovered a great deal both about my family and the wider history of the twentieth century. The horrors of the Holocaust became real in the context of the stories of loss and survival of family and the wider hostel. Despite experiencing terrible events they went on to have useful and fulfilling lives, many in turn creating their own families.

Postscript

Friends for Life

Dasha summed up her experience in 1998:

Often people ask me how I feel about the events of my life and how they have affected me as a person. My varied experiences strengthened my character and attitude toward my fellow beings. I feel no bitterness, I feel no hatred and to avoid being boring to others, I do not dwell on the past. I am very fortunate in having an innate positive and happy disposition and have not allowed my early disappointments and losses to affect my outlook and dreams of the future. My experiences have taught me that the best must be found in every situation. Every problem must have a positive aspect. I was always the one with the accent, the one without a home, the one that was laughed at when I was reading or reciting a passage from a book in front of a class. Later, when I lived on my own, I was the girl without a family. A situation which made me feel ashamed.

The hostel which was set up was supported by a Jewish committee who were appointed to be our guardian and they thought that this would be a temporary refuge for children fleeing from Nazi persecution. It was hoped that the parents would join their children as it was the case with my friends. Unfortunately, the children's home became an orphanage and we had to be supported for the duration of the war. Two elderly ladies were chosen to look after about 25 girls ranging from ages 4 – 18 years."

They deserve the highest praise for their invaluable work and the highest tribute.'

Speaking in 1998, Ilse was hugely grateful:

We can never thank them enough for what they did for us.

Perhaps, the last words should go to Annie, who so wisely said in 1999:

It does not seem like yesterday, some of my friends of those days are still trying to find resolutions, explanations and expiations for all those events. I don't, it was part of my life experience, to be digested - which was not always easy - to be incorporated, once you do the first, the second is not so hard, and then apply what you have learned as best you can to your daily life. It is part of me but I don't dwell on it, I often remember some detail or event or a picture flash through my head but never without an appropriate trigger and for better or worse it has deepened and, in some cases, enriched the way I see, experience and live life.

11111111111111111

Family Trees

Ticho and Sieber Family Trees

The Ticho Family 1807 - 2000

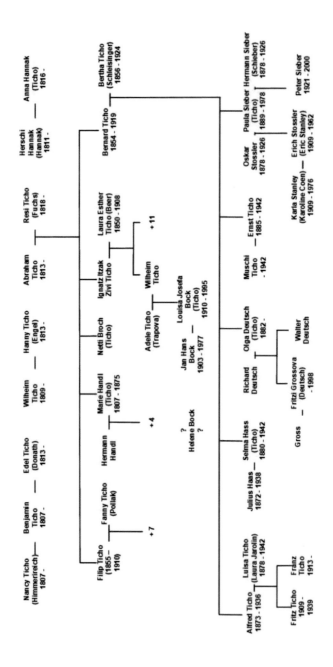

Ticho family trees 1938 and 1946

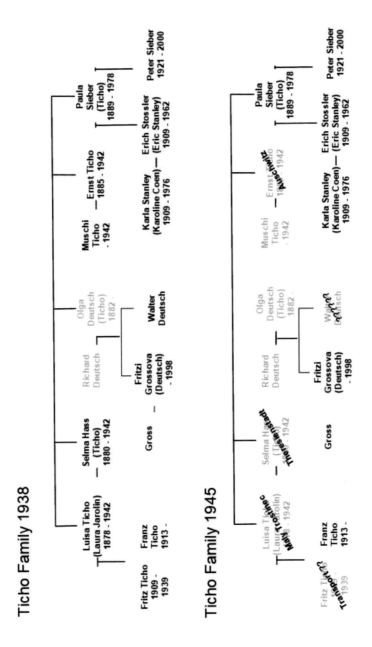

Ticho Family 1938

Ticho Family 1945

The Schieber/Sieber Family Tree 1850 - 2000

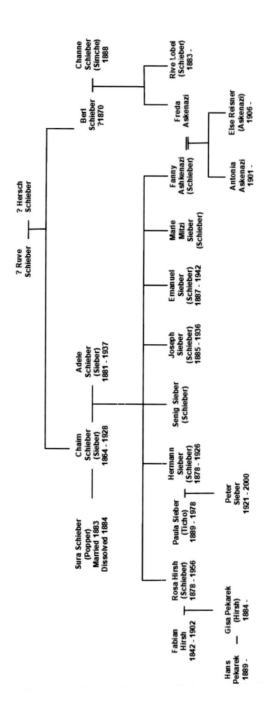

Appendix

Peter Sieber's Report on the Hostel

THE NEWCASTLE-UPON-TYNE

HOSTEL FOR JEWISH REFUGEE GIRLS

In recognition of the Hostel Committee who initiated the Hostel and managed it, and of the Newcastle Jewish Community who supported it.

As there are no known written records, these notes are based on living memories (including my own). For the purposes of this memoir, time has stood still and the 'girls' have remained to be the girls, including all the grandmothers. I am grateful to several girls who have kindly helped with information and photographs. I believe it will not be considered unfair if I say a special thank you to Elfie Reinert for her contribution.

To preserve confidentiality, the present names and addresses of the girls are not included. If contact with any of them is required, I will gladly forward any request, and for the future the whole file will be lodged with the Wiener Library.

Peter Sieber
March 2000

Wiener Library, London
020 7636 7247

Preparations

The persecution in Germany was at first mainly economic, depriving the victims of their work and living. In 1935 Gollancz published 'The Bloodless Pogrom' by Fritz Seidler (written by Marion Wieselberg under a pseudonym for his protection). Removals to camps were spasmodic and largely secret even inside Germany. Next to nothing was known about them in Britain or, indeed, anywhere outside Germany.

Increasing hardship in Germany led to more immigration here and to more personal accounts and greater awareness. The annexation (Anschluss) of Austria on 14 March 1938 brought a new wave of refugees and more first-hand reports. The horrendous outrage of the Crystal Night on 9 November 1938 was widely reported here. On 23 November, Britain recalled the ambassador from Germany and announced that the country would give temporary homes to refugee children. Woburn House in London, the centre of aid to refugees, sent appeals for help to all Jewish communities in the UK. There is little doubt that these reports, and the appeal, triggered action in Newcastle.

A committee was set up, quite informally. "We just got together," is a direct quote. Mr Summerfield was elected chairman. It would have been unusual then to have a woman in the chair. He was a leading jeweler in Newcastle's main street, well-known and respected in the Jewish community and beyond. He was the ideal spokesman, valuable in fund raising, generous with his time (in spite of running a business) and, in time, kindly and popular with the hostel girls.

All the actual creation, planning and running of the hostel was done by a small nucleus of committee members, the prime movers of the whole project. Apart from Mr Summerfield, there were Mrs Rita Jackson, also very active in the (then) Women's Voluntary Service, Mrs Rita Freedman (her husband and she also had in their home a little girl from Germany and me as well). Mrs Nolly Collins, Mrs Wilkes, with the moral and considerable financial support from their husbands Jack Jackson, Dr Wallace Freedman, Ike Collins.

We have no minutes of committee meetings; possible none were kept. The Jacksons, Freedmans, Collins lived within half a mile of each other. They must have just got together. There were a few other members of the committee, but we do not know their names. This was not a committee to draw a camel. It was an informal working group, and its achievement is awesome.

Funds had to be raised. Rabbi Rabinowitz at Leazes Park and Rabbi Drukker in Jesmond appealed for contributions in the synagogues and the Jewish community was generous.

Think of all the possessions and equipment your parents and you have collected, purchased, made over the years for families with, say, two or three children.

The committee hired a terrace house, 55 Percy Park, Tynemouth, within sight of the sea front, a pleasant environment, lower rents than in the town, easily reached by local train. Within a few months, they collected everything needed for 20 children from nappies to dresses, overcoats, and shoes. Curtains, carpets, linen, crockery and cutlery marked 'm' and 'f' (milchig and fleischig) the hostel had to be kosher, a cooker and kitchen equipment, furniture, 20 cots and beds. Coal, firewood, groceries, cleaning materials, food. Rooms furnished, however simply, for the matron and her assistant.

They bought it, got it wholesale, scrounged it, begged for it, got it given. Members of the community brought everything they could spare, vans belonging to Jewish-owned businesses took it to Tynemouth. Artisans were found to bring the house up to standard, adapt it for so many people, decorate it, make sure it could be heated, the Tyne is cold.

To house both boys and girls in the same building was unthinkable then. There was a fierce debate whether to have boys or girls. It was decided to have girls because it was felt they were even more vulnerable than boys.

A matron had to be found. In the dictionary a matron is 'a woman managing the domestic arrangements of a school, etc'. This one would have one assistant. They and the girls themselves would have to do everything. The committee asked Woburn House for recommendations. They gave one name above all others, Alice Urbach.

Alice Urbach was the widow of a Viennese doctor who had died young leaving her with two sons. To make a living, she was one of the first to start a cookery school. In time, she wrote 'Viennese Cookery' ('So Kocht Man in Wien'), the definitive book on its subject. Her two sons were in the USA. She was in London, housekeeper in a doctor's family.

Rita Jackson went to London to interview her. There was instant rapport and mutual respect. Alice Urbach moved into the empty hostel.

A deputy was needed. Alice Urbach recommended her old friend Paula Sieber. She also had two sons, my half-brother from an earlier, failed marriage, and me. My father, a solicitor in Vienna, had been killed in a road accident. She had been the leading spirit in buying and running a cinema in Vienna.

The hostel was ready to receive its guests.

The committee never envisaged a time-limit for the hostel. After the threat of war over Czechoslovakia, the Munich meeting on

29 September 1938 and Mr Chamberlain's famous "Peace in our time" it was generally assumed by the committee members that the girls' parents would before long get the necessary exit and entry permits and be reunited with their children. The hostel was thought of as a temporary refuge.

They were to run it for over six years.

The children arrive

They came in twos and three's early in 1939. If one of them was old enough, a member of Woburn House put them on a train at King's Cross. If all were too young, someone from Woburn House travelled with them to Newcastle. A member of the committee met them and took them on the local train to Tynemouth.

The children had left their parents and their homes in Germany and Austria hardly a week ago. Spent two days on trains and on a strange sea. Came to an alien country with a foreign language. Went by train to a huge city and on trains that go underground. Spent a night or two with people who were kindly, but neither could understand a word the others said.

They went on another long journey, were met by some other lady and now they were walking along a strange, windy road with a choppy sea at its end, all they had in the world in a suitcase or a bag. At least they could speak to each other, and to the two women when they came to the house. Except for one of the girls, Dasha. She spoke only Czech. Her only link with the world were the few words of Czech Paula Sieber remembered from her own youth in Brno.

The children were welcomed as well as possible, taken upstairs, two or three to a room, given milk or chocolate and good cake made specially. Some could not stop crying. One or two could not stop talking. The older ones were mainly silent.

Some were not used to sharing the bedroom. The food was different. There were dietary rules that were unfamiliar to most of them. For a few, they were not kept strictly enough. There were toys and games, but they were not their own. All the time other girls arrived and were helped to settle in. There were housekeeping jobs they had to do, depending on their ages.

Many could not sleep. Several had nightmares and Alice Urbach and Paula Sieber were up much of the nights in the first weeks. There was bed-wetting. Alice Urbach and Paula Sieber were kind and obviously meant well, they also had to impose order and rules which, sadly not coming from the children's parents, could be resented.

At least one of the committee came at least once a week, usually more. Rita Jackson, Rita Freedman, Nolly Collins supervised, organised, conferred with Alice Urbach, brought love, care, and fun whenever possible. Ike Collins could be found under the kitchen table playing with the younger girls.

Over the weeks, the hostel settled down into a routine and became a community. The children picked up English by osmosis as only children can. But always they missed their parents and prayed for a reunion. Every morning's post was a ritual of hope and disappointment.

At the end of August, Hitler made impossible demands against Poland in spite of Britain's pledge to protect the country. So far as was known then, only Lisl Scherzer and Helga's fathers and Ilse and Edith's mothers had got out, all the other parents had not. The children and the matrons with parents and other close relatives still in Germany did not eat, not sleep, not leave the radio.

On 1 September Hitler bombed and invaded Poland, unleashing WW2. Jews counted the hours. On 3 September, Chamberlain spoke. We were at war, our people trapped.

The older the girl, the more she understood, the worse it was for her. (Lisl and Vera Reiss's parents arrived at the hostel a few months later, and they left together.)

The girls, Tynemouth, approximately 1943.
Back row: Hedy, Ruth, Sophy, Lisl, Ruth
Middle row: Lore, Hilde, Elfie, ?, Dasha.
Front row: Frieda, Lea, Inge.

War

The war was slow to get going.

Food and clothes rationing began, bringing extra problems for kosher households. The older children started to go to the local schools.

There was this group with German names and German accents at the start of a war against Germany. The neighbours in Tynemouth, the tradesmen, the schools understood. There was never a word against anyone from the hostel

For the committee and the community who supported the hostel it meant that in addition to all the other anxieties and problems war was bound to bring, there was now also the responsibility for twenty girls, from three to fourteen, for as long as it would take. Not least, the need to raise the money when for many the war brought reduced or less certain incomes.

In April 1940, Hitler invaded Denmark and Norway. On 10 May, 2,000 German tanks started their lightning war (Blitzkrieg) in the West. Belgium surrendered within a week, the French army was in disarray, the British army was cut off around Dunkerque. By 5 June, 335,000 British soldiers were rescued from the beaches and brought home. France surrendered on 21 June.

The invasion of Britain seemed imminent. There was a campaign in the press voicing fears - real or imagined - of refugees having been planted here as a 'fifth column' to spy and sabotage. Male refugees were interned in England, and many were sent to Canada and Australia.

Coastal areas were designated as Defence Zones and 'enemy aliens' had to leave them at once. Tynemouth was one of the first. As a helpful concession, the committee was given three weeks to find another home and move the hostel.

The Lake District in the north-west seemed the best bet. With rail travel at its worst, Rita Jackson, and probably also Rita Freedman, went to Kendal, to Keswick, to Lake Windermere and there they found South Wood, a large country house set in a garden standing empty. They took it and had ten days left to move the children, the furniture and everything else.

Windermere

The house needed cleaning and putting to order. But there was more space, and the children enjoyed the garden and climbed the trees. The committee and the matrons faced new problems. The committee, how to run the hostel a day's journey away with an overloaded telephone system. The matron and her assistant, to manage on their own, a little way from the village. No more regular visits and the help the committee had given as a matter of course. Keeping kosher was difficult and meat was sent from Newcastle.

The matrons took turns in going to the village. Meeting the police, the shopkeepers, the schools, the doctor. With their softer accents, with their slower ways, without exception, they were kind and helpful and so remained. The headmistresses in Windermere, Ambleside and Kendal did their best to fit the girls into the right classes as they grew older. Teachers gave up their free time to help.

The matrons did not have to visit the vicar. He called on them and befriended them to the day they all left.

"South Wood", Hoo Lane, Windermere, Cumbria

The Battle of Britain started on 11 August and the future of Britain, quite likely of the whole of Europe, was being decided in the skies over England. By October, the RAF had won. The Germans switched to bombing English towns.

Everybody in the country lived a double life. First, to cope with the day-to-day concerns and the extra difficulties brought about by the war. And together with this was the constant concern for relatives in the forces and the ups and downs of the war as it unveiled history and taught a new geography: Pearl Harbor 1941, El Alamein 1942, Stalingrad 1943, the Normandy beaches 1944, Hiroshima and Nagasaki 1945.

For the hostel, there was a third dimension of fear. Not for a day could they forget about their parents and the other relatives and friends still in the enemy's hands.

But the species is adaptable, and life had to go on. Routines developed; friendships were formed. The older girls went to work, all did their duties in the house. And went for walks in the lovely countryside.

The girls, Windermere, Summer 1939.
Back row: Edith, Hanna, Elfie, Stella, Lore, Dasha, Helga, Annie*, Ruth, Marion.
Front row: Margot, Lore, Lisl, Ilsa, Eva
*The two little girls with Annie are visiting cousins.

Higher education was generally not common then, still less so in wartime, least for girls even from privileged homes. It could not be a high priority either for the committee in Newcastle or for the matrons. They did the expediently best. Several girls were apprenticed to learn trades, a few with their own initiative and help from the schools, beat the odds.

Anita and Lisl trained as dressmakers, Margot as a hairdresser, Ilse became a librarian and then a qualified dental assistant. Inge, Dasha and Lore went to grammar schools, Sophie and Eva qualified as nurses. Ruth Oppenheimer got a scholarship to London University, Elfie went to teacher training and taught in London.

Town by town, river by river, the allies were advancing. The allies landed in Normandy. Hope was rising. And then for the hostel came the worst horror of all. All the world was shocked when the camps were liberated, and the films were shown. For the hostel, it was indescribable.

The matrons heard that a film was being shown in Windermere. Alice Urbach gave the strictest instruction that no girl was to leave the house. One of the oldest sneaked out and went to the cinema. When the newsreel came on, she fainted.

The cinema staff comforted after her. The local policeman kindly brought her home in his patrol car. That was the contrast between those films and that policeman.

The newspapers and the radio could finally not be hidden from the girls.

May 1945 brought peace in Europe. Gradually, the girls dispersed to their further education, to relatives in other countries, Anita to her brother, Lisl Scherzer rejoined her father and wonderfully her mother who had survived the camps. Some went to private families.

Approximately 1944
Back row: Sophy, Elfie, Ruth ?, Lisl.
Middle row:? , Ruth A, Margot, Lore, Hilde.
Front row: Inge, ? Lea Freida.

When girls left, others took their place for short periods as hostels elsewhere were being run down, some only waiting for overseas passages.

With these comings and goings, in all over forty girls were given some sanctuary in the hostel.

The table below shows how they have spread around the world.

Mrs Urbach made her home in the States with her sons but often came back to Europe and stayed with Mrs Sieber. She lived to nearly a hundred.

Paula Sieber went back to Newcastle until 1947. Then she settled in London and lived to close on ninety.

Name on arrival	From	Age on arrival	Time at hostel	Living in
Inge Adamz	Breslau	5³/₄	1939 -1945	England
Ruth Adamz	Breslau	7¹/₂	1939 -1945	Israel
Dasha Deutsch	Prague	7	1939-1943/4	Australia
Annie Heufeld	Augsburg	14	1939-1942	USA
Lore Freitag	Konigsberg	7	1939 -1945	New Zealand
Sophie Goldschmidt	Lagenselbold	11	1939-1946	England
Ilse Gross	Vienna	13	1939-1942	USA
Edith Grossman	Dusseldorf	13	1939-1944	England
Margot Hirsch	Frankfurt/Main	14	1939-1946	England
Paula Katz	Berlin	14	1939 -1945	Australia
Eva Less	Berlin	14	1939-1941	Canada & USA
Marion Mandelsohn	?	15	1939 -1945	Australia
Ruth Oppenheimer	Near Frankfurt	10	1939-1946	USA
Elfie Reinert	Leoben & Vienna	10	1939 -1945	England
Vera Reiss (sisters)	Czechoslovakia	12	1939-1945	USA
Lisl Reiss (sisters)	Czechoslovakia	9	1939-1939	Australia
Helga Reiss (cousin)	Vienna	8	1939 -1945	USA
Hilde Roth (sisters)	Cologne	7	1939-1944	Israel
Freda Roth (sisters)	Cologne	5	1939-1944	UK
Lea Roth (sisters)	Cologne	3	1939-1944	Israel
Lisl Scherzer	Vienna	10	1939-1946	Israel

The girls' names, ages and places of origin on their arrival, the years they spent at the hostel, and final destination.

Hindsight in 2000

Some of the girls have disappeared from our screens, one or two wanted to forget and not dwell on the past. A few have died, one or two are ill. So far as we know, all were married, many had children. For example, Dasha two sons, three grandchildren; Anita three children, three grandchildren; Sophie two children; Ilse two and two; Eva two and two. Lisl holds the record, two children, six grandchildren.

Several of the girls have stayed in touch. Ten joined a reunion in London in November 1988, eight in June 1999, and found these meetings moving and rewarding occasions.

Reunion London 7 June 1989
Inge, Margo, Sophy, Ilse, (visitor), Ruth A, Lisl, Eva, Elfie.

Most have kind memories of Alice Urbach and of Paula Sieber and an understanding of their problems. One or two are not too happy about them, one is extremely critical. Some girls seem to think that the matrons were not ready enough to let them go outside the hostel to further education and training. But being responsible for the girls, the matrons would have to be cautious.

Reunion London 7 June 1989
Elfie, Eva, Inge, Lisl, Margot, Ilse, Sophie, Ruth A.

Faced with twenty girls aged three to fourteen, all torn from their homes, a present-day trained, professional social worker would demand compensation and counselling. Admitting my obvious bias, the two women at the hostel, used to running a cookery school and a cinema in Vienna, themselves refugees and worried about their sons in the services and other relatives, didn't do too badly.

In spite of the upheavals in their childhood, the hostel girls, their children, their grandchildren have lived and are living decent, fulfilled lives, thanks, of course, to their earliest upbringing with their parents and to their own qualities. But surely to a large part because of the sustained devotion of the committee and the others.

There is undying gratitude from them all for Mr Summerfield, Rita Jackson, Rita Freedman, Nolly Collins, Mrs Wilkes, for the rest of the committee and the Jewish community.

The girls should have the last word:

"They deserve the highest praise for their invaluable work and the highest tribute'

Dasha

"We can never thank them enough for what they did for us"

Ilse

341

Resources

Web References

Association of Jewish Refugees
Kindertransport survey includes responses from Windermere and Tynemouth hostels.
> https://ajr.org.uk/special-interest/kindertransport/

Austrian State Archive
National archives of Austrian papers.
> https://www.statearchives.gv.at/

Britain National Archive
National archives of British papers.
> https://www.nationalarchives.gov.uk/

Butlins Memorabilia
Albert Hall awards ceremony.
> https://www.youtube.com/watch?v=yUruT6FPl-w

Programme for Albert Hall event
> http://media.bufvc.ac.uk/newsonscreen2/Pathe/106270/NoS_106270_other.pdf

Czech Holocaust Portal
Searchable details of people by name, date of birth.
> https://www.holocaust.cz/en/main-2/

Findbuch
Documentation Centre of Austrian Resistance (DÖW). Provides links to databases and information about Austrian Holocaust.
> https://www.doew.at/english

Geni
Genealogy database with over 23,000 searchable, family information records.
> https://www.geni.com

Geni, Jewish Families from Boskovice, Moravia, Czech Republic. 2020. https://www.geni.com/projects/Jewish-Families-from-Boskovice-Boskowitz-Moravia-Czech-Republic/13125.

GenTeam
European collection of databases with free account needed for access.
https://www.genteam.eu/index.php

Historical Currency Calculators
Websites to help convert currency values over time.

Dollar to Mark Converter Harold Marcuse, University of Santa Barbara.
https://marcuse.faculty.history.ucsb.edu/projects/currency.htm

Historical Currency Converter.
http://historicalstatistics.org/Currencyconverter.html

JewishGen
Millions of Jewish digitized records, searchable by name or region on various databases.
https://www.jewishgen.org

Ellenbogen, S. W. a. I., History of the Jews in the Bukowina H. Gold. Tel Aviv. 1962.
https://www.jewishgen.org/yizkor/bukowinabook/buk2_084.html

Leigh, G., From Kretinga to Sunderland. A Jewish chain migration from Lithuania. Cause and Effect - 1850-1930s.
https://www.jewishgen.org/jcr-/Community/Sunderland_articles/From_Kretinga/introduction.htm#footnote-12.

Jewish Virtual Library
Online encyclopaedia website covering topics about Israel–United States relations, Jewish history, Israel, the Holocaust, antisemitism and Judaism.
https://www.jewishvirtuallibrary.org/

Information about concentration camps was passed to the allies.
https://www.jewishvirtuallibrary.org/when-did-the-world-find-out-about-the-holocaust

Article on what Chilean diplomats learned about the Holocaust.
https://www.jewishvirtuallibrary.org/what-chilean-diplomats-learned-about-the-holocaust

Municipal and Provincial Archives of Vienna Wiener Stadt- und Landesarchiv
Information about many aspects of life in Vienna.
https://www.wien.gv.at

Tracing relatives in Vienna.
https://www.wien.gv.at/english/history/archives/ancestors.html

Museum of Jewish Inheritance
New York based museum with virtual tours, survivor testimony and JewishGen.
https://mjhnyc.org/

Oral Histories
Oral histories referred to in the book:

Alisa Tennenbaum née Liselotte Scherzer.
https://digipres.cjh.org/delivery/DeliveryManagerServlet?dps_pid=IE10272116

Anita Fellner née Annie Heufeld.
https://collections.ushmm.org/search/catalog/irn531331#?rsc=132021&cv=0&c=0&m=0&s=0&xywh=-563%2C-190%2C3767%2C3767

Else Reisner
https://collections.ushmm.org/search/catalog/irn514604

Charles Ticho.
https://collections.ushmm.org/search/catalog/irn709457

Report of the liberation of Theresienstadt
https://bterezin.org.il/wp-content/uploads/2017/08/Liberation-of-Theresienstadt.pdf

Second Generation Network
Group for children and grandchildren of Holocaust families.
https://secondgeneration.org.uk/

Selma Hass Death Certificate Theresienstadt
https://www.holocaust.cz/en/database-of-digitised-documents/document/83290-haase-selma-death-certificate-ghetto-terezin/

Terezin Memorial
Holocaust museum at a former concentration camp with wartime exhibits & a replica dormitory.
https://www.pamatnik-terezin.cz/

The 'High' Streatham
Booklet written by residents: history of the flats.
https://thehighstreatham.files.wordpress.com/2017/12/the-high-a-history-of-the-last-80-years.pdf

United States Holocaust Memorial Museum
Digital collections, virtual events, survivor testimony, exhibitions.
https://www.ushmm.org/

Victims of the Persecution of Jews under the National Socialist Tyranny in Germany 1933 – 1945
Memorial book which allows you to search for people in a targeted way using a search form.
https://www.bundesarchiv.de/gedenkbuch

Video reconstruction of Brno 1919.
Brno 1919 showing the Ticho Shop at 2.40 minutes.
https://www.youtube.com/watch?v=GdDcwX8H4eU

Video reconstructions of Historic Vienna from the Austrian Film Museum, Vienna.
Video reconstructions of life in Vienna pre-1930.

Vienna 1900: Pictures of a Metropolis / Vienna Tramway.
https://www.youtube.com/watch?v=NOT-NSGlTjU

Colourized images of 1900 Vienna.
https://www.youtube.com/watch?v=qr-uqT5IYSc

1920s and 1930s Vienna videos by Stefan Weingärtner.
https://www.youtube.com/watch?v=OHG4xz95F28

Vienna Library
Discover historical books, manuscripts, posters and photos on the history of Vienna.
https://www.wienbibliothek.at/

Vienna Memento
Interactive city map showing last known address of those murdered.
https://www.memento.wien/

Wiener Holocaust Library
London archive of Holocaust materials, unique collection of over one million items.
https://wienerholocaustlibrary.org/

Yad Vashem World Holocaust Memorial Site
Digital collections, databases, survivor testimony, museums, exhibitions.
https://www.yadvashem.org/

Bibliography

Bonyhady, T., Good Living Street. Portrait of a Patron Family, Vienna 1900. New York, Pantheon, Random House. 2011.

Cesarani, D. K., and Kushner, T., The Internment of Aliens in Twentieth Century Britain. Routledge Taylor & Francis. 1993.

Clare, G., Berlin Days 1946 - 1947. London, Macmillan. 1989.

Clare, G., Last Waltz in Vienna: The Destruction of a Family, 1842 - 1942. London, Macmillan. 1980.

David, R. L., Child of Our Time. A Young Girl's Flight from the Holocaust. I.B. Tauris. 2003.

Golabek, M. and Cohen, L., The Children of Willesden Lane. Beyond the Kindertransport: A Memoir of Music, Love, and Survival. Warner Books Inc. 2002.

Henry, M., Fifty Years of Holocaust Compensation. The American Jewish Yearbook. 2002.

Hitler, A., Mein Kampf. Eher Verlag. 1925.

Kershaw, I., Hitler: 1889–1936: Hubris. New York, W. W. Norton & Company. 1998.

O'Connor, A. M., The Lady in Gold. New York, Vintage - Penguin Random House. 2012.

Orth, K., The Genesis and Structure of the National Socialist Concentration Camps. Bloomington and Indianapolis, Indiana University Press and United States Holocaust Memorial Museum. 2009.

Ovenden, R., Burning the Books A History of Knowledge Under Attack. John Murray. 2020.

Price-Smith, A. T., Contagion and Chaos: Disease, Ecology, and National Security in the Era of Globalization. Cambridge, United States, MIT Press. 2009.

Sands, P., East West Street. London, Weidenfield & Nicolson. 2016.

Stoppard, T., Leopoldstadt. Faber and Faber. 2020.

Ticho, C., The Jewish shop on Boskovice's Main Square. *Jerusalem Post*. 2020.

Urbach, A., So Kocht Man in Wien! Ein Koch und Haushaltungsbuch der gut bürgerlichen Küche. Wien, Zentralgesellschaft für buch gewerbliche und graphische Betriebe A. G. 1936.

Urbach, K., Das Buch Alice: Wie die Nazis das Kochbuch meiner Großmutter raubten Berlin. Propyläen Verlag. 2020.

Waal, E. d., The Hare with Amber Eyes: A Hidden Inheritance, Vintage. 2011.

Whiteman, D. B., The Uprooted: A Hitler Legacy. Da Capo Press; New Ed. 2001.

Williams, A. T., A Passing Fury: Searching for Justice at the End of World War II. Jonathan Cape. 2016.

Index